Rescued

By Death

By R. L. Hegstad

1

Disclaimer

This book is a work of fiction. Off shore bank account numbers, Characters, Places and incidents are products of the author's imagination or are used factiously. Any resemblance to events or locales or person, living or dead, is entirely coincidental or intentionally disguised.

Raymond Lee Hegstad

Chapter 1

Someone was stealing children. We were on their trail and I was in no hurry to leave town, but you know how it is when the relatives invite you to their summer home. I was also sure that Rudy and I were close to nailing the pair of murderers that had been terrorizing the neighborhoods of Fountain Hills. No, I'm not a cop, but I often think I missed my calling. I'm a novelist who has a fetish for criminal investigation.

The media had labeled the pair by the uncreative term 'Puppy Killers', not because they were killing puppies, but because they used 'injured' animals to attract both children and adults. This information came from a traumatized ten year old who managed to escape when his captors got careless. He was found wandering about in the evergreen crowded woods near Prescott, Arizona. His clothes were streaked with a combination of woody dirt and pine needles that looked like short porcupine quills. With scratches and bruises covering his skinny frame, he looked the part of any Hollywood's version of a war orphan.

I was sitting at my desk; studying the police department photos that Rudy had given me. The gaunt face and the hallow, vacant, coffee-colored eyes of Raphael Martinez pulled my attention away from any other features spread upon the indifferent eight and a half by eleven inch Kodak soft gloss Picture Paper. My hands seem to move of their own will as I shuffled to the next picture: it was taken at the spot where Raphael was found curled up in the middle of a clump of small evergreens that were ailing from beetle rot. I wondered what he must have been thinking as he lay between life and death. The nights were cold as soon as October, but this was early May. He had not eaten for five days. Dehydration had taken him to the point of death. Did he dream about a warm bed and hot food? Or maybe the gruesome death of his mother as she was killed and left in the park for others to find her, like some discarded wrapper from a fast food restaurant.

"How's it going?"

I raised my head and pursed my lips. With a soft movement of my head, I looked up at my wife of fifteen years. She was holding a large coffee cup that featured the smug face of an adult polar bear holding a bottle of Coca Cola at the end of his crossed arms. "That for me?" I gave her a pleading, smiley face and wrinkled my forehead while I put out my hand imitating the look of a surviving seaman who was just rescued.

Waggling her pretty head, she laughed, "No sugar, no cream. Must be yours, Mr. Malone"

Even after our many years together, I sometimes look at her and she looks different. Like someone once said, 'take time to smell the flowers'. I like to take time to appreciate how lucky I am to have Julie for my wife. She's not only pretty, and smart, but a true friend. Not for the things she does but for how she makes me feel about me.

"This kid should not have made it." Holding up his picture I gave it a wag of the wrist. "Five days...no real food or water." I paused, noting the pain that flicked though Julie's eyes. I knew she was thinking about our children. I pulled back the picture as I mumbled, "Plus we think he saw his mother killed." I slurped my hot coffee.

She put a hand on my shoulder. "What about his family? Where's his dad?" Her eyes moved as she struggled to hold back ensuing tears. "Has he got any brothers and sisters?" She gave a short sniffle, as if it were a period at the end of a typed sentence.

I knew, if our eyes met, we would both start dripping tears. I looked away and pretended to be studying my computer's display screen. "The department is desperate for information, but the kid's throat is almost raw from lack of moisture. He's not doing much talking, but he can nod and shake his head." I shuffled the stack of photos and added, "So far they're just asking basic questions. I'll know more when Rudy comes by...we're going to the spot where they found him." I held up the photo for her to see.

Julie's blue-gray eyes examined the picture, but she would not find the answer to 'what kind of people could be doing these Puppy killings?' Without comment she handed back the photo. "How's Rudy holding up? Bet he wishes he had stayed retired."

Strangely, I hadn't thought about that, he always seemed so confident and professional: that probably came with his twenty-one years with the Federal Bureau of Investigation. His white shock of wooly hair seemed to be the perfect crowning for his friendly persona. Because his specialty was placing 'bugs' and stealth communications, the local police had asked for his help in bugging the woods and several unoccupied cabins that were in the area where Raphael was found. Thinking there might be a good story in this case, I was tagging along with Rudy.

I presented Julie with a grin, the kind kids give when they have an innocuous secret. "Naaa. He seems to like it." I put my hands behind the back of my head and looked like I had just sprouted wings over my shoulders. "Rudy feels useful, and he wants to get these guys just as much as I do."

Julie sat on the edge of my desk;, her face had a serious look, like someone getting ready to convey bad news. "Well, he couldn't have liked that article the newspaper put in the Sunday paper." Now Julie's face took on a mask of a person who just opened a container of rotten meat. "It made him seem like a professional mercenary instead of a crime fighter. And why did they drag your name into that story?" She leaned toward me and spoke as if she were betraying the answer to a mystery. "Don't they know people who like these murderers read the papers too? They might decide to come after both of you just too…make a point." She seemed close to panic.

"Not their style, sweets, they prefer helpless women and children." I knew I fell into 'it' even before I ended the statement.

"You mean…like me and our three kids?" Her eyebrows were pinched together: not a good sign.

I flipped out my palms from behind my head and took a defensive pose. "Don't get paranoid on me, Julie! We are the least of their problems, and besides, they will probably have them in jail by the time we get back from New York." I sort of winced. I really wanted to be in town when they got these two lowlifes.

In response to the noise outside, we both looked out the office window. *Saved by the truck.* Rudy's white pickup truck was slowing to a purring halt next to our driveway. I was sure it would be an interesting day as I watched him placing his sound-traps in the buildings and discrete places in the woods.

"Guess you think you just got saved by the bell, huh?" With a feminine snort, Julie exited stage right.

If I said one word I knew I would regret it, so I jumped up and gave her a cheek kiss. "Be back by five, Hon." Feeling like a convict with a death reprieve, I hotfooted it out the front door. I hoped she wasn't right!

Chapter 2

Rudy had the look of a fighter pilot waiting to charge down the deck of a World War I aircraft carrier. His fingers were clenched on the steering wheel: making sure it would not suddenly escape just when he reached the end of the deck. His eyes seemed narrowed yet as alert as a hunter attempting to find a concealed enemy who was at the edge of a deciduous forest.

Attempting to ignore his preoccupation, I jumped into the passenger side of the pristine Dodge. I talked while I plugged in my seatbelt. "Were you able to get everything?"

Contemplatively he slipped the truck into 'D'. "Just about." The truck moved smoothly away from the curb. "I got some stuff coming from Virginia, but we should be able to get an idea of where to set some ears."

I gave in. "Okay Rudy, what's bothering you?" I tried to sound friendly; he wasn't one who liked to talk about personal things.

Rudy took a deep breath, like he was getting ready to swim under water. "I just stopped by the hospital to see Raphael and get a file that Charlie Port put together for me." He did a flash-glance at me. "These guys are really a couple of sick..." He hesitated, "…bastards, Eddie." He took a quick breath and expelled it, hopefully driving the revolting thoughts from his mind.

Puzzled by his words, I asked, "You've seen a lot of bad stuff, Rudy, why does this bother you so much?

We had reached Highway 17; he turned north and punched the accelerator. "I don't know, Ed. Maybe I'm just getting old, but the things these guys are doing to innocent people and animals, is…well, barbaric." He rolled down the driver's side window and a gust of cool fall air swept through the plush cabin. Maybe it would clean out all the tormenting memories.

We moved northward at a legal sixty-five miles an hour, the tires hummed as rhythmically as four strong horses pulling a wagon. The outside air was getting cooler; I zipped up my jacket, but stayed silent while Rudy mutely wrestled with his thoughts. Finally, we dropped down from the highway and turned west toward Prescott.

Rudy wasn't the only one struggling with untellable things; I had a few of my own. "Does anyone really know how far he traveled… or where he might have been kept?" I could almost picture my words floating out of the window, they looked like cartoon balloons.

He shook his head. "Not really, but I think he was either in a cave or in a cellar."

I was about to ask him to explain, but he continued. It was like listening to a different person as he shifted into the voice of a college professor.

"Too much dark earth in his hair, and pieces of fresh tree roots were found wedged into his sneakers." He paused as he pulled off the paved road and onto a dirt one lane that abruptly continued west. "Small pieces…like the bottom of a root…lots of root hairs!"

The truck bounced, swerved, and bucked from side to side as we kicked up billows of yellow-brown dust behind us. Bare rocks and large tree roots lined the pathway like reefs attempting to rip open the bottom of our ship.

"Aren't you afraid they'll see us coming?"

"Don't worry, Ed, if they're here, they know we are here. This kind don't care, they think that no one will ever catch them." Using his head, he pointed with his chin, "We'll slow down when we get closer to the spot where they found little Raphael. The police think the Puppy Killers won't use this spot again, but I know they will…they can't help it. It has been working for them and they think they are in control. They have to think that or live in fear, and they're not willing to do that.

Twenty minutes later we slowed to a crawl. We were almost there. I could recognize the trees from the pictures I had. They looked bigger now. Clumped together like the bars of a jail cell, their bars took on the appearance of rusted steel. "This is the spot?" I knew it was but I had to say something before the pounding in my chest shot through my lungs.

We sat in the truck like two shipwrecked men afraid to step into the shark-infested water. It wasn't hallowed ground, but putting our feet on it would make it too real. It would make everything true and us part of the horror. "Where do you want to put your 'ears'?" Rudy had a lot of pet terms he used for his eavesdropping snoopers. Some of them looked like rocks, some like logs, others were just loose and ready to be placed anywhere an ant could walk.

Rudy moved quickly as he opened his door and planted his foot on the pine needle earth that surrounded us. "Won't know until I see it …first things first. I need to find out where they might be staying and where they are spending their time. Maybe a cave…or some abandoned mine." He reached into the back of the truck and grabbed a knapsack and slung it onto his back. "Let's make some tracks."

Chapter 3

Rudy and I spent a good three hours scouting the area and placing listening devices in caves, abandoned homes, out houses, camping areas, and trail paths. It was the same kind of work that is often done to catch criminals who choose to hide out in remote areas. I served as a pack rat while

Rudy set the 'ears'. Years of experience had trained him to think like the culprits we were tracking. Even though I was born and raised in Alaska, I felt like a cub scout learning to tie advanced seaman's knots.

On the ride back home we tried to free our minds about the Puppy Killers. I knew Julie and I would soon be taking the kids to Fire Island, just off the east coast of Long Island, New York. It's an area that boasts of famous industrialists, movie personalities, and others who are just plain rich. Julie's sister-in-law had inherited a home in a part of the Island called Saltaire.

"Ever been to New York?" I was sure of Rudy's answer, but I needed to start the conversation at some point.

Rudy gave me a quick glance that could not have looked more puzzled if I had asked him if he had ever seen water. "New York, New York?" He shrugged, "Of course...lots of times. Does this have to do with your vacation to Fire Island?" He now resumed studying the rutted road. "I thought that wasn't until June."

"Yaa, that's right, but...well, I hope we have this case wrapped up by then. I'd hate to not be here for the end." The words kind of hung in the air; I never thought they would sound so self-centered. I hadn't said I wanted the killing to stop, just that it might be bad timing for our vacation. I made a face like someone who had smelled his own egotism. "That didn't come out right. I meant I

13

wanted to see this vile team caught as soon as possible."

He gave a sympathetic chuckle. "I know what you meant. You want to be able to include the capture in your new book, but you want it to be first hand. Understandable, Edward." Rudy's tone shifted to a chill that was ethereal. "I want these guys sooo bad I hope I don't get my hands on them." He sucked in a deep breath and calmed his voice. "Don't worry, Ed. We'll get them…soon, I hope." We hit our last bump on the dirt road and swerved east toward Highway 17.

I looked out the back window of the truck cab and wondered what out little traps might tell us. How soon would we be able to hear the voices of the sick Puppy Killers? Where they really living somewhere in the woods, or were they someone's 'loving' neighbors? My neighbor? Rudy's neighbor? Did people pass by them everyday and not know their dreadful secret? Like Rudy, I didn't like the inhuman thoughts that came to mind when I thought of what I'd like to do to them. "Ya, me too."

Chapter 4

Like soft black fluffy shadows, the evergreens silhouetted the evening sunlight as it dropped into the desert southwest. A dark-blue paneled van moved over the unpaved road that snaked from side to side up the south side of a deserted mountain area which had once been a ranch for wealthy people. Long gnarled branches scraped against the dust painted sides of the truck as it rocked over the worn outcroppings of rock and wood.

In the front of the truck sat two figures dressed in jumpers covered with Disney characters, their faces were smooth and angelic. The figure in the passenger seat turned sideways and studied the small child laying on a mattress that was encased in a blue bottom-sheet.

"She's still out. You give her too much either?"

For a young person the voice was throaty from years of smoking and alcohol. The sound better suited a person who was in their late sixties and dressed in a flowered housedress.

An answer was slow in coming. *Jesus, she's still after me just 'cuz I screwed up on that damned kid.* "Give me a break, Lena!" The heavy young man jerked the steering wheel causing the van to tilt slightly to the right. Lena flew backwards, hitting her head against the panel. "The Martinez kid was an accident, we were running low on either." To himself he muttered, "It wasn't my fault."

Rubbing the back of her head, she lashed out with her left hand and punched her brother in the shoulder, "Watch out where you're going!" Again she glanced at their latest prize. "What if he tells them all about us? He can identify us, ya know."

Harold scoffed, "No way, dumb one…I gave him a shot of 'the stuff', he's probably dead by now. No one has ever lasted more than a week before." He snapped a quick look toward the back of the van. Images flashed though his sick mind. He changed the subject. "Don't forget to give the dog some food."

The dog was a mutt, but kids and adults both seem to gravitate to him as if he were Bengi, the famous Disney dog. Long ago he learned to lie quietly in the back of the truck. He raised his head as a handful of dog bones came flying at him.

Lena Pepper crossed her hands across her slightly swollen stomach. Somewhere in their fooling around she had gotten herself pregnant. At quiet times like this she began to brood about their life: it was exciting enough, but the baby was beginning to put a cramp into her fun. For a short time it had even seemed 'kind of cool'. Now, all she could think about was getting rid of it. "You found us a doctor?"

"You know that's too risky right now. They're looking for us." Harold tried to use his best voice, one that sounded caring and wise. "Maybe we should leave the state." He raised his voice as if he had just discovered one of life's great truths. "Ya! That would do it. We'll leave the state and let them chase their tails for a while." His broad grin confirmed how brilliant he was.

The child in the back of the van was moving. She let out a soft groan as she fought for consciousness. Tentatively, Lena was distracted. She grabbed a can of either and a cloth and headed for the back. She snapped at her brother, "Not taking any chances this time." She moved on her hands and knees as the rocking truck continued toward their latest home. Applying some liquid to a cloth she held it tightly to the child's face.

"Is everything okay?" Harold's voice sounded anxious: like a concerned parent asking after a coughing child.

Lena loosened her grip on the cloth, "Sure! She's fine!" Her voice trailed off: she was having one of her 'spells', she liked to call them. Something was happening to her. Lately, she found herself having feelings about their abducted trophies, this never used to happen. She had really enjoyed the games they had played with their victims. Probably most people wouldn't have understood some of the feelings that seem to come over them when they switched from one game to another: parent, lovers, hunters, doctors, undertakers, and whatever passed through their minds. The more stimulating, the better, but lately the games didn't seem as exciting as they used to be. She had tried telling Harold how she felt, but he hit her so hard she had to cover her face with wads of makeup.

"Hey, Lena?"

"Ya?"

"Did you get a look at that guy's face when I hit him with the gun butt?" Harold snorted one of his laughs that caused Lena to shiver. She knew how he was when he got like this. "I'll bet he was surprised. D'ya suppose he ever realized that the dog was just bait?"

She knew it wasn't a genuine question…he just wanted to rant and relive the kill. It was his favorite part, it always had been. "Ya, I'll bet he was really surprised." Lena stroked the girl's forehead, she even considered giving her too much either, but Harold would have really given her a whopping. *I wonder what it's like being a real mother?*

Harold yelled from the front of the truck, "What 'cha doing back there?" He lowered his voice to a threatening tone, "Are you having one of your moods?" He flipped his face toward her, his dark brown eyes flashed to the color of engine burnt oil. His chin tensed and he pushed his lips together, his nose flared. "So help me, little sister. You better snap out of it!" He hit the steering wheel and shifted the truck down to first gear. He pulled behind a large stand of trees, and the truck seemed to be swallowed up. "We're here!"

Lena clutched her bulging stomach and moved to the side door and waited for Harold to open it. With a loud metallic screech, the door opened revealing a string bean of a young man with a scraggly three-day beard growth. His eyes were red rimmed from poor meals and alcohol. With very little stretch of one's imagination, he would have looked like a German made marionette that had been painted by a preschooler. "Get the girl ready." As if to clarify his words he barked, "Give her a hot bath."

He climbed into the back of the van and, from a hunched over position, looked down at the little girl. His body responded with a hot wave that shot through his loins. Effortlessly he picked her up and headed for the small three-room log cabin that was enveloped by trees and shrubs. So well enclosed was it, that it resembled a large pile of dead branches.

"Karl won't like it." Lena was pumping water into a copper tub that was used for bathing. Knowing her brother's touchy disposition, she spoke softly: it was more like she was talking to the copper tub. She flinched and held up her arm as the blow she was expecting struck the backside of her arm and caught her just above her left ear. Defiantly she shouted, "Well, he won't!" Anticipating another blow, she ducked her head.

"That tub of lard can get his own women...this one's mine. Now clean her up!" Whenever Harold hit his sister he remembered how his mother used to beat him with a rolling pin for 'being mean' to his little sister. Even now, he flinched at the prospect of being whacked unconscious. The last time his mother beat him, he killed her with a hatchet, but the fear still hung about in his mind like some daytime nightmare. He could picture the

19

wild wide eyes that lifelessly shot hell and damnation flames at him while she struck with every ounce of force she could manage. Sometimes, when she beat him, she would call him by his father's name. His father had deserted the family just after Lena turned ten years old. "Now get her cleaned up!"

Chapter 5

Karl Harley Boss was fat, but he was also good looking. Besides his wavy blond hair that looked like it belonged in a barber's magazine, his piercing eyes bordered on electric blue. He was the kind of pretty boy all the girls looked at when they entered the room: they never seemed to notice he was 'over weight'. He had earned his name from his bike riding father who was the boss for a crew of crop pickers in California: his mother thought the term 'boss' was his last name. Besides being gullible, his mother was eleven years old when he was born in the back of a Volkswagen Bus somewhere in Colorado where his mother stayed after his father dumped them, and then headed for Mexico with another woman.

Besides hating women, Karl considered chickens more useful; his favorite pastime was killing barroom drunk men. He met Harold in a bar and had just been prepared to take Harold Pepper outside to kill him when Lena came into the bar to haul him out before he got into trouble. For some unexplainable reason, Karl seemed to like Lena better than chickens. He certainly liked her better than her hotheaded idiot of a brother.

Unconsciously, Karl checked his rearview mirror as he approached his turn off: there was a king-cab white truck coming toward him, he road past his exit. After five miles he turned around and slowly returned to his turnoff. His eyes flitted about like a hawk looking for his evening mean. *No traffic...good.* His dark green 1995 Honda was not really made for off the road activity, so he had to drive slowly and be sure to miss any of the outcroppings of rocks and roots.

God, I hope that idiot is passed out. He stretched his neck in an effort to better see the road. "Someday I'm going to kill that crazy bastard." There was no passion in his words; Karl seldom felt anything like what people called anger or fear. His thoughts just 'were'. One shrink at the detention center told him he was a psychopath...whatever that was. He just knew he was different from other people.

Ahead he could see little puffs of gray smoke coming from the cabin; it looked like a small brush fire was beginning behind the billows of dead branches. Lena was standing in the doorway. He liked seeing her, she was a good kid, maybe a bit hair brained, but then she couldn't help it...she was a girl. He raised his hand and waved to her, he had to laugh, his arm moved back and forth like a skin windshield wiper. "Hi, L. how's it going? Any good hunting today?"

She shrugged and raised her hands to stretch in a way to match the sides the doorway.

Chapter 6

"'Scuze me, maim. My girlfriend is about your size, and…ah, would you like this dress?"
Julie Malone knew she was being paranoid. At first she had felt flattered that the young blond man had asked her about a dress he said he was buying for his girlfriend, she felt her mind racing like bolts of electricity; she felt obliged to respond.

"It might be a bit too old for her, if she is your age." Julie ended with a perfunctory smile and continued looking at the rack of blouses.

Karl moved closer to her, as if she had opened the door to her house and invited him in. "Why thank you, maim. I would never have thought about that." An 'ah shucks' expression slipped easily onto his face, "I'd like to buy you a cup of coffee for your kindness." With a practiced smile that would melt the heart of any mother, he flashed an expectant grin.

"I appreciate the offer, but I'm rather pressed for time." Julie used he most firm voice as she chided herself for even talking to the stranger. Maybe he was harmless, but she had the feeling she was looking at a glowing red hotplate that was coaxing her to grab it. Afraid that taking time to check out an item would make her vulnerable; she slung her black purse over her shoulder and headed for the exit.

The pleading voice called out to her, "Sorry if I bothered you, maim." Karl took several steps in her direction, "I didn't mean any harm." Karl Boss felt a self-satisfying grin slowly form beneath his ice blue eyes. He didn't blame himself for the way she reacted; it was obvious the fault was with her. His eyes narrowed as he watched his prey dart out of the discount clothing store and cross over to her car. Karl chuckled as he spoke so softly that his lips barely moved, "This will make the game much more interesting, Mrs. Malone."

Julie fumbled around in her purse, "Where are those damned car keys?" Her head popped up and down like a bird dining on a patch of wild seeds. She was watching the door to the store and fishing into all the corners of her bulging purse. "Ah!" She clutched the keys between her trembling fingers, hadn't she just warned Edward about the consequences of their off shore bank account numbers appearing in the newspaper? Of course she knew she was being ridiculous, but she couldn't seem to help herself. She opened the door and slid into her car seat, with lightning fingers she locked the car doors and began breathing deeply. A tremor erupted from the center of her swelling chest as she watched the 'young man' come out of the building and stop to look around the parking lot.

With a sense of control, and a feeling of power, Karl stood at the exit door and glanced around the parking lot. He even looked up at the sky and used his hand to shade his eyes from the piercing sun. He knew she was watching him…and he enjoyed the fear he imagined she was experiencing.

Trying to calm her, Julie started the car and thought; *he probably doesn't even know who I am.* After placing the car in 'D', she made a sharp right and headed away from the building. At the far side of the lot she again turned right and began her trek to the safety of her home. She hated the trembling that was wracking her body, it was like the feeling she had when she stole a candy bar from the neighborhood grocery store: she had been ten years old, but it was days before she could shake the panic of discovery. At the first traffic light she almost drove into the trunk of the car in front of her.

For the first time she began to hear the talk show host which was chatting about the advantages of eating at a local Hispanic restaurant. The station made a break for local news. The man's voice settled into a tone that seemed too professional to the point of being mechanical. "Today the police continue to investigate the Puppy Killer murders. The police refuse to issue the exact count of the number of victims, but urge the public to be alert. It is rumored the witness-victim now recovering at a local hospital has slipped into a coma. The rumor is unsubstantiated and the police department denies there is any truth to the rumor." *BE ALERT*, that's what she was being. She was just being ALERT. The announcer had switched to another subject just as she turned off of the main road and coasted into her driveway.

The garage began opening before she activated the remote switch: *Edward must be home.* With cobra speed, Julie's hand darted across the seats and snatched her purse from the passenger seat. Controlling her anxiety, she pulled the car into its birthing spot and shut off the car. As if sensing her panic, Edward stood at the entrance to the kitchen, the door held open as if he were guarding the moat to their castle.

"What's wrong, Hon.?" He was reading the tension that overlaid her usually happy visage.

"Oh, Edward!" She felt foolish, even embarrassed for her feelings.

Chapter 7

Rudy Tracker leaned back in his high-backed black leather office chair. After flipping the handle on the side of his chair, Rudy rubbed his aching feet: particularly the joint at the base of his big toe. Not wanting to disturb his wife, he put on a set of earphones and started flipping through his channels that were monitoring the audio traps he and Edward had set that afternoon. Each one had been carefully labeled and tuned in to maximize the reception.

The level of nocturnal activity was surprising for the high desert. A couple of the cabins he had bugged were now occupied; they could be owners up for the weekend, or transients who got lucky. It was not unusual for some of the road bums to use the same places year after year. Some used them as drop off places and others used them to hole up during the entire winter.

Sometimes his listening 'ears' turned defective, and sometimes they got banged around, but almost never were they discovered. It was now after ten o'clock at night. He stretched and grabbed the cooling cup of coffee he had strategically placed just within his reach, but away from the electronic gear. The coffee was cool, like the final sips one takes at a winter ball game. The sugar tasted like weak syrup.

There were raised voices on number 17. It resembled the sounds parents hear when kids are fighting in their bedrooms. With his left hand he attempted to improve the sound but all he got were bits of words resembling some people talking under water. "Somebody's really ticked off" The words slipped from his coffee stained lips…intended for no one but himself. He switched to number 18: it was a sensor mounted at the under edge of a weather worn cedar shingle just outside of the bathroom. The bathroom window had a very serious crack in it and was located close to one of the bedrooms.

"Are you coming to bed?"

Rudy almost jumped out of his skin. A shot of static electricity seemed to touch every nerve in his body. His first response was to turn down the volume, but he glanced up just in time to see his wife rubbing her eyes. She was a small woman of Irish linage and the disposition to go with it.

"Sorry, Kate…I just got caught up in these traps we set today. Right now I'm listening to one hell of a row." To most wives he would have sounded like a sports nut reeling off a game winning play.

Kate shot up her eyebrows and stepped forward, her feminine curiosity was peaked. "Oh! What are they saying?" She held out her hands hoping to enjoy a little eaves dropping.

Handing her the ear phones he blithely said, "Can't really make out a word, its more like watching a TV movie with the sound off. I can't tell if they are either really excited or mad as hell."

Grabbing the earphones she bounced her head as if listening to music. She rolled her eyes with a gesture of impatience. Pulling one of the ears away from her head she said, "Mad as hell, Rudy." She giggled, "At least she is!"

He glanced at his computer to make sure everything was getting recorded. Later he would be able to enhance the sounds and probably make out what was being disputed…just as likely they were arguing about money or sex: at least that was what most of these conversations turned out to be. "Probably just a couple of migrants that are 'squatting' for a few days."

Handing Rudy his headphones she asked, "What are you hoping to hear?" She swished her nightgown under her and sat in a matching overstuffed chair. "A confession, gunshots, cries for help? She knew what the answer would be but she wanted to help him get a few words out. This case was really eating at him.

"A confession would be nice, but for now I'd settle for a few words that would tell me a child was being held against her will…kidnapped." He made a face at his cold coffee…a hint that he would like 'Kat' to get him some hot stuff. "I just have this real sick feeling in the pit of my stomach. You know, like when a doctor tells you you've got terminal cancer, or that your youngest kid has just been run over." He squeezed his lips together and blinked his eyes. He didn't want to cry. Not in front of Kate.

She picked up his coffee cup and peered at the bottom. "Cold?" Her grin was that of an all-knowing Cheshire cat. Tipping her head like a mother addressing her young child, "Would you like some hot coffee?"

He nodded and ran his fingers through his flurry of white hair. "I think I'll be up for a while, Kat. We really need to get these guys." His words were apologetic, but his tone was laced with agony. That's the way he was...he cared. "Would you make sure the coffee stays hot? Just press the button." He smiled as he picked up his headset and started surfing the audio channels. Eight of his channels were showing some activity, but five of them seemed to show the most promise of all the channels which were being recorded.

Channel 8

It was late at night, probably around three in the morning. I had gone to bed with a burping condition that was really annoying. Seeking to escape some of the heat generated by the bed covers, I dangled my leg outside of the blankets. It seems ridiculous now, but at the time it was how I chose to deal with the way I felt.

About three-thirty I got up to go to the bathroom. I really felt lousy! The room seemed out of balance and my eyes felt tight and like they were trying to follow the rotations of a roulette wheel. Even the toilet sheet was moving. The next thing that

29

happened is the experience anyone who has ever thrown up hates to feel coming on.

I began to sweat. The kind of sweat that comes with a chill that makes you feel like the frozen Thanksgiving turkey that has just been trust into a preheated oven. I was going to barf, and there was no way I could stop it…I only hoped I wasn't going to pass out the way I had done so many times in the past. I headed for the tile-covered bathroom floor when all of a sudden the room went quiet.

There was blood seeping from my nose; at least I hoped it was my nose. Apparently I had passed out and hit my face against the cold tile floor. The jig was up; everyone would know that I was not a superhuman. I had a problem and it could be my heart valve. I set about cleaning up the mess on the floor, but I was pretty sure that when Julie saw me in the morning my face would be starting to turn black and blue.

Maybe it was really nothing…just the latest bug going around.

I was weak from the various attacks on my body, but I managed to make it back to bed. I slept, but fitfully.

By the time the morning alarm rang, I had my alibi all worked out. I was the 'criminal' with a secret. I was sure I could pitch my version of what happened, perhaps, by now, I had even convinced myself.

"What happened to your nose, Ed? Does it hurt?" Julie was squinting, her face a picture of sympathy more than concern.

Dismissively I touched my ailing proboscis and did what most red-blooded men would do, I lied. "I was getting up from the toilet, and I slipped on the tile...I really whacked my nose." Notice that I did not mention any of the other peripheral situations: nothing about spinning rooms, nothing about sweating, nothing about passing out and bleeding.

She responded in kind...nothing really important, just like a stubbed toe. "Well, I bet it's going to back and blue your eyes." She peered closely at the swelling bags beneath my eyelids. Her forehead wrinkled, "Sure you're okay?" She shook her head and continued preparing for work.

Julie is a well-credentialed private school teacher, and a Doctor of Education. Julie teaches at the elementary level. She loves the work, and adores 'her' children.

I nursed a cup of hot tea and set about dismissing the events of last night from my mind. That became somewhat difficult on the occasions when I passed by a lying mirror. By ten o'clock I was busy working at my latest book that would be based upon the hunt for the 'Puppy Killers'. I wasn't sure it would be a number one best seller, but it might make it into the top ten if my agent and publisher were willing to spend the promotional dollars.

Before noon I would need to call Rudy and see if he had anything, at any rate, I was sure we would end up going back into the woods to check on the 'traps' he had set. Last night was forgotten.

Chapter 9

The pieces of wood felt cold to his hands. Harold Pepper cussed as he picked up the pieces of dead limbs that lay on the forest floor. A large bundle of twigs was loaded on top of his left arm as he turned to carry his load of firewood to the small cabin. He sucked at another cut on his right hand. Harold was almost to the door when he stopped and turned his head toward the sound of a vehicle that was making its way up the incline to the east.

The cabin door opened. Lena stood at the entrance and looking irritated, "It's about time you got your butt back here, the fire's almost out." She popped up her head and looked in the same direction as Harold. Her face flashed a message of danger, her body tensed like a doe in the forest when it hears the approach of a predator. "Reckon that's Karl come back from town." Still looking down the road, she stepped back and spoke softly to her brother, "Better get inside."

After several long strides, Harold dropped his load of wood on the floor to the right of the aging rock fireplace. The clattering seemed to go unheard with the prospect of Karl Harley Boss's arrival. Harold was bigger than Karl, but lacked the badger instincts that made Boss so dangerous. The way that Lena saw it was, Harold was cruel because he was brainless. Karl was vicious because he had no heart: he killed or tortured not because he liked it, but because he didn't care. She liked him because he was handsome and could charm a pig out of her favorite hog wallow and he had a certain kind of power about him.

"Put some more wood on the fire, little brother, you know how Karl hates to be cold." Mixed feelings zipped through her as she anticipated Karl's unpredictable moods. Sometimes he was jovial when he returned, but other times he was spoiling to hurt someone…and she was usually the target. Harold would make a lot of words and fume about the house, but he wouldn't do anything to try to protect her. "Hope he's in a good mood."

"Yeah." He put a pile of logs on the dwindling fire, then he blew some air at the base of the pile and watched the grayish sludge turn to small glowing coals.

Together they waited on the other side of the door: like frightened children wondering if their violent father was coming home drunk or sober. Lena watched the door while Harold tended the fire and tried to still his thumping heart. They both tensed as they heard the car's engine stop: he would be coming in soon.

There was no preamble, no knock, and no shout. The door flew open and the smiling face of Karl Boss came bounding into the room. He was half laughing and half talking as he began speaking. "You wouldn't believe where I just was." He shook his head and his blond curls bounced about like yellow meringue. He moved next to the developing fire and slapped his hands together. "I was at the Wal-Mart, or was it a K-mart; I never can keep those places straight." He gave a quick chuckle and looked around to make sure they were paying attention. Ever since he left the department store he had been smiling and hooting.

Lena could tell he was testing their interest. She didn't want to set him off, "Well, what happened?" She leaned forward feigning uncontrollable interest.

Imitating the actions of a father telling a bedtime story to his two infants, he spoke softly, "I just had a fun time with Kate Tracker." He giggled.

Harold and Lena exchange confused glances. "Who?"

Karl pretended to be crestfallen. Slowly, as if speaking to a child who was mentally challenged, "The wife of that old cop who is helping the police to find us." He snickered, "It was a real hoot."

"Did she know who you were?" Harold inquired as he nonchalantly stirred the fire. "I don't mean to be critical...just curious."

With a face that reeked of compassion, Karl shook his head and replied, "Of course she didn't know who I was…I'm here aren't I? He used his knuckles to rap Harold on the head, "Jesus, boy, why don't you use that noggin for something besides eating?"

"He didn't mean no disrespect, Karl!" Lena interjected.

"Yeah, yeah…I know." He frowned, but just as quickly changed to a smile. "I even asked her about a dress I was picking out for my girl friend." (Giggle!)

"For me?" It was a dumb question, but Lena spoke before thinking.

"Come on, you two. You miss the point! It was fun! She'll remember it later when I kill her."

"Did that store have a security camera?" Harold acted as if he were speaking to the flaming logs. "Someone, like her husband, might pull them."

Karl fell silent. Slowly, his face seemed to change. It was like watching the special effects of a movie, as his eyes grew cool and narrowed. Harold had been right; the dummy had actually shown some brains. "Lena, get me a beer!" Of course he was changing the subject, but even more importantly, he was reaching out to control someone: it was what made him feel a sense of power. He pitched a small log toward the fire: it sailed over the left shoulder of Harold: glowing red sparks scattered about landing on Harold's hand.

Harold pushed back from the fire, "Hey! Watch it! You almost set me on fire!" It was a bit dramatic considering the few sparks that really endangered Harold, but it had frightened him. He had expected some sort of outburst from Karl, but the limb sized log had caught him off guard.

In a mocking tone, Karl said, "What's wrong, little girl…did the sparks scare you?" Karl snatched the bottle of beer from Lena's hand; he gave her protuberous belly a look of disgust. Grasping the neck of the beer bottle, he was prepared to break the bottle over Harold's head if he made any threatening movements. "You know, Dumbo, you just might be right." He pitched the bottle to the back of the stone fireplace: the bottle shattered spreading shards that fell to the bottom of the hearth.

Lena flinched as she watched the bottle explode. "We gave the girl a sedative, Karl. I think she will be out for some time."

Karl seemed to be preoccupied. "You think that we can get some money for this one…we're really broke. We need some money."

She felt like cowering, but knew that it would probably make things worse. Her eyes flicked toward Harold, but she knew he would be of no help…he was all talk.

"How about it, Hal? You up to a little night business?" Karl's words were measured, perhaps challenging.

Harold knew he had hit a nerve when he had mentioned the surveillance tape, but he had enjoyed barbing Karl: he was a real horse's ass. Without looking up from the fire, Harold asked,

"So, what 'cha got in mind?" He knew that Karl would want to get the tape or disc.

"Your sister says we need money. I say we keep the little girl for a bit longer…might need her." Karl squatted next to Harold and spoke next to his ear, "Let's dump the safe at the Wal-Mart and get the tape at the same time…two birds…one stone, so to speak."

Harold looked over his shoulder and into the worried eyes of his sister, Lena. For a second he wondered what she would ever do if she didn't have him to take care of her. Not that he was the best brother in the word, but at least he had some feelings about her. "You'll be all right?" Her answer didn't really matter, but it was his way of saying yes to Karl.

"Sure." Lena folded her arms across her chest and rubbed her arms as if trying to warm them. "Bring back some milk, will ya?"

Harold nodded and then he stood up. He looked down at Karl: he felt big, but he knew he could never take Karl in a 'fair' fight. One day one of them would end up killing the other. "I 'spose you know how to open a commercial safe?"

With a dismissive snort, Karl smirked and began walking out of the room. "Wake me at seven o'clock." He opened the door to the refrigerator and snatched another bottle of beer as if he were grabbing it from the hand of some defiant person.

Both Lena and Harold listened as Karl's footfalls went up the wooden stairs and down the upstairs hallway. They remained silent as if by not speaking Karl would not exist. Their eyes met, unspoken words were exchanged. Harold was sorry for ever introducing Karl to his sister and she was sorry for 'falling in love' with Karl.

Harold tipped his head, indicating they should go outside. Lena followed him, being sure to make as little noise as possible. After they had walked a good distance from the house they stopped behind a large stand of dry brush.

Lena spoke first. "I know what you're going to say, Hal, but he really isn't that bad. He doesn't mean anything by it." For one of the few times in her life she realized where her life had taken her. She was pregnant, and caught between two angry men. Her life wasn't looking too good.

Without preamble, Harold Pepper wrinkled his forehead and began breathing deeply, almost exhaling like a rabid bull. "I'm gonna kill him, Le. That SOB doesn't deserve to live."Harold now started speaking conspiratorially: fast, but still hushed. "If we don't do something, one day he is going to kill both of us…when he decides he doesn't need us anymore, or that we know too much." He took a quick breath.

Lena used the opening to interject. She tipped her head, in a pleading manner. "You know…Harold… that he might be the father to this lump."
She used her fingers to pat the pregnant bulge that housed her forth-coming child. "Doesn't that mean

anything to you? She placed her hands on her hips and tried to look motherly: it had worked on her father.

Chapter 10

"Ed?"

"Yeah?"

"Rudy's on the line!" Julie fought off an urge to listen in on the conversation. She punched the 'hold' button and hung up the phone, but her eyes were studying the wall hanging phone as if it would magically reveal its secrets.

I snatched the white remote-telephone and smiled, "What'cha up to?"

"Six-one, the last time I checked."

We both eked out a short chuckle: it was a common joke we liked to offer to each other. Rudy continued, "I've been giving some thought to that creep that was talking to Julie the other day."

"Yeah?" I knew that I sounded curious. I had related the details to Rudy as best I could, but I had not wanted Julie to get too concerned. Alert, but not worried. "Sooo?"

He responded with a tease. "How would you like another chapter to your book?" He paused just long enough to sink the fishhook a little deeper. "Let's go to that Wal-Mart and see if they caught that little encounter on tape. At least we might be able to find out who has been sending you those messages…at worst, we will able to get me a new book to read."

I hesitated. Not because I was reluctant to go, but chided myself for not having thought about it. Of course I didn't have the credentials that Rudy had, but I could have suggested it to him. "Sounds great, pardner. When do we ride?"

"I'd like to catch Farley before he goes home or locks up for the night."

"You know the manager?" I wasn't really surprised; Rudy made it a habit of meeting people who were in charge. ' Never know when you're going to need a friend.' He always said.

"We go to the same church." He glibly let the words flow out as if he had rehearsed the answer. "Likes basketball, too."

"Figures." I returned an obliging snort and asked, "How about after dinner?"

"Yours... or mine?" Rudy always ate at a much later hour.

Ignoring the disparity, I responded before he came up with another idea. He frequently did.

"Six…sharp." Before he had a chance to hang up, I wanted to pose another question. "Do you think this has anything to do with the traps we set? You know…the Puppy Killers?" I was hoping he would 'poo-baa' my inquiry.

"Wouldn't be surprised, Ed." He paused in order to soften his tone. "I know you didn't want that answer, but I don't think we ought to dismiss the

40

possibility, Buddy. If, and I mean IF, these are the same people, then they are capable of anything."

I really didn't want to discuss the subject, especially where my worrywart wife could hear it. "Get your point. See you at Wal-Mart at six." I waited and then asked, "Okay?"

"Sure, I'll have Kate fix up an early ceremonial dinner." The line went dead. I could picture him badgering Kate to fix an early meal. Ha!

Surprisingly, Julie didn't say anything when I told her Rudy and I were going to do some work on the book. She simply nodded, as she often does, and continued grading papers. I wanted to ask, but thought it better if I didn't know if she had been snooping at the phone.

My eyes flipped back and forth from the table to the wall clock: like someone watching an up and down tennis match. Have you ever had the feeling someone must have Super-glued the minute hand to the face of the clock? I don't know whether I was apprehensive or impatient. Julie and I just pecked at our dinner as the time parade-marched on. At six o'clock I found myself supernaturally transported to the department store. Rudy was waiting.

"This shouldn't take too long; Farley is a pretty succinct guy. A man of few words, one might say."

I could tell Rudy had something else on his mind, but I didn't bite. "It's okay. I've got all night." We passed through the first set of tall glass doors. As usual, we were welcomed to the establishment by a set of smiling elderly people who resembled the standard family pictures of a pair of grandparents.

We had just passed the display of 'on sale' garden hoses when we spotted a thin, dark-haired man who was sporting a navy-blue vest that must have had more round metal stickers that a freshman working at aTGIF restaurant. He had something in his hand; it looked like a VHS tape.

As if revealing a national secret, Rudy spoke out of the side of his mouth. "That's Farley…the store manager. I think he has our tape."

If he had 'our tape', it was obvious that it had to be a copy of the department's surveillance tape, but then, it made sense: Julie would have to pick out the guy. I hadn't thought of that. I wasn't even sure she would want to. I waved to Farley. Were we about to see the face of one of the Puppy Killers? I wondered.

Chapter 11

For several days Julie had been bugging me about making the final plans for out trip to New York. I had the tickets, but there were clothes to buy and plans for our kid's activities.
Christine, our ten year old, would be interested in fun and games. She's just coming into that age

where she enjoys watching boys fall all over themselves when she flirts with them. Both of our girls are real beauties, (no prejudice in our family): they take after their mom. Christine in the one with the copper colored hair and puppy eyes.

Dell, eight years old, has honey-blond hair and hazel eyes: she's the athlete. Dell is a bit tall for her age and loves to dance. She doesn't like to flirt as much as she likes to be the one in control.

And then there is Joel. Donkeys could learn the art of stubbornness from him. If it can be disassembled, Joel has taken it apart: putting things together will have to wait until he cares if one of his latest projects works or not. There are days when we think that the movie *Toy Story* had Joel in mind when they characterized the bad boy next door. For being only eight years old, he can be a charmer, ask the constant victim of his 'sweetness': his mother. I'm not too sure what will interest him the most about the Island, but I am certain it will require the combined services of the fire department and the local constabulary.

The Puppy Killer couldn't have come at a more difficult time, but I had to put my part of the investigation on hold until we return. I could still write, but that would mean my on-hands feelings and experiences would be limited. We only had two weeks left before we fly out of here and got to JFK.

I was working on a draft concerning our trip to the woods, when Rudy called me to tell me Farley had been killed last night. "What happened?" It was the only thing I could think to say. I thought I knew the answer, but I sank into a pool of sick feelings. Farley's smiling face popped out at me; I could still see his smile as he walked toward us.

The pause was pregnant. I was certain Rudy was trying to compose himself. He always gave the impression of being a tough guy, but anyone who knew him could not escape the kindness which was in his soul. "Money was taken…and so were his video tapes from the surveillance VCRs. The police are operating on the premise it was just a normal robbery, even though the robbers didn't get much." I heard him swallow and clear his throat.

I had to ask my question. "What do you think? I mean, do you think it was our guy coming back to get the tapes just in case Julie could identify him?" That sick feeling was moving about in my gut like the propeller of an outboard motor. *Was Julie in danger? Maybe a trip to New York wasn't so bad an idea after all.*

"He doesn't know we have a copy, Ed. Hell, he probably doesn't even remember talking to Julie."

Rudy struggled with the words. I could tell it. I had listened to enough cops and reporters to know BULL when I heard it. I snapped back at him. "Don't give me that Bull, Rudy…not me." I tried to keep my tone civil, but even I could hear the tremor in my voice. "I'm sorry, Rudy. I know it's

44

not your fault." I shifted my voice to cordial, "We wouldn't even have our copy of the tape if you hadn't thought about it." I would have to get Julie to check out the tape before she found out about Farley.

"Has Julie seen the tape?" Rudy sounded remote and clinical, but there was also a flavor of concern.

After a split second of guilt, I answered. "Na. Sorry, but I didn't want to scare her. I'll show it to her when she gets home." After my outburst I felt a bit foolish.

"Where is she now?"

I didn't like the edge in Rudy's voice: it sounded like panic. "What are you **not** telling me, Rudy?" I waited for a few seconds before I asked the real question that was bothering me. "Are we in some sort of danger?" The inquiry was sort of like asking if I might get stung for jabbing a stick into a functioning beehive. The answer was obvious: eventually the bees were going to attack.

He gave his pat answer. "I wouldn't rule it out."

I knew he was right, these types of things had happened before. After all, criminals don't always appreciate all I am doing is writing a 'harmless' book. "Other than there was the stupid newspaper article...how did they get our name?"

"I don't know, but it's reasonable to assume they consider us as a different threat than the police."

This is where, being a writer, my mind began to run wild with various tragedy plots: people breaking into the house and killing my family while we slept, that kind of thing. I couldn't seem to shake the attack of the plot people. "So, what shall we do?"

"I doubt they will do anything right away, but we should be on the alert. You know, watch out where the kids and Julie are and keep the house buttoned up." Rudy switched to his sinister voice: low and pensive. I always hated it when he did that. "I haven't heard anything on traps we set out, but then…we could have missed them."

"Should we check on them tomorrow?" I wanted to fell like I was doing something, anything, proactive.

"Sure, we can do that…how's eight?"

"Sounds good, reluctantly, I hung up the phone, I wanted to keep talking, but I knew it wouldn't help. Instinctively I began to look around the room, half expecting to see Puppy Killers filling the room, hanging from the ceilings, or even peering through the windows. For now, I decided to hold off telling Julie until tomorrow: I was sure Rudy would do the same for Kate.

"What was that all about?" Sometimes I wonder what God had in mind when he created women; they have the curiosity of a paranoid cat, but only when you want to keep something from them. The rest of the time I can pilfer Julie's purse right in front of her and she pulls a sergeant Schultz on me: 'I see nothing…NOTHING.'

Casually I rearranged some papers on my disk as I eloquted with my most relaxed voice. "Oh, that

46

was just Rudy. We were discussing the progress of my book." My demeanor then turned politely dismissive.

Julie responded with guileless innocents. It was beginning to feel like a chess match. "I thought I heard you ask him if we were in any danger."
As casually as a housewife wiping her hands on a cooking apron, she asked, "Are we?"

I suppose a hundred responses flashed though my mind, but I knew none of them were going to work as much as the truth, so I 'wimped out' and told her the truth, but just the highlights. She was okay until I mentioned we should keep an eye on the kids. I could see a soft shade of rose pink beginning to form on her cheekbones; it was a hot red by the time she spoke.

"You mean those Puppy Killers might actually, intentionally, target our children?"

An African lioness had nothing on Julie, she was not just being protective, she was in the third stage of anger. I was happy to find out she was not mad at the book or me. I comforted myself with the assuring words any man would understand how I felt. I quoted Rudy, "Well, Rudy thinks it would be wise to not dismiss the thought."

She spoke softly, as if reflecting on every word. "Why would they come here?" Her wheels were turning.

"Rudy thinks the same guy who killed the Wal-Mart manager might be the guy who was bothering you the other day." That's as far as I wanted to take the conversation unless she said the magic words.

Her eyes widened, "I can identify him, Ed." Her face changed to understanding. "Why would Rudy think that bum would remember me?"

"He thinks he pestered you on purpose. Maybe he was just casing the place, but also, maybe he knew who you were and he was counting cue."

"Cue?"

"Yeah, the Indians used to sneak up on a potential victim and either take something or leave a mark on the person just to let them know how vulnerable they were." I studied her worried face, "You know…'look what I could have done to you.'" I didn't like what I saw in her eyes: it was a kind of sickening fear. "We got a tape from the store; we hoped you would be able to identify the guy talking to you in the ladies' department. Do you feel up to it?"

Her voice sounded like she had just drunk boiling hot coffee, "Yes!"

Chapter 12

I think everyone remembers certain events in their life: some are happy, some are sad. It's not unusual for people to try to forget those events which were traumatic.

As I remember it, it was just after three o'clock in the morning. I looked at the electric alarm clock: its red digits glared back at me. Somewhere in my mind I had heard the sound of breaking glass. As many times as I had watched scenes like this unfolding from a TV scene, I was not really prepared for my feelings. The first thing that occurred to me was to freeze, you know... if I don't move the boogieman won't get me.

I'm not sure how long I played ice cube before I looked over at my sleeping wife. *Maybe I was dreaming*. The room looked strange until I realized what the problem was. The night-lights in the walls were not on. The alarm clock was on operating on battery backup. Conclusion: the power was off which meant our remote phones would not work. An unfamiliar chill shot through my body. The feeling of stark fear began pounding through my nerves; my face was hot from increased blood pressure.

"Julie?" I knew I was speaking quietly, but even my softest words sounded like an angry school principal using a crowd control bullhorn. I was really concerned she would bark back something like, 'I'm sleeping'.

Sounding like a war-wounded patient on her last legs, she mumbled through closed lips, "What?"

Okay, she was awake, now how do I tell her someone has broken into our house and not have her shout out or break out with a panic fit. Thank God the girls were spending the night with one of

Christine's friends. Joel was across the hall, but he could sleep through paramedics passing a body-ladened gurney over his bed, and actually had. "I think I heard glass breaking down stairs."

"Is Joel down there?" She was only mildly alerted.

I dropped my hand into the stiff leather briefcase that is next to my side of the bed. My hand slipped neatly into the case and grasped my nine-millimeter Glock automatic. The clip was full and in place.

"I'll be right back. I'm going to check on Joel." I flipped back the covers and moved next to the wall: using it to cover my back.

I didn't notice, but Julie reached for the phone. If someone were down stairs they would have seen the light come one. "Ed? The phone doesn't work…not even a hum."

I could have sworn she had stolen my bullhorn. "I know." Suddenly it occurred to me. We have a cell-phone. "Use you cell-phone. Call 911."

"It's in my purse."

"So?" I challenged.

"It's downstairs."

I shook my head and hurried across the hall to get Joel. He was so deeply asleep that, when I picked him up he just flopped on my shoulder like a tired puppy. I checked the hallway and then silently dashed across: it felt like it was the width of a football field. I also noticed the noise downstairs was becoming less muffled.

Julie almost ripped Joel off my shoulders. We put him on two pillows behind my heavy wooded dresser. Julie and I crouched against the wall and waited. There was little else we could do.

The horrible thing about waiting was the pounding of blood that was rushing through our fragile bodies. Our frights were so numerous it was impossible to fixate on any one of them. I was sure I was going to forget to breathe. A cloud-shadowed moon broke through and cast a clinical white glow into our room. I looked at Julie and Joel, I could feel my bowels loosen as I realized I might be the only chance to save them.

"Do you think it's him?" Julie whispered into my ear and I felt the wispy warmth from her vibrating body.

"Don't know, but we had better be quiet." As I tightened my grip on the Glock I was surprised to notice my hands felt like frozen meat. I had left the door to our room slightly open: we could hear movement in the hallway. Stealthy feet slowly creeping in the direction of our room: it sounded like more than one person. *Maybe it was Rudy, or some policemen.* Julie seemed to read my mind.

"If that's the police, wouldn't they yell out?" Her breath was getting cold. "I mean, isn't that what they're supposed to do?"

I wanted to answer her, but I had to wait until the strange sensation left my head. It was strange, like a numbing darkness that was incasing and pressing against my brain. It passed. "Yeah, they should." I

51

took a deep breath and whispered, "It's not the kids, our friends, or the police, Julie." My heart was pounding; skipping beats, and seemed to be shutting off at intervals.

She clutched my left arm with the strength of an Olympic weight lifter. "I can hear them, Ed. They are checking the kid's rooms."

I think it is impossible to relate the amount of relief we felt because none of our children were in those rooms. I was focused on the hallway activity: they had stopped moving, or al least I couldn't hear them. My pistol was in my right hand or I would have patted Julie's white-knuckled fingers.

Julie tightened her grip on my arm, something I would have believed to be impossible. "Ed, they're coming to our room."

I was certain that, if I could see her eyes, they would be as big as two fried eggs. I raised the Glock and made sure the safety was off. I think my stomach was making noises.

Julie was totally fixed upon the door into our room, so she didn't notice when Joel moved from side to side. Abruptly he sat up and attempted to look around, but the only light was from the intermittent moon. "Hey, what's going on, Dad?" The words exploded into the room like a TV set that had just come on.

In spite of myself, I turned to face the frightening words: the hallway people would now know we were in the room waiting for them. In the hallway I could hear their voices but I could not make out the words. The tension in the sound soon stopped.

"Okay, you guys…we are leaving. We wouldn't hurt you; we were just looking for a few things to sell." Under other circumstances the speaking would have been comical because the words had been spoken like some junior high school kid auditioning for the lead roll in Romeo and Juliet: unconvincing, and clumsily delivered. They still managed to cause a lump in my throat.

By now Julie had put her hand over Joel's mouth and he had seemed to grasp something of the situation. I rotated my left arm and broke it loose from my wife's vice grip. To both of them I indicated they should do nothing and say nothing. I was having another brain freeze, but managed to fight it off. It was when the doorknob began to turn that I felt the warmth from a shot of adrenalin course though my veins. The hammer on the Glock was in the back position, ready to fire. I was breathing in short fast gasps, the pistol was doing a nervous dance, but I was focused.

I could hear Julie and Joel, perhaps it was breathing, and maybe it was just the movements of hugging one another. The bedroom door began to move, like when a CD movie is on *still* and *slow advance*. There was a faint outline of a body, but there was no back lighting. I began to squeeze the trigger, but suddenly I got a pang of conscience. "Go away! I have a gun, and I'm prepared to use it." My mouth was dry and I was experiencing tiny quivers.

The voices conferred with one another then the one in the back said, "WE don't believe you, mister. We don't want any trouble so just give us what we want and we'll go away." The tone was practiced-persuasive, not like the junior high auditioner.

"Go away NOW!" I shouted.

The door moved. They were coming in. I fired…four shots at the man in front. The sound bounced off of the close walls: it was ear splitting: a strong smell of burned gunpowder drifted about the room.

"Jesus!" Someone shouted.

The man in front moved backwards as if he were going to lean against the wall, his handgun dangled from his left arm. *Was he going to fire at me?* I could hear the racing footsteps of the other man as he beat a hasty retreat down the hallway. I raised my weapon and prepared to fire, but the man's body seemed to turn to sawdust as he slipped effortlessly to the floor. *Could he be faking?*

"Stay still!" I barked as quietly as I could. Julie and Joel froze. I couldn't see their faces. I was sure they were just like mine: pained, dry, and painted with panic. "I'm going to check on this guy and then get your cell phone. We need to call the police…maybe they can get the other guy."

I knew the right technique for approaching the dead man. Just in case. As soon as I could, I kicked the revolver from his hand. Even in the dimly lighted room I could see the bullet holes in his chest, one had caught him in the throat. If nothing else, Harold Pepper had bled to death. From what I could see of him, he looked like a poorly painted mannequin. My stomach felt sour: I wanted to throw up, but another side of me felt proud: I had protected my family, vanquished the evil invader. My hand was shaking uncontrollably.

Chapter 13

Lena paced the floor; she was nibbling on her already cropped fingernails. For the fifth time she returned to the dust covered glass pane that gave her a view out of the south side of the wooden cabin. She no longer paid any attention to the creaking of the wooden floor. There was someone out there, a white headed man who was snooping about. Randomly he would dart in and out of the brush or kneel down by a pile of rocks. *Who is he? What does he want?* She wished that Harold and Karl would get back from town. *Karl would know what to do.*

Rudy moved about as if he had not one care in the world. There were no cars at any of the cabins in his route and it was early in the morning. For early June it seemed a little cooler than usual, just the way he liked it. The air seemed cleaner and the animals were already busy scurrying about for their daily bread. Most of the nighttime predators had returned home to enjoy their hunt and share with the family. Rudyhad only seen two late night coyotes loping about like a couple of teen-agers slinking home after a night of stupidity. So far, everything seemed in order: loud and clear signals from all stations.

Rudy found a log that was hidden among some Juniper trees: a perfect place to open his Thermos and enjoy some of his ' fully leaded' coffee. Rudy slipped his backpack off of his shoulders and rested it against the trunk of an undernourished tree that had been scorched by a flash of lightening. For amusement, he watched a colony of ants that were diligently searching for nourishment. Their long lines of workers were oblivious to the giant who was pouring liquid into a metal cup.

Lena bobbed and weaved about the window. The man had disappeared behind a bunch of short trees. Turning her head, she scoured the room for some sort of defensive weapon, and then there was the little girl upstairs. For now the girl was controlled by a drug induced sleep. She decided she must take some sort of action: her eyes locked on the double-bitted axe that rested against the cobble-stoned fireplace. A pang of guilt stabbed at her: she wasn't a killer like Harold or Karl. She had killed, but only once and that was in self-defense. Lena's fingers latched comfortably around her brother's nicked and soiled Louisville Slugger baseball bat.

Even with her bulging stomach her tiny feet moved gracefully along the high desert land: being raised in the woods had to have some advantages. In the fashion of a medieval knight, the bat was clutched tightly in her two hands: it covered her front and her face. In only a few minutes she could see the man, he was sitting and drinking something. The path to his back was not very clear, but it might be doable. Lena stopped as she heard the sound of an approaching car, it was to her left: toward the highway.

Rudy was still sipping his coffee when he heard the sound of an approaching vehicle. Rudy's eyelids flipped upward, not that he would see anything, but it was one of those involuntary responses that we all make. Next he stood up and attempted to see between the bushes. It wasn't likely it would be Edward, so it might be any number of people who were squatting in this area, maybe even the Puppy Killers. He jerked as he felt movement behind him.

Because of the closeness of the surrounding trees, Lena could not get as full a swing as she wanted to, but the bat whizzed through the air catching the tall man across the back just where his shoulders met with his neck. The cup slipped from his hand as he collapsed to the ground, his body bridged across a thin trail of coffee. The car was getting closer, she hesitated, the bat held high above her head. Her body seemed frozen in indecision, should she hit the man in the head? The approaching car might be Harold and Karl coming back, but it also could be some strangers or even the police. She looked down at the sprawled form: ants were already crawling over his hands and into his white hair.

Karl was almost to the cabin. He wasn't sure he wanted to be here but he couldn't just leave Lena and the girl at the cabin, they knew too much to allow them to fall into the hands of the police: especially if Lena found out about Harold. Maybe he would have to kill her, he really didn't want to, but he was going to have to travel light now that they had botched the job at that author's house. His fingers tightened on the steering wheel beyond the point where they hurt him. Just thinking about the way things went made him long for some violent outlet. He needed to kill someone.

Chapter 14

Lena watched as Karl slammed the door to his rattletrap. She had seen him like this before: he was in the mood for one of his cruel streaks. She wanted to be strong, even tough, but her body began to shake as she anticipated that she might easily become his target. Maybe Harold would be able to distract him…but where was Harold? With her eyes fixed upon the car, she watched as Karl marched toward the cabin. She decided on a bold plan. Moving out of the woods, she left Rudy lying on the ground.

High in the air a set of four F16 fighter jets streaked though the sky; their engines pierced the high desert silence with a roar that was bone shattering.

Since Lena had just come out of the cabin a few moments ago. Her timing was such that it looked as if the noise had come from her opening the door.

Both Lena and Karl placed a palm over their eyes as they looked to the disturbance in the sky.

"Where's Harold?" Lena tried to act nonchalant as she continued to follow the path of the jets. She knew how Karl hated to have anyone question him.

Curling his lips in a gesture of disgust, he barked, "Damned jets!" Ignoring any kind of eye contact, he said, "Hal wanted to get some supplies before we left town. He'll meet us in Kingman." Something about lying made him feel better: a flush of calm caused him to make a deep sigh.

"We're leaving?" She caught herself in time, just before her tone was questioning.

"Yeah, this place is getting too hot, Le." Karl was scanning about the room. Either he was distracted or he was taking inventory and deciding what to take and what to leave.

Should she tell him about the man she had clubbed with the baseball bat? If she did, there was a good chance Karl would kill him just for the amusement. On the other hand, he would be proud of her, it might even boost his feelings for her. Lena always sought the approval of men. She was about to tell him when he stopped pacing about and cast his eyes toward the upstairs.

"We're going to have to get rid of her...she could identify us you know." He moved his mouth about. Karl was considering the best way to get rid of the little girl. He rubbed his scruffy chin with the hand he had cut when he broke the glass window at the Malone house. Dried blood colored his palm.

"You're hurt." Lena sounded alarmed, not just for him, but now she had questions about Harold: she kept them to herself. She wanted to distract him from killing the little girl. It seemed her maternal instincts were beginning to influence her mind. Now was not a good time to talk about the stranger she had clubbed. "Here. Let me clean up that cut." Gingerly she held his hand, "What happened?'

Karl had always been a sucker for medical attention. It had been his favorite thing his mother had done for him, whenever she was sober or not shacked up with some rummy who bought her latest bottle. Lots of times he had picked fights at school just to get some cuts and bruises. Mom would always take his side, 'that nasty bully' she would say. Yeah, Karl was always the sweet innocent boy that others picked on. "Hal and me were trying to talk some reason into that writer and his pal. The writer pulled a knife on us." Karl held her hand and moistened his eyes: he could fake tears anytime he wanted to.

"What?" Lena sensed the bad news before it was spoken. "What?"

"I lied to you, Le." He gently tightened his grip on her hand as if he were trying to strengthen her. "That writer guy killed Hal…for no reason, Le. He just killed him. Shot him dead." Tears seeped from his compassionate eyes. "I was lucky to escape, Le." Karl swallowed as if the news was too horrible to even speak the words. He had intended to tell her at another time, but he had learned to trust his timing when it came to dealing with women.

Her mind seemed to go blank. Nothing seemed real; it was as if she ceased to exist. She took in short shuttering breaths as she stared blankly at the mouth that had spoken such inconceivable words. *Harold's dead? Harold's dead?* "That's a cruel joke, Karl. I don't appreciate it." She grinned, "Did Hal put you up to this?" It all made sense now; the guys were always trying to pull jokes on her. This was just a cruel joke. Harold would soon come walking through the door. It was a joke!

Holding Lena by the shoulders, Karl tried to focus on Lena's eyes, but she kept shifting them as if to avoid the reality of what had happened. He watched as her words of denial flowed from her lips. It was just like his mother had acted when she had learned of the first person Karl had murdered. Denial!

"Where's Hal?" Lena's face contorted as if, finding some particular shape it would crack the code that would make Harold magically appear. Her voice faded into a sobbing string of words that were incomprehensible. As her body sagged to the ground a new look flashed onto her face as a gush of fluid appeared from between her legs. Dazed, she said, "My water just broke."

Karl's eyebrows pinched together as he dropped his vision to the wet spot on the floor. "You peed on the floor!" He could not have sounded more confused if she had suddenly sprouted two heads. "What's wrong with you?" Karl's face became a mask of disgust.

Unable to believe Karl did not know what she meant, she responded with a joke, "Oh, yeah, I do this every once in a while…just for fun." She paused and then, she realized he was not joking. "I'm having the baby KARL!"

She sat down on the already soiled couch, "I need to get to a hospital, and NOW!" Before the words even left her mouth she knew he was never going to agree to the exposure they would get at a hospital. "Jesus, Karl, I need some help here." She watched as he just stood like some Alaskan totem pole.

"Don't you know someone who can do this?" Karl shook his head from side to side: a picture of disbelief. "Can't you wait?" Now his head made little nods, "Maybe until we reach Kingman." He gave her a forced smile to encourage a 'yes'.

A birth pang fired through her insides. She was certain her intestines were being ripped out by some demon with a garden rake. Her eyes narrowed as she forced in a deep breath, "Damn it, Karl! This is your kid! Don't you give a Damn?" It was not the best time to bring up the subject: it would most likely turn into some sort of debate. "If Hal was her, he would get me some help." Her eyes scrunched together as another pain ripped through her determined body.

Karl's mind was racing in all directions. He could not take her to a hospital: that was out of the question. Delivering the baby was not his thing: it wasn't going to happen. Maybe the best thing to do was to leave her here...she would probably die and it would not be blamed on him. The little girl could not survive without someone to take care of her. He grinned. It was perfect, two for one and he would be in the clear. "Tell you what. I'll go for a doc, I can force him to come here and take care of you. If the kid wakes up, give her a double dose of those pain killers...I'll take care of her when I get back." Karl actually felt some ripples of conflicted feelings, but by now he was used to ignoring them.

He grabbed his car keys and headed out the door, "I'll be back in a jiff." The door crashed shut like the top of a wooden coffin. Karl felt relief, all he wanted to do was run, run, run, as far as he could from this horrible thing that had been thrust at him.

The car jumped to life, the aging muffler belched carbon monoxide through a plethora of rust holes. The balding tires slipped over the thin coat of earth as Karl made his escape.

Inside the cabin Lena was drifting into a sea of disbelief. She knew Karl's character: he wasn't coming back. He had acted so quickly her mind could not deal with the birth pangs and his silver tongue at the same time. What was she going to do? Despair! Pain! Panic! Could she deliver the baby? If she couldn't, she and her baby would die. Between clenched teeth she wailed, "You son of a bitch!" Her hands clutched her tortured uterus. As a flood of tears began to cascade over her hot cheeks, she began to sob and fight for breath.

Chapter 15

Pain exploded through his right shoulder, his neck throbbed with pulsating flames that resembled darning needles. Rudy was lying face down on the desert dirt; he could feel the ants attempting to feast on his unconscious body. Rudy moved his eyelids and wondered what time of day it was. How long had he been out? He was pretty sure he remembered some movement just before he was struck from behind. He had a million questions, but first he had to get himself upright. Painfully he moved his head about as he looked for the noise that had awakened him: it sounded like an old truck. Maybe it was the person who cold-cocked him. He worried, was the person coming back? Voices? Where were the voices coming from? With a Herculean effort, he rolled himself over and began brushing the annoying ants from his exposed body. Reaching across his chest, he grabbed hold of his nine-millimeter Glock that was in his shoulder holster. Why hadn't his attacker taken it?

Lena wiped her sweat-drenched forehead. The pains seemed to have passed. Maybe she had just experienced false labor. She sat up and took several deep breaths. *Karl will be back...boy, will I feel foolish.* Feeling like a baby hippo emerging from sucking mud, she got up from the couch. Would Karl really bring a doctor here, especially with the little girl still up stairs? She didn't think so; unless he was counting on her making sure the little kid would not yell out or something worse like coming downstairs. She would have to kill the girl if she wanted Karl to help her. Using her free hands, she held onto her stomach as she slowly moved toward the stairs to the girl's bedroom.

His head was throbbing, he felt like a bull rider who had just been thrown and stomped. Rudy made a quick assessment of the cabin. Part of him wanted to just hike to his truck and get out of there, but he was certain he had heard a woman moaning in pain. There were no vehicles close to the cabin: could she be one of the Puppy Killer's victims? He moved closer.

With determination, Lena stood at the bottom of the steps with her hand gripping the knob of the railing. She felt light headed; a warm, wet, dark cloth seemed to be enclosing her brain. Her vision drifted while she fought to take deep calming breaths. Her heart leapt with excitement as she heard the front door close. "Karl?" She turned her head.

It was Rudy's turn to question his eyes. The young woman before him was poorly dressed, like someone out of a Stienbeck novel. Her hair was long and resembled long, wet, desert grass. There was a good chance that her dress was made from department store imitation gunnysacks. She was either fat or very pregnant, he guessed, the latter. Still holding his weapon, Rudy glanced about the room. "Are you all right, lady?" It was a dumb question considering her appearance.

"Are you the doctor?" The words just slipped from her mouth like saliva escaping from her lips. Lena could feel herself slipping to the floor: maybe from relief, but just as likely from exhaustion. He was coming closer to her, but she didn't care. As she drifted into darkness, she thought she recognized the man. Her arms fell to the floor making a soft pasty sound like flapjacks plummeting to the floor.

With measured caution, Rudy rushed to the girl and felt her pulse: she was alive, but definitely pregnant. The large wet spot on her dress told him the real picture, she was ready to deliver a baby…and she was alone. "Hello?" He yelled up the stairs, perhaps she was trying to get to her husband. "Lady, did your husband just go for the doctor?" No answer.

Just in case, he rushed up the stairs. The rooms were much smaller than he had thought. There was a smell of unwashed clothes and bottles of open beer. The first room had a standard size bed that was covered with an old brown sleeping bag that had so many rips and stains that it looked like a cloth pattern. Pieces of clothing were strewn all over the floor and on a useless rocking chair.

In another room he found a urine-stained mattress placed in one corner, nothing else but broken floorboards and dust. In the last room he gasped as he looked to the floor and saw a little girl who was clothed only in her underwear, a gray blanket lay at the foot of the bed. He could feel his pulse begin to race as he moved closer; she looked so still he was beginning to fear the worst. He had stumbled into the lair of the dragon. "Margarita?" His voice was tentative, soft, questioning. His steps were slow, fragile, as if he were afraid he might damage her just by awakening her. She was breathing...he could see that. "Margarita?" He knelt by her side and checked her pulse and pulled back her eyelids. "Drugged!"

Rudy wrapped the girl in the soiled blanket and carried her downstairs and placed her on the couch. He would have to act quickly. It was obvious there were no phone lines into the cabin and a cell phone seemed out of the question. Would that other person be coming back to the cabin? Did he have time to drive the lady to a hospital, he didn't think so. A sick feeling pierced his stomach as she looked at the two 'victims' who found themselves depending on him.

"Mister---can you---help me? I'm---pregnant." Lena did not even open her eyes as she spoke by separating her words with deep breaths. "Doc?" She was still hanging on to the hope that Karl had cared enough to bring a doctor in order to save her life. "Karl?" She asked, half hoping, half not expecting.

Avoiding the questions, Rudy said, "I have a phone in my car. I'll get you a doctor. I'm taking your daughter to the car. She'll be safe there. He was not sure she heard him, her face was ashen and her eyes were rapidly moving under her eyelids. At this point he did not know if she was victim or criminal.

Chapter 16

Karl felt uneasy; it was not like him to leave so many loose ends. Lena and that little girl could easily pick him out of line up. Karl slammed the heal of his palm into the rim of the steering wheel. The wheel was like his life: covered with blotches of dirty grease. Interstate seventeen was slipping beneath his speeding truck as he rocketed south towards Phoenix.

Lena would be dead pretty soon, and the little girl? Well, even if she survived the drugs, she would not make it out of the wilderness: she was already too weak. He pushed harder on the gas pedal, escaping from the crime scene like he had always done. His mother had always accused him of running away from his responsibilities.

Karl first noticed the patrol car when he sensed a movement in the rearview mirror. As if by some strange cosmic power, the moment he looked at the cruiser, the dome strip jumped to life with flashing red, white and blue lights. His first response was to try to outrun the car or pull off on some side road and try to lose him in the woods, but he knew that neither of those plans not only wouldn't work, but by now the cop had called him in.

Most people would have experienced pangs of guilt or fear, but that was because they dreaded the power of the law. For Karl, it was an irritation, like a fly that had crawled on the dinner table, or a pesky ant at a picnic party. Spotting a pullover up ahead, he signaled his intention to exit the road and submit to the patrol car. In a few minutes, he pulled off the highway and under a group of overhanging elm trees The shaded area was equipped with four weather beaten, dried out wooden tables which had once been painted dark red. Pieces of trash lay about the ground just inches away from the trashcan.

Karl sat in his car and watched his mirrors as the trooper collected his ticketing equipment. It was evident the officer was alone: the passenger seat was empty and the metal cage that separated the front from the back was unoccupied. Karl looked around the park area: it was deserted. At first he considered placing his gun on the floor by the door, but then he considered that the officer might do nothing more than a lecture. Like a cat watching the movements of a small bird, Karl studied the strides of the policeman as he crunched over the dirt surface.

His face was craggy, like a man who had spent most of his life out in the sun: probably a great deal of time on the water. He fumbled with his paperwork as if Karl were not even in front of him. "License and registration, please." Now his eyes, shielded by his aviator sunglasses, examined Karl.

Karl pulled at his wallet; it was wedged in the back pocket of his tight jeans. "Sorry, officer. I believe I was speeding." He smiled, "Was I going very fast?"

The thin lips of the Highway Patrolman did not seem to move as he said, "'Bout ten over, son." He was waiting for the documents, but he gave no indication of alarm or hostility.

After gripping his wallet from his back pocket, he leaned toward the glove compartment. The officer tensed as Karl popped open the door. He took note of the man's responses. With his left hand he handed the trooper a folded piece of paper, with his right hand, Karl pulled out his pistol and emptied three shots into the shirt button that covered the trooper's solar plexus. Karl was about to shoot the man again because he made a motion toward his own holstered pistol, but instead, the man dropped to the ground. From the pool of blood that was staining the front of the officer's shirt, it was evident he had not been wearing his bulletproof vest.

Karl opened the door to his car and got his drivers' license and the piece of paper from the dying man. The paper was just a market flyer that was in the glove compartment but it had his fingerprints on it. Quickly he pulled the officer back to his car and opened the door. Using the paper to hide his prints, he jerked out the wires to his radio and then grabbed the trooper's gloves. After placing the body in his car, he locked the door and closed it; the car keys went flying into the distant brush. From a distance it would look as if he had pulled off of the road for a nap.

After Karl returned to his car he released a few shudders. His mind and body surged with life, continuously his mind replayed the time when he shot the officer: the thrill was intense. For several minutes he just sat and savored the moments, it was good…but it had been too brief, just enough to wet a man's appetite. Like taking one lick of an ice cream cone, it left him wanting more. Now his nerves were trembling with excitement as he continued to soak in the flash visions of the noise and the blood. He started his car and then took one last look around…just in case. Slowly he pulled up to the highway and headed north. Leaving Lena and Margarita to chance was not a good idea. He knew he would feel better once he had eliminated the possibility they would one day turn him into the police. Karl could feel his hot blood pounding through his veins as he considered the possibilities. The old car belched a cloud of gray-black smoke as it picked up speed.

Chapter 17

I had planned to go with Rudy to check his audio traps, but getting ready for our New York trip was taking more time than I had thought. At times I thought I might have to send a UPS package to

Julie's brother. There was no way I was going to be able to get all of the clothes changes that Julie, Christine and Dell wanted at their disposal. Joel and I had all we needed in one medium bag each. Joel had a backpack with a slew of electronic gear, even some stuff he bummed from Rudy. I had a carry-on bag that was for my laptop: I needed to keep up with my writing while it was still fresh in my mind.

"Ed, dear, I 'm not going to have enough room to pack my swimming suit, do you have any space in your bag?" She was slouched on one hip, a pose she used when she was really irritated. In her hand she held a pile of clothes that would have filled most desk drawers. "Did you hear me?" There was an edge to her inquiry.

I was slow to answer because I knew my answer, anything other than 'yes' was going to cause another discussion. *"I'd love to help you out, dear, but both Joel and I have our bags full."* Beyond these words was a minefield of trouble, but I opened my mouth anyway. "Maybe you girls could leave some of your things here; after all, we will only be there ten days." Mechanically I moved the corners of my mouth up to form a clown like smile.

She huffed, she puffed, and she was getting ready to blow the house down. "Edward Malone, you know perfectly well that I have no idea how I am going to feel when it's time to dress for something special. **You're not a girl**...you just don't understand." After an ear splitting snort, she whirled and left the room, I was certain she was headed to the girls' rooms to get reinforcements.

After scrubbing my face with my palms, I went back to writing my story before the three of them returned to affect a frontal assault. Right now I was wishing I had gone with Rudy, but I was sure he wouldn't need me just to do something as routine as checking his electronic eavesdroppers. I was writing about the death of the Wall-Mart manager, Farley Wilson, and the invasion of our home by Harold Pepper. Both Julie and I were still getting flashes of him standing by the doorway: it was difficult to escape the guilt of killing a man in our own home. We could remove the blood from the wall and off of the floors, but washing our memories was much more difficult.

I leaned forward, toward my computer screen; perhaps the three 'Enemies at the Gate' would have mercy on me and go away.

"Dad, we need more luggage." Christine had a way of getting to the point. Her tone was soft and syrupy, like bait for an anteater. "We've tried to take only what we needed, but, well, there is just not enough room in our bags…what should we do, Dad?"

It was a trap. Well planned and executed. They weren't fooling me. Any second now, Dell was going to zap me with one of her famous barbs about how little I cared about how they looked.

Julie would remain quiet while her troops were waging guerrilla warfare.

Dell was right on queue, "Dad, you're not going to make us wear the same old things, are you? What will Uncle John think about us? She paused to reload, "My suit is too small, I've grown you know. You don't want me hanging out of my last year's suit, do you?" She moved closer, in for the kill. "Dad, Christina is almost a woman." ...

Yeah, thirteen years old. Don't remind me!
"...you know how the boys will be looking at us."

I should had given them my suitcase and taken a paper box. Now I knew where this conversation was going. There was only one way to end this discussion. It was time to let them knew who was running this family. "I understand your plight, ladies." I paused for masterful effect. "When we get to New York...why don't you just buy some new suits? I'm sure they have all of the latest styles and maybe even your favorite colors." Once again I had proven who was in charge of running things in the Malone family. Well, anyway, Julie had taught me that a woman would rather shop than pack, and I am a good student. "Now, let me get back to writing. Go" I smiled.

"Dad, you're the greatest!" They giggled as they triumphantly disappeared.

I went back to my writing, but...you know how you can get one of those uneasy feelings and have no idea where it came from, well, I was having a hummer right now. At first I thought it was about the New York trip, but I soon decided it was about Rudy being alone in the woods where we thought that the Puppy Killers might be. *Damn, I should have gone with him.* I considered giving him a call on his cell phone, but put it aside as my being a worrywart.

Chapter 18

Rudy's 911 call had gotten immediate action, especially when he told them he thought this cabin was being used by the Puppy Killers. After making his call, he returned to the cabin and settled Margarita on a ratty looking rug that was in front of the fireplace. Lena was either asleep or had passed out. He pulled back her eyelids and checked her pupils: she had probably just passed out from exhaustion.

The Prescott police led the way for the emergency medical truck; Rudy watched the columns of dust billow toward the pristine blue sky. Occasionally he cast a worried eye toward his temporary wards.

Pointing inside, Rudy directed the EMT team and then waited for the patrolmen. "You guys got here pretty fast." Rudy held up his FBI badge and displayed an approving smile. He was not on active duty, but that was not the issue here.

The older officer displayed a grim face as he said, "Yeah, I used to hunt this area. Turkeys." He stopped and appraised Rudy. "I didn't know the FBI had been called in on this case." He didn't look surprised as much as he looked confused. In the silence that followed, he listened to the idling diesel engine of the emergency vehicle.

"I'm retired. But I'm helping out Captain Caterous…as a favor."

There were no formalities as the EMT team came charging out of the cabin. Anyone in their way would have been knocked down. "We've got to get these two to the hospital…stat."

* * *

Karl pulled off of the highway and saw the column of dust. He drove slowly until he saw the patrol car and the ambulance parked by the cabin. At first he thought it was because of the officer he had just murdered, but there was no way they could have tied that killing into this cabin. The ambulance had to be for Lena. How had she called them?

The old car moved slowly as Karl put it into reverse. It was not a time to send up a dust cloud or be heard by the men at the cabin. The best thing to do was to pull on to some side road and wait for them to leave.

* * *

After the ambulance started down the road, the patrol car pulled in behind until they reached the highway. Rudy wanted to do some looking around at the cabin but didn't want to step on the toes of any of the local police, besides he wanted to go to the hospital to see how the little girl was doing. He made one last glace around the cabin; the smell was caustic to his nostrils.

Now that he was in his pickup truck and following the ambulance, he reached for his car phone. It rang twice before I answered.

"Hey, Rudy, I was just thinking about you. How's it going?"

It was a strange experiences listening to him relate all of the things that had happened to him in so short a time. Hit over the head, rescuing a pregnant woman, and maybe finding the little girl that had just been taken… probably by the Puppy Killers. Rudy had yet to find out how the young woman fit into the picture. "Ed, do you know of any young women who have been taken by the Killers?"

I thought for a moment, but I was certain none had been reported, so far. "I don't think so." I lowered my voice, "Could she be part of the gang? I think Raphael is still trying to recover…he hasn't really said anything."

Rudy pressed down on his accelerator. "Yeah, Ed, I think you might be right. I'm following them to the hospital." The line went dead. I felt ill; we all were still in danger if the man from Wall-Mart was not yet apprehended. For the first time, I couldn't leave soon enough.

Chapter 19

As the ambulance pulled up to the emergency entrance, a flurry of activity began to take place. A gurney equipped with a small incubator, intravenous pouch and an oxygen tank came dashing out as if it were on an Arabian flying carpet. Lena had delivered her baby girl while she was in route to the hospital. At the same time the EMT team wheeled Lena out and rushed her to a cordoned off area where they began to give her blood and a water/glucose mixture.

Abandoning his pickup truck, Rudy, holding his ID badge high, rushed into the emergency ward. While he had a genuine concern for the mother and her child, he was equally interested in anyone who would come to visit her. Anyone studying his eyes would have thought he was in a war zone sweeping the area for snipers. He was tense, his face drawn into the mask of predator.

In a voice filled with irritation a young nurse swept forward and stood in front of Rudy, "Sir, can I help you?" It was not really a question, it was a challenge: he tensed as he studied her.

Flipping open his badge, he barked, "If anyone comes to inquire or visit that young lady, let me know." Without further comment, he moved around the startled nurse and followed the gurney that was taking the baby to the infant ward for examination.

"Officer, are you here about the little girl we just brought in?" The voice was behind him. It was a scruffy beaded man who looked like he needed a shower, but his white coat identified him as Robert Harmon.

"Oh, yeah!" Rudy couldn't believe he had actually forgotten about the little girl. Undoubtedly she was a key piece to this puzzle. Rudy glanced at the white rectangular badge. "Are the police putting her under protection?"

"Yes, but they haven't told us why." He gave a nervous shuffle to his Nike gym shoes.

Rudy studied the young man and narrowed his eyes, "You don't need to know, son. Just do your job." In long strides, Rudy walked down the hallway. The baby was being pushed to a hallway on the right.

Karl Boss shook his head as he watched the retired agent disappearing down the hallway. He wanted to laugh; his face broke into a grin. *Here I am, mister lawman. What a dope.* He glanced over to where they had taken Margarita and Leah. It was too risky right now, but he would keep an eye on them to see where they would be sent. He would have to deal with them before the police had a chance to get information from them. *Later!*

In the trunk of a new Chevrolet Malibu, the lifeless body of a young male nurse lay on its side in a fetal position. Robert Harmon's life was over. He had had the misfortune of pulling into the parking lot next to Karl. After a quick exchange about the arrival of the emergency ambulance and the police, Karl had swiftly struck the man with a tire iron and then put him in his own trunk. For good measure, he slit the throat of the nurse and left him to bleed to death in the trunk of his new car.

Leah was taken to room 202 on the second floor, which happened to be the same floor as the entrance level. Two officers pulled up a set of metal chairs that looked like they belonged in the cafeteria. The metal seats and backs were covered with what used to be maroon vinyl now stained from sweat and food spills.

When she was lucid, Rudy planned to interrogate her. Again he flashed his badge; the two officers gave him a resentful look. "When she is feeling better, I will need to interview her." He considered telling them more, but they looked neither interested or informed. "I'm going to go to the cafeteria…you guys want some coffee?"

After a brief exchange of blank faces, the officer who had his chair tilted against the wall responded. "Na, but thanks, I'm sure we can get one of the nurses to get us some." He gave Rudy a knowing wink.

Again he glanced at the room number. Two hundred two…he would have to remember that number. Slowly he walked down the hall, he felt uneasy, but couldn't put his finger on the creeping feeling that was running up and down his spine. Pictures of the Wall-Mart manager, Farley flashed in front of his eyes. Someone out there was an aggressive killer; he just hoped he could stay ahead of him long enough to protect the lives of the three people he had brought to the hospital. He paused…he doubted it.

Chapter 19

I arrived at the hospital just as the morning sun was beginning to burn its way into the western side of the Desert Mountains. Swatches of golden red followed behind the soft blue that was so clean and brilliant it scoffed at Hollywood's silver screen. In the seat next to me, I had a large bottle of hot coffee and a chilled food bag Kate had asked me to give to Rudy. My friend had spent the night on a small cot in room 203, next to Lena. Her newborn baby girl was still in the 'preemie' ward, while dehydrated Margarita was recuperating in another secured ward.

The two sleepy officers that sat uncomfortably on metal chairs eyed me as I passed them and pushed open the door to room 203. Immediately, I recognized Rudy's shock of hair, it blended so well with the pillow cover that he appeared to have sprouted a massive white wig during the night. Not wanting to jolt him to consciousness (I did not want to be shot for my efforts to bring him his breakfast); I made an exaggerated throat clearing sound.

"Jesus, Ed! Are you trying to get yourself killed?" Rudy's red-rimmed eyes popped open and flashed a quick inspection of the room. "Is that my coffee thermos?" A grin the shape of a slice of cantaloupe formed on his face even as he squinted his eyes closed. "Kate makes great coffee; I tell you, Ed…she's a great wife." He quipped as he stretched his hand out while mimicking the gestures of a desert stranded miner reaching for a bottle of life giving water.

"She says, 'Hi!' and sent you some goodies in your freezer bag." I dropped the blue canvass bag on the chair next to his cot. "Anything new about the girls?" I avoided his eyes just in case he was going to give me some bad news.

He sat up and ran his fingers through his unruly hair, and then began to open his thermos "I was about to ask you the same thing? Any more break-ins at your house?" Circles of white steam drifted up from his stainless steel cup.

I think I was trying to forget about that incident, at any rate, I felt a small stab in my stomach and a quickening of my pulse as I thought about Julie being at home alone. "Na. Nothing new, Captain Cateras says the man's prints match a file on a guy named Harold Pepper; his prints were also found at the cabin where the girl was found."

The smell of the hot coffee filled the room. I have always been amazed at how much better coffee smells than it tastes. Rudy closed his eyes as if he were savoring a treasured memory. "Yeah, I heard that." Sip, sip. "I think these guys are the Puppy Killers we have been chasing…God, I hope so." He looked over the top of his cup, "Want some?" He gestured with his hand.

Lord knows I would like a cup, but I knew he was just being polite. I didn't have the heart. "No, but thanks." I made a pause in order to change subjects, "So…the girls? How are they?"

"Oh, yeah. Fine…last time I checked." His eyes moved up and to the left, "About three this morning. Are the guards still out there?" He wrinkled his forehead as if he feared they were not on duty.

I was about to answer when the door burst open with such force that it sounded as if it were being ripped off of its hinges. A panting police officer, his shoelaces dangling on to the floor, jumped into the room. His face was red and looked to be in pain, "FBI man, we just found one of the male nurses…" he forced in a gulp of much needed air. "…Dead…in his car."

It didn't take a giant leap to guess what everyone was thinking. 'There was a good chance that someone was in the building, imitating the male nurse, and it was a good chance it was the other nut that was with the gang.' Rudy flipped back the covers and jumped to his feet: he was fully dressed. "Check on the girls...all three of them...go!" He whirled and snatched his Glock from under his white pillow. "Damn it!" He grumbled in a low voice.

"What's wrong?" It seemed like a dumb question, but I sensed, rather than knew, something else was bothering him. I pulled my own weapon from the ankle holster on my right leg.

As we headed for the door Rudy barked, "I met that son of a bitch in the lobby about ten hours ago. Scruffy, dirty shoes...damn, I should have listened to my instincts. I thought he had just gotten called in to cover the emergency. Damn!" I followed Rudy as he moved along the hallway. The two guards were just coming out of Lena's room next door. The look on their faces answered the question before it was asked.

An older patrolman stopped at the open door, grief and anger seemed to glow from his face. His weapon seemed to dangle from his fingers, "She's gone." He struggled for a quick breath, "She's gone!" He looked up and down the hallway giving the impression he expected to see Lena casually walking toward him. It was obvious he did not have a clue about what he should do next.

Rudy and I checked the room. No Lena Pepper. "When did you last check on her?" It was a simple question, but I watched as the two guards exchanged looks like two teenagers looking for the best lie.

"Has anyone checked on the girl and the baby?" Rudy yelled at them, shocking them back into reality.

They both chimed in by holding up their cell-communicators. "They're okay." The thought seemed to make them feel worse. The others had done their job but they failed.

"What happened?" I tried to sound as calm as I could.

There was a short pause, they didn't want to tell, but it was going to be told at some point. The old man, his face still beet red said, "One of them male nurses came by and said he was going to be in the room for about a half hour." He hesitated, his Adam's apple moved as he gulped down the obvious truth. "He said he could cover us... we could take a coffee break."

The younger officer interjected, "We didn't know about the dead guy in the parking lot. We just thought he was the real thing." He offered a weak smile; "You suppose he just took her to the cafeteria?" He winced at the sound of his own stupidity.

All we could do was rub our palms against our faces, a useless gesture for a hopeless cause. "Get out an APB and let's get some men to do a thorough search of the parking lot and this building."

"And for God's sake tell the guards watching the little girl and the baby to NOT leave their stations!" I was yelling so loudly that I sprayed saliva in their direction. I'm sure they wondered whom I was to yell at them.

Chapter 20

Julie stiffened when she heard the sound of a car pulling into their driveway. Using her tiptoes, she popped up over the stainless steel sink and strained for a better look at the unfamiliar car. She glanced over her shoulder, a gesture that indicated her anxiety as she considered calling for the female officer that was with the children. She had been reluctant to accept any protection from the police, not that she felt safe, but she did not want to unnecessarily alarm the children.

Christine was stretched out on her bed, reading the latest edition of Harry Potter. Her slender fingers were whipping through the pages, her mind a million miles away from the cares of today's world. Dell and Joel were in the back yard taking turns being pushed by Officer Warner, a pert young lady who had just finished her training at the police academy. They giggled and made sounds of delight and approval as the swings shot higher and higher.

The darkly tinted windshield made it difficult for Julie to identify the person in the driver's seat. She felt the tension rising, her shoulders were like the roots of a giant oak tree. An auditable gasp escaped her lips as the car door began to open.

Kate! Julie's arms went limp. *Are Rudy and Ed back from the hospital?*

With a bag of groceries in one hand, she waved to Julie. Kate Tracker was so small she was often mistaken for a college age girl. She and Rudy did not have any children, not that they didn't want any, but they had been busy with their careers as FBI agents.

It seemed like ages since she had talked with Kate. Julie rushed to the front door and released the bolts and alarms in order to let her friend enter without alarming half of the police force of Phoenix. "Kate. Are the boys back?"

After a short, gusty snort, Kate shook her head, "Not that I know of. They're still chasing the bad guys." She held up the bag she was carrying. "Brought some snacks and a German chocolate cake." She gave Julie a one armed hug, "A little treat to help pass your time in confinement." She laughed and continued walking past Julie as she headed for the kitchen.

Julie opened her mouth to begin some small talk, but they both snapped their heads in the direction of the telephone as it emitted its familiar demand to be answered. Kate and Julie exchanged looks of concern; they always felt that way when they knew their husbands were pursuing trouble. After the second ring, Julie snatched the phone from its perch on the wall. "Hello?" Again her eyes met with Kate's.

The tension in Julie's body alerted Kate. She looked away as if expecting bad news about Rudy: it was always a possibility, a situation to which she had never become accustomed. She pursed her lips and began to unpack the grocery bag.

"What makes you think that?" Julie's eyes were drifting about the room, eyes that were looking for something that would not be found in her suburban kitchen. Her chest heaved as she nodded and moved over to look out of the back window where the children were still swinging. They were still there...unharmed. "Yes, I'll tell her. She's right here." Julie's frightened eyes were on the verge of tearing up. "He is?" Julie took a deep breath and spoke in hushed tones, "Okay, Ed. Get here as soon as you can."

The only hint that Kate was bothered could be seen by her trembling fingers that were aimlessly moving items about the kitchen table. "So...what was that all about?" She seemed intent on evading eye contact. Kate was the kind of person that most people labeled as 'up tight'. She had a heart of gold, but was flooded with feelings of impending doom.

Attempting to change the tone that was overtaking the kitchen, Julie slowly and deliberately replaced the phone. "Ed says that the girl that just gave birth...was kidnapped from the hospital." She placed a hand on Kate's arm, "He is concerned she was taken by the same man that was in our house the other night." Julie tightened her grip. "Rudy and Ed are concerned he might be headed in our direction." She bounced her head about as she attempted to smile, "Of course that is just a guess…he wouldn't tell me why they believed that." Julie laughed, "You know the boys… they worry about everything. What do you say…shall we get the kids to join us for some of your treats?" She turned and started toward the back door, "Oh, by the way, Rudy was talking to our 'guest agent' in the back yard. He says, 'HI'."

Kate lightened up and joined Julie as they walked, arm in arm, "Well, I'm happy the boys are all right." She gave a brief sigh; "I suppose you're happy you'll be leaving town in just a few days." Without changing her verbal stride, she asked, "How's Ed's new book coming? Is he getting what he wants?" Now that she was talking, she began to calm down, but she was still worried about the man who had taken the new mother.

"Ed seems to be making good progress, but this case has got him more involved than he usually gets. I suppose that's because of his friendship with Rudy." Her voice turned serious and she stopped in order to make a point. "Let's not scare the children, Kate. To tell you the truth…I'm a little worried that man could show up here…God knows, I'm scared!"

Chapter 21

Karl reached up and adjusted his rearview mirror: she was still asleep. Taking Lena from the hospital was easier than he had thought. He chuckled to himself as he imagined the looks on the faces of the officers that had gone on break while he had used a wheelchair to calmly take Lena out of the room. He waggled his head and grinned like a nightclub comedian seeking applause for his latest joke.

Interstate highway 10 was busy for nine o'clock in the morning; at least that is what Karl thought. Eighteen-wheeler trucks whined as they pressed their weight into the asphalt covered roads that, less than one hundred and fifty years ago, used to be narrow pathways for hopeful pioneers who endured months of painful bouncing over rutted dirt on cow paths to America's west. Karl made sure he did not violate any laws. He could easily kill the police officers, but that would attract attention.

"Where are we?" Lena's mouth was dry and felt like it was loaded with Elmer's glue. She needed a bath.

Her voice caught Karl off guard; he tensed as if he had just been stabbed. Nervously, he looked into his mirror. "Well. Well, I was beginning to worry about you." The statement was only partly true…he had plans for her. "How do you feel, Le?" He moved his stolen automobile into the far right lane.

By now Lena was used to Karl's games. There was no doubt in her mind but what he had more concern about his next hamburger than he did about her. She chose to ignore his superficial questions. She coughed, it was painful. "I need to ask you a question."

"Sure, Le. shoot." Karl flicked his eyebrows in an effort to make eye contact with Lena.

Groaning, she moved to her side. "Who told you my baby…died?" It was a difficult statement. She felt like throwing up just for having spoken the offensive words.

He made a very serious face. It was important to feign sympathy if he were to gain her trust. For a flash of a second, he looked into the back seat and made intensive eye contact. "I got you out of the hospital by pretending to be a male nurse." He paused to consider his next words. "I planned to take your baby at the same time that I got you out of there, but…when I went to the delivery room, they were talking about her death." He paused, "I'm sorry, Le. I guess she was just too weak."

As the enormous tears slowly trickled down her face, Lena sobbed, not just because her baby had died, but somewhere, in the back of her mind, she had wished her entire life could change: she could be a respectable mother. Pictures flashed in her mind as she pictured the joys of being a family: herself, Harold, and her little girl. She would buy soft little dresses for her. They would go shopping together. Spend nights by the fireplace playing board games, but…that stupid book writer had spoiled all that when he had killed Harold, and now…her daughter was dead before she even had a chance to have happiness.

"I'm sorry, Le, I know she would have been real special to you." This was a good chance to start putting his plan in action. He sighed as if he had just experienced a surge of sympathetic pain. "You know…she might have made it if that writer and his buddy had just been more interested in saving her than they were in capturing you and grabbing that little bratty kid, Margarita." Karl shifted his voice, "Hey, we better find a motel so you can rest up."

"Is that the same SOB that killed Harold?" There was no mistaking the venom that was in he words.

He almost laughed. She was so dumb. This was going to be easier than he thought. "Yeah, that's the same guy that shot down your brother, in cold blood. He never gave him a chance…even when he stood there with his hands up in the air." For emphasis he lowered his tone and repeated himself, "Yeah, shot him down like a mad dog."

Her tone was so filled with hate it sounded unearthly. In spite of himself he could feel the penetration of the words as they moved out of her mouth like drips of witches' poison." I'm going to

kill him. I'll kill him and everyone in his family."
Lena seemed to gain strength with the dripping of
each word.

Sympathetically, Karl sighed and pitched his
tone to reflect a feeling of regret, "Too bad, Kitten.
They are going to New York."

"I'll still get them, Karl. Damn it, Karl…I'll get
ALL of them."

Expecting to sear her mind with hatred, he spoke
softly. "I don't know, Lena…people like them
folks have got a lot of powerful friends. I don't
think we can do anything."

So powerful was her hate she could feel a surge
that sent a shock wave of anger into every cell of
her aching body. Her heart began to beat fiercely,
her fingers twitched in a gesture that resembled
strangulation. "How many kids do they have?" She
groaned at the loss of her daughter, Lena could still
feel the soft warmth of the child as she lay upon
her chest.

The way she measured her words told him she
was ignoring every word he had spoken to her: he
was very satisfied. "Three kids for the
writer…none for the FBI puke, just an FBI wife."
Pretending to be indifferent to her pain, he made a
quick turn toward the back seat. "There's a motel
up ahead, I think we need to lay low for a while."
He took the exit to Quartzsite, Arizona. "Can you
handle this?"

Lena barely opened her mouth just enough to
mumble, "Hell, Karl, I don't care." Her chest was

rising and falling like a bellows feeding a hot fire for a blacksmith. Resolutely she announced, "I'm going to kill the youngest first."

"Are you going to make the rest of the family watch?" Karl was excited by the thought. "Are you going to make them watch?" His head bobbed as he looked from the rear view mirror and back to the road. His pulse was rising as he began to decelerate in front of the motel.

Lena's eyes glazed over. Before her was a motel that looked like the one used for the movie, Psycho. The series of abutted rooms were coated with splinters of faded yellow wood. It had probably been built during the time when route 66 had been popular; this portion of the road was still covered with a coating of rutted sand. The setting seemed appropriate for the way she felt.
Tonelessly she replied, "Yeah. That's a good idea. Yeah, I'm gonna make them watch." She leaned forward, "Let's go to New York!"

Chapter 22

The airport shuttle would be arriving at our house at 5:00 a.m. for our flight at 7:15 a.m. We would get into Kennedy airport at 4:44 p.m. Still plenty of time to catch the ferry to Fire Island, just off the east coast of Long Island, New York.

At 4:00 a.m., I put on a pot of hot tea and started some toast. I always liked the smell of toast and tea in the morning; it seems to perk up every sense in the human body. Our two Schnauzers padded their way into the kitchen; it was too early in the morning for them to wag their tails. With the dream of sampling some peanut butter and jelly toast, they sniffed at the ceramic tile floor, inspecting every inch. I was feeling a bit guilty about leaving them for ten days, but we had arranged for a professional 'dog sitter' to keep an eye on them while we frolicked in the Atlantic Ocean. "Good morning, boys." I stroked their recently groomed hair. "See you in a couple of days." If the experts were right, dogs can't read calendars.

After the usual complaints and pleas from my three girls: "I can't find my" --or "There's not enough room in my suitcase." Joel and I kept watch while we waited for the arrival of our airport shuttle. It was running late. I always hate times like these: when our imaginations start working on us. Undoubtedly our minds come up with every life and death panic handed down from the beginning of time; I could just imagine a morning with our 'Mother Eve', "Adam, why is God so late this morning? Don't you usually start your walk before sunrise?"

We arrived at the airport at 6:15 a.m., plenty of time to catch our 7:15 flight. Well, it should have been! I goofed! I had booked with an online agency, but the airlines had changed the departure time to 6:45. It wasn't life or death, but it felt like it. Here I was trying to act as calmly as I could when, at the other end, we had to catch the last ferry of the day, and now, maybe book a room for the night. Not a good way to start our trip; a bad sign?

After a session of self-castigating and pleading with the airlines, we managed to get booked on a flight leaving at 11:30 a.m. We would be late. I was tired of feeding on guilt and inadequacies so I suggested an alternative diet. "Let's get a good breakfast!" Five simple words, but it changed the environment from Island Gloom to Temporary Purgatory. Little did we know, but that delay in departure was about to make an exponential change in our future.

The breakfast food was typical airport fare, but the pause was healing. Julie was gracious to my little fau pas so, as long as I kept feeding the kids from the airport trough, I had hopes of fading away the dungeon brand of INCOMPETENT that was blazing from my forehead.

After working our way through the endless lines at the security x-ray unit, where I thought they were going to disassemble my carry on laptop computer, we settled into a row of black chairs. It was difficult to tell if the chairs were black because of the soiled vinyl, or just in the need of a good scrubbing. We cautioned the children to not get lost and then they charged into the nearest book and candy store. Julie and I began killing time by scanning the other travelers.

Julie stood up and placed her carry on cosmetic case in her chair. "I'm gonna check on the kids. God only knows what they are planning to buy." This decision left me alone at the end of four other reserved seats. If someone took any item lying in a seat I would either have to let them go or leave all of the other reservation bags for another thief. I shifted my laptop from the floor to the left side of a vinyl seat: it was then I noticed the man in the next chair.

I didn't give much thought to my words; they just fell out of my face. The statistical probability was remarkable. "I see we have the same laptop case. Do you work at Intel?" We both had a forest green Port case. It was brown leather trimmed on canvass: very sturdy. Here were these two bags, only inches apart. They could have been as common as M&M candy, but I had never seen another one since my friend who worked at Intel gave me this one.

The man was probably only in his late thirties, but he looked old for his age. He had the stubble of a Don Johnson beard and gold-rimmed glasses like John Denver used to wear. Actually, he looked as if he were in ill heath, but that could well have been because of his pasty white complexion: unusual for Arizona. He responded with a labored smile, "No". His head moved about as if precariously balanced on a red licorice stick. "I don't work for Intel."

I told him the story of how I had acquired my laptop case. He nodded and pulled a magazine from the outside pocket of his Port case and began flipping pages. I guessed the conversation was over. I shrugged and then returned to my hobby.

"I got there just in time to keep the kids from buying out the news stand." Julie verified no one had absconded with her cosmetic bag. "I'm going to the restroom. Watch my bag."

I wanted to tell her about my great laptop bag discovery, but she was all ready weaving her way through the hall traffic. I resumed my hobby; watching people and place watching. I like to see things and wonder how I would describe the people or events to someone who was blind; because that is the way my readers are when they work their way through one of my books. It was then I sensed, rather than saw, the nervous tension that was oozing from the man on my left. At the time I just wrote it off as someone who was fearful of flying. Big mistake!

When Julie returned, I took my turn at inspecting the restroom facilities: if you've seen one, you've seen them all. Surprise…surprise. When I returned to my seat, Julie was deeply engaged in talking to the nervous man. He was leaning over my Port laptop case that was in my empty seat: Julie was in the seat to the right of my vacant seat. He was laughing at something that Julie had said. As I

approached he withdrew to his seat as quickly as a
fly jumping to avoid a swat.

"Guess he prefers women." I informed my wife.
Of course I kept my tone hushed. "He wouldn't
talk to me." I probably sounded hurt or jealous.

She made a face. The kind every man on this
planet recognizes: you have just said something
that only befits a person of low character or who
belongs in a mental institution. "We were
discussing the coincidence of his case and yours.
He laughed and told me you had just said the same
thing." She paused and looked away, "I think he's
ill…he seems worried." She batted her eyebrows,
"And he has the pastiest skin I've seen." She did a
full stop in the conversation and abruptly stood up.
"I better get the kids. We'll be boarding soon."
Typically, she vanished like a whiff of smoke in
front of a house fan.

Chapter 23

The Crime Scene Investigators had finished their
work at the cabin and the Prescott hospital. There
was no doubt but what Harold Pepper and his
sisters, Lena were part of the Puppy Killer team.
Just how they fit in with a career criminal like Karl
Harley Boss was still being put together. Rudy had
gone over his tapes and tried to find some answers:
only a few popped up. He took a deep breath and

released it slowly. He was bothered. The same question kept haunting him. *Where had they gone?* The trail was not just cold, it was nonexistent. He feared that Lena was dead: Karl was like that.

"Hey, Rudy!" Captain Cateras was talking even as he just came out of his office. In his right hand he had a fist full of facial tissues: he had a bad case of desert allergies.

Rudy pitched his pencil onto the desk: it rolled to the base of his desktop computer. "Ya, Cap?" He welcomed the relief from his thoughts.

"I've got a three day old inter state message in my office...I want you to see it." He gave a sweeping gesture with his free arm. "Office!" He managed to gasp out before he was seized with another nose gush.

The room was new: nicely furniture for a police department. After snatching the paper from the Captain's hand, Rudy took a seat close to the door, glanced at the paper and asked, "What do you want me to see?" Moving the message like a fan, Rudy read it. "So?"

"That guy who was murdered at the airport." He blew his nose. "He was in the waiting area for people going to New York." He raised his voice, "They say he was a maintenance engineer for the Palo Verdi Nuclear power plant."

"Yeah?"

Cateras was becoming impatient: his runny nose didn't help his already prickly personality. "Witnesses said he was talking to a man and woman who had three kids with them." He paused to thrust his chin forward. "Man, woman, three kids, going to New York!" He rolled his eyes.

Rudy frowned.

"Could this guy have been talking to your friend, the writer?"

Rudy passed his hand through his shock of white hair. He smiled, "No, Cap. Not them." He flipped the paper on the desk. "Wrong time of day…they had a 7:15 a.m. flight."

"Maybe they missed it."

Rudy laughed, "Never happen, Cap. Ed's a stickler for punctuality; organized, to a fault."

After a sneeze which triggered the captain's dog to jump high enough ,if he had wing, the hound would have been flying "Okay, okay, but would you do me a favor and check it out for me. If it was them, maybe they know something." He pitched a hand full of tissues into an overflowing waste can.

In disbelief, Rudy shook his head. "Just for you, Cap." He turned to leave the room. "Better see a doc about that cough." He chuckled as he plucked a Washington Delicious apple from the ageing wicker basket perched next to the departmental coffee pot. "I know a guy at Sky Harbor; I'll get him to show me the boarding area surveillance tapes." *Better call Kate and tell her I'll be late for lunch.* Working as an independent contractor had its ups and downs; Rudy wasn't yet sure which one this was going to be.

Chapter 24

The kids sat three across, on the other side of the isle. Christine made sure she was in what she considered as the prime seat: next to the window. Dell took the middle seat. That left Joel in the isle seat where he could converse with anything that moved and bug us to take him to the bathroom. By now I had recovered from my feeling as an idiot for not having verified our original departure time. I made a mental note to be sure to check all future departures, but, knowing Julie's personality, I was sure to receive ample interrogation and scrutiny for at least the next twenty years. *Mental note: do not fly for the next twenty years!*

After a brief stop at Cincinnati, Ohio, we charged east toward our final destination of JFK airport in New York. At thirty five thousand feet in the air and the constant hum of the jet engines, you would think it would be easy to blot out some of the events surrounding the Puppy Killers, but I found it was impossible: too many unanswered questions. I looked out of the ovoid window and watched as the world slowly slipped away. Don't believe everything you think you see: below us the earth is spinning at one thousand miles an hour. I was not looking forward to handling my baggage. For some time I had been keeping a dirty little secret: I was having a problem with shortness of breath.

For a mere one hundred and twenty dollars per room per night, we were able to obtain two rooms for the night. Julie and I had finally gotten the kids to agree to go to sleep. The girls finally condescended to allow their little brother enough space to sleep in THEIR room.

I fired up the TV set and examined the weather forecast for the next ten days. "Looks like decent weather, on." Julie was brushing her teeth so I doubted she really heard me. The phone rang…it surprised me; must be a call from the front desk.

"Hello?" I didn't appreciate being interrupted.

"Ed? Rudy." He paused. "Sorry to bother you, but I need to ask you a few questions." In the background I could hear a number of phones ringing. He must not be at home. But I had a bigger question for him."

"How in the hell did you get my phone number?" I had an idea, but I wanted him to say it.

An elfish chuckle tickled my ear; "I've got friends in high places. You used your credit card, Ed…your government at work, Buddy."

I rolled my eyes and sighed, "I knew it." Julie stepped out of the bathroom and squinted at me. "Rudy" I mouthed to her.

"Just before you boarded your flight, Julie and you talked to a man at the airport."

I recalled the funny, sick looking man, "Yeah?"

"The guy from Palo Verde? He sat next to you."
Rudy was being specific and redundant.
Something was up.

"Yeah, Rudy; I remember! What's the
problem?" While I was curious, I was tired. Why
didn't he just wait until tomorrow?

He lowered his voice, "He's dead, Ed. Killed in
the men's room at the airport. Stabbed and throat
slit."

"Wow!" I mouthed the story to Julie. She
dropped her mouth to indicate her surprise. "So
what do you want from me?" I shrugged.

"The airport tape shows you talking to him…did
he say anything unusual, or that would cause you
to be concerned?" His tone was peculiar. There
was something he wasn't telling me. "Did he seem
worried?"

I could picture the expression on his face; the
guy's brows were wrinkled and he was nodding his
head. "He seemed…preoccupied, at least when he
talked to me. Cautious, not sociable, but a little bit
less on guard when he chatted with Julie." I
wanted to change the subject, "Besides the fact he
was murdered in the Phoenix airport, why are you
involved?"

Rudy hesitated. "Can't answer that yet, Ed.
Sorry?" He went back to his question, "What did
he talk about with Julie?"

"She says they just talked about the same thing I
talked to him about…we had the same laptop case.
I thought he might work for INTEL. He said, 'no'.

I got mine from a guy I know who, works at INTEL."

Rudy's voice jumped to life. "You had the same kind of laptop case? A green Port?"

"Rudy? Was the FBI interested in this guy?" Silence on the line, "Why?"

"I'm checking this out at the request of Captain Cateras. I'm not aware of any agency interest." Rudy paused, "I thought you would like to know we haven't got any kind of a trace of Boss or Pepper. They just seemed to disappear."

I was pretty sure he was not telling me everything, but, for now, I'd cut him some slack. "Okay, I'll buy that for now. What about my laptop case? Why does that interest you?" I glanced down at my case; it was leaning against the dresser which was supporting the TV set.

"I just found it interesting…but his case was found in the men's room, in a stall. It was cut to shreds. Apparently someone was looking for something they thought he had." The next words were predictable. "Are you sure you have **your** case?"

"Just a second…I think so." I tucked the phone under my chin and dragged it to the dresser. With a quick glance inside it was apparent it was my material and my laptop. "Yep, it's all mine." I returned to my prone position on the bed. "What are you looking for?"

I've known Rudy for quite a few years and I pride myself that I can read most people like open books...something smelled.

"We haven't a clue, Ed. It's just the way the case was cut open. We believe the killers were looking for something." He cupped his hand over the phone and continued. "We don't think they found it...whatever they were looking for."

"So you thought he might have given something to me?" I gave my case another glance as if by eyeing it again it would change.

I could tell something else had his attention. "Well, it was possible so it seemed like a good idea to check." He changed his tone, "He was probably killed just about the time your plane left the terminal."

"Well, we don't have it."

Rudy interrupted his silence, "Okay." More silence ; "I'll keep you posted on the Puppy Killer thing. In the meantime, enjoy yourself...and both of you be careful."

That's Rudy "Puppy Killers...or Airport Killers?" I gave Rudy a forced laugh.

I can still hear his words bouncing around in my brain. They were words from a friend who had saved my life several times. Like parental concern bordering on a warning, he said, "BOTH". The line went dead, almost as if it were an eerie warning from a prophetic specter. I read the concerned look on Julie's face. I shrugged and gave her a wry smile, "Rudy...he hung up."

She was giving her hair a vigorous rub with a towel, but stopped…waiting for my reply. I had one of those yucky feelings we all get when we have to come up with a phony story; "Nothing much. He said that the guy we met in the airport was murdered. He had the same kind of laptop case as I have. He wondered if the guy had switched cases." I walked past her and closed the bathroom door. I didn't want her to ask too many questions because, right now, I could hear Rudy's words, "Both!" I wondered how safe my family and I were, even here in New York. I was feeling nervous and light headed.

Chapter 25

Cash was getting low, and so was their tank of gas. Lena was between consciousness and spasms of post delivery pain. Her lips were pushed tightly together in order to 'tough it out'. Karl switched to highway 15 and headed for Las Vegas, Nevada. Every time they passed a patrol car they could feel a suffocating tightness in their stomach.

Maybe it was male pride, or just waiting for the right words, but Karl knew he was going to have to say something. "Leah?"

Her response was weak and disinterested. "Yeah."

He sniffed, not because he needed to, but it gave him a pause to do some thinking. "We're low on gas, Le. I'm going to stop pretty soon. Can you sit up?" He was going to need her at the gas stop. "Just for a little while." His tone was as soft as an aging grandfather with a history of concern.

Lena may have been weak, but she was not yet stupid. As a surge of pain shot through her wounded organs, she squinted. "Karl. We need cash?"

Karl smiled. Not bad. She was just as smart as he thought she was...and tough. "Yep; we need some cash...and we need gas." He glanced back at her, he was surprised at how peaked she looked. "And to answer your next question, I plan to heist the place." He meant <u>rob</u>, but he could not bring himself to say the words.

This would not be the first time she had participated in a robbery. She always loved them. Her heart began to pump with the anticipation. Ignoring the pain, she sat up, "Got a gun for me?" This could be an opportunity if she played her cards right. She liked Karl, but she didn't trust him. One moment he could be warm and loving, then, in a flash, he could cut your throat. It might be a good idea to have some protection. *God he's cute.*

"You okay? I mean, you just had a kid, Lena." In the rearview mirror, he met her eyes. Her face still looked flushed. Her eyes were incased by a rim of red and pinkish flesh: she was weak and tired.

A forced smile displayed her coffee stained teeth. She leaned forward and placed her hands on the back of the cloth-covered seat in front of her. "I'm okay, Karl...just a little tired." The truth was, she was experiencing something that surprised her: she was thinking about her newborn daughter. Her breasts seemed to be throbbing, aching to be sucked by the baby she had left at the hospital; "Really."

Karl nodded as she was speaking, but Karl Boss was not a man to trust anyone. She didn't even realize he had kidnapped her in order to have a hostage and, at the same time, to stop her from testifying against him. "Lookie, lookie;" Karl's voice was animated. He pointed at the road ahead. There were two people, apparently hitch hiking toward Los Vegas. They had their coats tied about their waists and walked without looking behind them, with their left hand held out in the manner of one who did not really expect to be picked up. "Straighten up, Lena...we've got company." She could feel the car begin to slow down. "Cops are looking for two people traveling alone. They aren't as likely to look at a car with four people in it." Karl was thinking far beyond that simple statement as he pulled over in front of the two young hikers.

With jubilant smiles the two road weary kids trotted toward the sedan, their backpacks bounced, their canteens rattled as they drew nearer. After a cool night of sleeping in a concrete culvert, they had been walking for the last three hours. Tired, foot sore, they had visions of sitting down and sleeping. Maybe they would have to be friendly and chatty: that was the price of a pick up. The girl had been keeping pace with her boyfriend, she let out a soft sigh when she saw there was a girl sitting in the back seat, her fears of being assaulted or kidnapped disappeared. She would have a woman to talk with: that would be a relief.

The back door flew open and Lena slid across the seat so she was behind Karl. "Hi!" Her voice sounded cheery and homey. Karl clicked open the trunk. He apprised the young red headed girl who slid into the back and extended her hand to Lena. "Hi, I'm Tammy." She did a quick unassuming glance at the handsome man in the front seat. *He's hot!*

Lena gathered her blanket about her chest. "Lena". She smiled. "How far are you going?" "Vegas."

The trunk closed and the girl's partner came dashing toward the back of the car, but Karl reached across the seat and opened the front door. "Come on up here…less crowded." He used his most friendly tone, the one that assured people he was not a person to harm a fly. As the man settled into the front seat, Karl studied the man's movements. He was athletic, but probably not too difficult to handle. Well dressed: probably had some money. "Headed for Vegas, huh?" He held out his hand, "Karl".

"I'm Tom. We really appreciate the lift. It's been tough getting a ride. A lot of people just don't stop now a days." He held out his hand to Lena. "Tom."

Lena didn't know for sure what Karl was up to, but she had a few hunches. The man holding her hand was good looking, probably a nice guy. It had probably been a few days since he had had a bath. "I'm Lena". She noticed his eyes slip down to her blanket. "I'm recovering from a little minor surgery." Quickly she shifted the conversation, "So, going to Vegas, huh? Hoping to strike it rich?" She chuckled.

Karl put the car in gear and moved out into the traffic.

"We're getting hitched!" The young Tammy held out her hand displaying an inexpensive diamond ring. She followed with a short shrug, "My folks think I'm too young, but Tom and I just can't wait any longer." She blushed and grinned at Tom. "They'll lighten up once we're married."

It was time for Karl to work his famous charm. "Yeah, it was the same for Lena and me. We've been married for five years". He slapped at the steering wheel. "Best damned thing we've ever done." He tipped his head toward the back seat. "She's not quite telling you the truth about the surgery."

Lena's heart jumped. What was he up to? What was he going to say?

"She had a miscarriage. It's been really tough for her, but she's a fighter." Karl was a born manipulator, he knew the miscarriage story was partly true, but at the same time it would cause the kids to relax. "It was our first, but the doctor said we still have a chance at another one." He reached back with his hand and patted Lena's knee. Tom and Tammy were silent in sympathy. They exchanged glances, each one wondering how well they would handle this catastrophe if it had happened to them.

"Hey…I got to stop for gas. Do you guys need anything?" Karl sounded like a World War II fighter pilot blowing off the death of several of his buddies. He fixed his eyes on a service station that was situated at the top of the hill. His smile was not due to happiness; it was because of anticipation.

Chapter 26

It was like sleeping in a room filled with ghosts. Every time I closed my eyes I could see the man with the green laptop case. In life he had seemed gaunt, but in my dreams he was red eyed and wispy like Morley from Dickens's Christmas carol. His hand moved up and down as if he were slowly beating a green snare drum with one hand. There was an oversized monocle in his left eye.

The room felt hot. I was so covered in sweat that I felt like I had just left the hotel swimming pool: which I had not. Tomorrow was going to be a long day: we had to catch the morning ferry from Bay Shore to Fire Island, Saltaire. Then there were the words with which Rudy had ended or last conversation, "Both". So where were Karl Boss and Lena Pepper? I got out of bed and opened the adjoining door to the kid's room: the three of them were sprawled all over the king sized bed. Safe!

After a trip to the bathroom, I returned to my wet side of the bed. Julie was still sleeping as soundly as a newborn puppy. With only three hours left before we were to get up, I laid down. Determined to deny any ghosts into my dreams, I closed my eyes and drifted into some place that abruptly ended when the motel phone rang. It was time to get up.

After paying for a family breakfast that should have put a dent in the national debt, we finally got to the ferry. If you've seen one, you have seen them all. A flat-bottomed slab with an upper deck: noisy diesels that spew fumes in every direction while they shatter you eardrums. The weather was cooling, for which I was grateful. The view of the city was blurred by morning fog; all in all, not a bad trip.

At our arrival in Saltaire we became aware of a
situation which was to change my life forever. I
had not considered it important at the time but
then; I had no way of knowing that. Julie's brother,
Jake, and his wife, Janet met us at the dock: Janet's
son, Roland, topped off our welcoming crew.

My instincts prodded me to look about for any
suspicious strangers. "Both". Everyone was a
stranger to me, and they all seemed to have
someone to greet them. It would have to do for
now, but at least I didn't see Karl and Lena.

"We got you guys fixed up in a little guest
house; it has its own bathroom; Janet bubbled as if
we were long time friends who were finally
reuniting; a gracious hostess who was proud to
share her childhood home with us. Indeed it was a
nice little house, perfectly suited to Julie and me.
The kids were to stay inside: Joel with Roland
together, and the girls in a spare bedroom.

After the obligatory travel questions, we settled
down to talking about friends and family: from
Julie's side of the family. My mind was still
spinning with various scenarios of danger.
Unconsciously, I found myself glancing out of the
windows: expecting, at any moment, to see killers
at the door. I didn't want to spoil Julie's vacation
by unduly alarming her; after all, I could be
worrying about nothing. But…what if I were
wrong and we really were in danger?

My nightly ghost dreams were getting to be a
real drag. I decided I should take another look at

my laptop case: maybe I missed something. It was possible. I vowed I would do that in the morning.

On day three I got hackles on the back of my neck when we returned from the east beach. I was chatting with Julie, "That's really a nice beach. Hot, clean. The waves were just right." It was just small talk, but I was just, finally, relaxing.

She snuggled against my arm as we walked on the wooden sidewalks. The kids were moving like a batch of mice huddled in beach towels. It was a good feeling, something like a Currier and Ives picture taken at a beach rather than a field of snow. We moved right and left in order to dodge the infrequent bicycles. When we reached the main home, we separated and walked arm and arm toward our cabin.

"My God!" We looked inside the cabin and stiffened as we stared at an unbelievable sight. Blankets, clothes, everything was strewn about. Naturally, our first thoughts were that some kids had made the mess. Our second thought was that some criminals had decided to check out some new tourists.

Before I touched anything, I went over to the main house to use the phone and talk to Jake. I expected to see the main house suffering the same attack. I had not even closed the door before I realized the main house had not been ramshackle. "Jake!" He was in the back room. "Someone has trashed our cabin." I tried to sound calm, after all we were guests. I was talking to Jake, my mouth was moving, but my mind was playing a different tape. I could hear Rudy's words like a haunting voice from beyond, "Both!"

Jake scanned the surrounding area of the main house...it was in good shape. He headed for the back door which led to our cabin. "I have no idea who would do anything like that, Ed." I could hear the rest of the house following us. Jane, Roland, and our kids brought up the end of the column. I was thinking of calling the local police when I opened the door to the cabin and saw Julie sitting on one of the beds...she was near tears.

I can still remember when the whole thing seemed to change. My mind became clear. Janet asked, "Is anything missing? Did you have anything of value?"

"No, just our usual stuff." Julie's voice was sullen. I could tell she felt personally violated.

Again Rudy's words came back to me, "Did he give anything to you?" I wanted to rush to my laptop case, but felt I had best wait until everyone left our cabin.

"Not really" I said, "I have no idea what they might have been looking for." I was so anxious for them to leave that I could barely stand it. "Well, we better get this mess cleaned up and see if anything is missing."

Finally we were alone. Julie was still sitting on the bed looking as if someone had stolen her favorite doll. I had spent enough time with Rudy to be suspicious about bugs. Maybe someone had

117

done all of this just to distract our attention from a bug that had been planted in the room. I moved close to Julie and whispered in her ear, "They might have left a bug."

She looked at me as if I had lost my mind. "What are you talking about?" Her eyes flared. She looked at the floor expecting to see a local version of the cockroach galloping over the floor.

I tried again. "The people who made this mess might have planted a bug, a listening device. So watch what you say."

"Honestly, Ed. You've been spending too much time with Rudy. This was probably done by some kids looking for drugs or money." She got up from the bed and began picking up her clothes which had been scattered on the floor.

I went to the closet in the corner and reached for the top shelf. I had put my laptop computer and its case in a spot that would discourage the kids from snatching it in order to play computer games. I grabbed it and pitched it onto the bed. Unlike the last time, this time I began to search every inch of the bag. I removed everything and began a thorough search.

Julie placed her hands on her hips and gave me the scolding look of a mother who was about to lecture her unruly child. "Now what are you doing?" Without waiting for a reply, she continued. "Is that stupid computer all you can think about?"

I held my finger to my lips and gave her a threatening frown. "Stop it!" I began flipping through the pages of the manuals I had in the outside pocket. From between the pages of the operations manual, a computer disc dropped to the bedspread. It so surprised me I could not have flinched more if it had turned out to be a snake. I could not recall putting a disc in this laptop.

"What's that?" Julie turned her head from her clothing pile. She was reacting to the way I had tensed up.

"A computer disc, Julie;" I was still convinced there might be a bug in our room, "It's my start up disc, Windows 98+…it just startled me. I forgot I put it in that pocket." I picked up the disc, it was duel sided, and most certainly not anything I had ever seen before. Every inch of my being wanted to put the disc in the laptop and run it. What was on it? I continued searching the bag but found nothing else. I had been wrong; the man had dropped the disc in my bag. Why?

"Come on, Ed. Stop fooling around with that computer. Honestly, you are just as bad as the kids. Help me get this place back in order." She closed the suitcase she had been filling and started on another one.

"Well, I just wanted to make sure I would be able to do some writing done while we were here." I made an effort to lighten up the situation, "Maybe they wanted to steal my latest book." It was a nervous laugh because I was now not only worried about the Puppy Killers, I was now wondering if the men who killed the man who put the disc in my case; had actually tracked us to Fire Island. I would need to talk to Rudy. Maybe, by now, he had some answers. My next concern was…what if they returned?

Chapter 27

"You didn't have to kill them, Karl." Lena squeezed her lips together and folded her arms over her aching breast. "They were nice!" She turned her head to look out of the passenger side window.

Karl returned an affable smile. "How can you be sure I didn't just tie them up and leave them?" He shrugged. "You didn't see anything…you didn't hear anything."

Lena muttered, "Just the way you like it, huh?"

Slowly, Karl's head moved from side to side, "Give me a break, Lena. I have a heart you know." While he was talking, mentally he reviewed the image of the two hitch hikers lying on the floor of the motel: their life's blood moving over the floor like an aggressive ameba. "They **are** nice kids." He knew she would believe him. She wanted to believe him. People always did.

120

Lena softened and turned toward Karl; "Really?" She looked skeptical, but smiled; "Really, Karl? Really? I'm so glad!" She moved to his side and tucked her knees under her. Her small hand moved to Karl's forearm. She sighed, "I feel much better." She giggled, "I bet they have a great story to tell to their kids." Putting her hand to her face, she laughed with relief.

The feeling come over him with great surprise. Right now he was experiencing a new feeling...he cared what she thought. For a short flash of time he even considered regretting his actions, but the foreign feeling quickly waned. Karl returned a practiced laugh then he turned toward her and said, "So...do you think we should forget about the Malone's? After all, they're nice people too." He furrowed his forehead in a comical gesture.

Lena was a serious thinker. She weighed her feelings. The man had killed her brother, Harold. Admittedly, he was always in trouble, but he was her brother. Edward Malone had killed her brother...that was a fact. Her eyes teared up, she sniffed, "He killed Harold, Karl. I know he was bad, but he was my brother...I have to do something about it."

He nodded and grinned. He had a better idea, one that would be more satisfactory to him. "Why not trade him misery for misery?"

"Well, I figure, if you kill him, that's not much of a punishment to him. Why not make him suffer like you have to?" He almost laughed with delight.

She shuddered as she took in a few quick breaths and dabbed at her wet eyes. "What? What do you mean?" Her eyes were turning red.

Taking on a cavalier attitude, he shot off a quick reply, "Ah. It's probably not right." He waggled his head but tried to act humble.

She turned angry, "Stop it, Karl!" Her voice echoed off of the walls of the car. The noise pierced his ears.

"Jesus, Lena. Calm down!" He waited for some silence. "I was just thinking."

"Thinking what?"

"Maybe you should not kill him."

"Why not?"

"Kill someone who matters to him. Then he will suffer just like you are suffering." The poison arrow had been released. Would it pierce its target?

Lena sounded mellow. "Does he have a brother or a sister?" The words rolled out of her mouth, but they even sounded strange to her.

"How about his kids, or his wife?" Karl could not recall another time when he was having so much fun manipulating someone. "If they were to die, he would live the rest of his life suffering the same way you are. Kill him and it is all over;...no time to suffer." He had just reached the top of a hill, maybe it was symbolic.

Lena nodded, she could not speak. Flashing though her memory were pictures of her brother, home, the beach, the mountains, school, and the holidays. Her words were brief, "You're right, Karl." She blinked tears out of her eyes, "I want him to suffer...just like I have to."

The car seemed to become quiet. Karl and Lena stared at the road ahead. It seemed to lack shape: just asphalt with little yellow rectangles or reflective markers that floated under the car. Karl reflected upon the two young people he had killed. Lena was swimming in a pool of self-pity: her brother dead, others to die. She was feeling miserable.

"Then he shall suffer." His words sounded phony, like a poorly delivered from some Elizabethan movie. He extended a sympathetic hand to Lena's arm, "I know it's hard for you, but your brother was a great guy. He deserves to have his life mean something." His voice was soft and silky. "I'm with you."

Driving northeast they continued in a silence, each person was in their own little world. Karl's need was to disappear for a while. It would be best if he could kill the Malone lady before she could testify against him. He didn't think she had really seen him, but why take any chances?

Chapter 28

An electronic squeal polluted the morning air. Its intrusive sound seemed to echo off every item in the room. *Now what?* Without answering the phone, Rudy had a feeling it was something important.

A sunburned arm protruded from under a pile of blankets. If possible, he was going to answer the phone without ever opening his eyes. His arm, a stubble face, and a shock of white hair stuck out of the blankets. Kate was shopping, things were slow, and he had stayed up late watching an old John Wayne western.

He cleared his throat: it felt like dry grass. "Yeah, it's Rudy."

A chipper voice bubbled back at him. "Mr. Tracker?" She didn't wait for an answer. "Captain Cateras asked me to give you a call. I hope I'm not too early."

He glanced at the clock, eight forty-five. Any other day it would be fine, but this was his 'sleep in' morning. "No, it's fine." He was awake now: he moved back the covers and rubbed his eyes. "What's the good Captain want…Mrs.?"

"Sergeant Bird, sir." There was a brief pause while she apparently answered a question asked by someone who just approached her. "Ah, he thought you would want to know the Lake Powel police just reported finding a couple murdered at a motel in Boulder, Nevada."

"Bolder? Boulder, Nevada." Confusion was the flavor of his words: black, dark and murky. He searched his brain for any connection: he could find none. "Did I ask him about a couple?" He ran his head through his hair as if looking for a clue that might be lurking there. A thought occurred to him. "The Boss kid and Lena Pepper?" That would be great. Ed and Julie would be glad to hear that.

She snapped back, "Nope!" She paused, making Rudy think he was to guess again?

He pressed his eyes close together. It almost pained him to even ask the question. "Ed and Julie Malone?" He was beginning to be irritated with this game.

She sensed his anger, "Captain thinks, from the description, that it was the work of your Puppy Killers. He's going over to the scene to check it out."

"They don't usually kill adults, sergeant. Why does he think it's the Puppy Killers?" He was wide-awake now. Boulder, Nevada would put Karl and Lena on a path for the northwest: maybe Seattle by way of Las Vegas.

At first the sergeant had sounded like a young lady, but now her voice seemed old, maybe even tired; "The way they were butchered. Throats cut...bodies posed like children sleeping. He's going to have your ME check the knife cuts for comparisons."

Rudy was up and starting to dress himself with his free hand. "When is Cateras going up there?" He hobbled on one foot while slipping on his socks.

She laughed, "He thought you might want to come along. He says he could use some of your input. There is a helicopter leaving from the Scottsdale airport. Can you make a ten thirty flight?"

Swinging his head in every direction, he selected his clothing. "Yeah; I'll be on the road in twenty minutes." He plopped on the edge of the bed, "How about the ME?"

"He'll be with you. Captain will join you at the Prescott airport." After a short hesitation she put a smile in her voice, "Any questions, sir?"

"None, Sergeant, but thank Cateras and tell him I'll be there." He hung up the phone assuming she had nothing more to say. He would have to leave Kate a note. Should he call Ed? No...he didn't have enough facts yet. *Better let him spend a relaxing vacation, besides this could be just a copycat killing.* Rudy wondered, his eyes fixed on his telephone.

It would be one thing to tell Ed that the Puppy Killers were headed west and not after him, but it would be another thing if it turned out they were on an easterly track, alive, and killing their way as they went. After splashing some gel on his face he began to give himself a quick shave. He met his own eyes in the mirror: they had the look of a man who was deeply troubled. If anyone were to ask him what it was that bothered him, he couldn't say. Somewhere in his gut he felt unsettled, worried about his friend and his family. He brushed off the feeling as he headed out the door. Rudy wondered if he would ever get used to examining crime scenes, he hoped he wouldn't. He headed for the 101 east to Scottsdale.

Chapter 29

I wasn't sure what the disc might contain, maybe nothing. The manual in which I found the disc had come with the laptop. It was entirely possible it had belonged to the previous owner. It was two sided so it could have contained a lot of information…probably computer games. I had to smile as a thought formed in my mind. I'll bet the kids were looking for something like this. It's probably some game like the Dungeons and Dragons, or maybe some war game.

After we returned from dinner, I'd make a point of examining it, if I could access it. Sometimes computer games were password protected so I didn't want to spend the evening at dinner with my brain fumbling through possible passwords. It had not occurred to me there could be anything on that disc which had cost a man his life. Undoubtedly, the man at the airport had given us that disc but why. Maybe it had cost him his life, but I really doubted it. Just the thought seemed ludicrous. Things like that are statistical anomalies and belong in a James Bond movie.

Getting to the restaurant was accomplished by a long, but pleasant walk down several back streets rutted and covered with sand and diagonally cut wooded sidewalks. Jake and I took the lead while Julie and Janet sauntered behind us. We were headed for one of the two most popular eating-places in Saltaire, the Inn and Out; it was everything as advertised...great food, nice atmosphere, and my favorite, reasonably priced.

The walk back to the house and our cabin was a little more awkward because it had turned dark. We had just passed into a spot where the walkway was hedged in on both sides and the ground was packed sand. At the risk of acting paranoid, I bent down to retie my Nikes and look behind us. I was rewarded by seeing two men stop just at the edge of where the road made a ninety-degree turn behind us: they were now concealed behind a row of hedges. My heart did a slight flutter as it switched from labored to panicked...my pulse rate must have jumped from eighty to one hundred.

"Shoe laces loose?" Julie chuckled as the ladies walked past us.

"Go ahead...make fun of a shoe challenged man." I joked.

I watched Jake as he began telling me more about the history of the great storm that hit the Island in 1912. Besides the severe damage, many lives were lost. I listened, but my mind was dashing through so many alternatives I really didn't hear. By the time I stood up, I was torn by a feeling that I should tell Jake, but also I was concerned by what reactions I might get. Should I tell Julie? It would probably ruin our vacation. Suppose I was wrong and just being jumpy. Realistically, I had just come off of a murder case that would make most people look over their shoulder. Two men had even invaded our house and I had shot one of them. My guts were churning with a fire that was making my head feel light.

"You okay, Ed?" Jake had stopped and was making a face that was rittled with concern. His brow was wrinkled and his eyes narrowed to the intensity of a magnifying glass.

"Just nerves, Jake. I was on a murder case in Arizona just before we came here." I took several deep breaths and tried to relax. "We had a break in at our house...I killed one of the intruders." I paused, anticipating Jake would back off and let me continue my worrying.

Up ahead the ladies had stopped, waiting for us. It was the perfect chance to change the subject.

Another group of people were headed toward us. That gave me some relief. Jake used their arrival to continue walking and exchange greetings with the couples. When they had passed I was sure that he would come back to the break-in at out house. "Julie, told me about the break-in. Did they ever get the other guy?"

I had hoped they had, but I had not yet received any word from Rudy, or anyone else for that matter. I certainly didn't want to alarm Jake by inferring that the man and his crazy girlfriend might be headed for New York. "No, not yet, but it's only a matter of time. They'll get him." I put a period on my talk by giving him a manly chuck on the shoulder and an 'everything is great' smile. I didn't think he bought it. I surely didn't.

Chapter 30

It was a six-inch hunting knife and it was pushing into my chest. The man holding the blade studied my eyes: he was looking for something that would measure my fear. I was afraid, but I was more concerned about what to do to prolong my life. Beads of sweat were beginning to trickle from my forehead. Behind the man was another figure; it was a young girl; featureless.

From the far end of the room came a familiar voice, "Ed, are you all right?"
As colored clouds whirled about my mind, I struggled to identify the voice. "Ed!"

Like a drowning man surfacing from dark, green seawater, my eyes opened. I coughed. The concern on Julie's face was enough to urge me into another level of panic.

"Are you all right?" She placed an ice-cold hand on my brow: her hands were always cold.

I blinked my eyes in order to determine which picture was a dream. "Yeah, I'm okay." Then I asked a stupid question, I think I was intending to divert the subject. "Why? What's wrong?" I moved my pillow up higher on the bed so I could sit up.

After squiggling her face into a look of reproach. "You were having a hard time breathing, Ed." She took a deep breath and narrowed her eyes. "What's wrong?"

My head hurt. "I was having a bad dream. I think it was that talk with Rudy." I pushed my wet fingers though my soaked hair. "Those kids, Tom and Tammy, must have been scared to death when that Karl and his girlfriend killed them."

We had just walked in from our evening out at the Inn when I got the fifteen-minute call from Rudy. He told me about the discovery of the two bodies at a motel in Boulder, Nevada. It sounded grizzly. I had not told anyone about the details or that Rudy urged me to be vigilant. The dream was in line with the horror scene in Boulder.

Julie put her hand to her mouth as if to block the painful words that she was thinking. "Why couldn't he wait until we got back?" There was a powerful lot of anger in her words, but I knew they were only said because of her fear for my mental and physical health. "You scared me!"

She was not the only one who was scared. I didn't like the pounding that was going on in my chest or the swallows of air I was being forced to take. "It was just a dream, Julie." I patted her hand, "Nothing to worry about." *Yeah, nothing to worry about. People following us, wanting to kill us. Mystery discs and crazed killers from Arizona.* Now...I was beginning to worry about my heart. *Nothing to worry about.* Was it serious...or was I just being spooked? Maybe I'd find out soon.

As an answer, I shrugged and smiled. "Rudy just wanted to keep me up to date. He thinks I need the information for my book." The explanation was partially true, but he wanted to warn me.

"Okay, I guess I'll forgive him, but you need to calm down...night sweats can't be good for you." She moved back to her bed on the other side of the room. "You're sure you're all right?"

"Sure." I watched Julie as she turned off the lamp which sat on the nightstand in between us. "Night;" The bloody thoughts continued to display at the back of my eyelids. If I had known the forcers working against us, I would have had even more trouble getting to sleep.

Chapter 31

It was dark outside. The night air was wet from the rolling salt sea surf. Ships moved about the dark bay, their white lights that undulated in the moving surf outlined travel lights of red and green. High above, aircraft moved about like alien craft inspecting the blue planet below.

Two men sat at the beach side combination deli and grocery store. The fanny packs concealed their weapons as they sat in silence and sipped from white plastic containers of coffee. Occasionally a bicycle would rumble past them, sometimes sounding antiquated bell ringers at each other. The larger of the two men stretched out his arm and looked at his wristwatch. "It's about time we did something. We need that information and we've got less than a week."

"No argument." The other man spoke quietly, his eyes darted furtively checking for eavesdroppers. "What are you suggesting...kidnapping, murder, arson...what?" He took a quick sip of his coffee and studied his large partner. "Don't forget, the information is only good if no one knows it's missing." He leaned forward and snarled, "The Sky Harbor killing was a huge blunder...just because you wanted to get the material without paying the guy. DUMB."

"I didn't hear you screaming when I first mentioned it."

"I didn't know you were going to kill him before we knew where the discs were, Peter."

The big man leaned forward and wrinkled his nose in a gesture of hate. "We agreed, no off shore bank account numbers, Bill." The threatening face was replaced with a smirk. "We still don't <u>know</u> where the disc or discs are. What I'm trying to get across to you is … our informant <u>thinks</u> the disc was dropped into the other guy's laptop bag."

"Okay, Peter…what do you want to do?"

"Hell, Bill…I think they ought to meet with an accident, you know… in case."

Tossing his empty cup into a nearby trashcan, Bill shook his head. "Okay, that might work, but do we do that after or before we know where the disc is?" He leaned forward and shifted his eyes from side to side, "Do we 'accident' the whole family…or just the guy?"

"Hum. I'll have to think on that." Peter leaned closer to his coconspirator and whispered, "Definitely, we need the disc first."

Without another word the two men got up and mounted their bicycles. The night was turning cool. They zipped up matching forest green jackets and headed toward the beach and the public dock. (Just two more tourists, enjoying a summer stay on the island.)

"Mr. P, I think we'd better make a call and make sure those guys are still going to pay us…then, we'll decide what to do."

Chapter 32

It was dead. D-E-A-D; no matter what Karl tried to do, the car would not start. Maybe he had left some electrical thing on or the coil had given out, he couldn't remember and he didn't know, but there they were in a rest stop: Stranded in Goodman, Mississippi. He had wanted to stay on the road until Memphis, Tennessee, but Lena had insisted on staying near a rest stop.

She tucked her legs up underneath her: her feet were cold. "God, Karl. What are we gonna do?" She whined as she added, "I'm cold and I need something to eat, Karl."

He wasn't listening. He was thinking. They would need a car. He would have to steal one, but it was going to be risky with so many people lolly gagging about the parking lots. A small motor home would be neat. It could be missed, but not if he could take the owner with them. There were three of them in the lot. Two of them were okay, the other one was too large...too risky. "I'm working on it, Lena. Just give me a few minutes and you'll have food and be warm. Trust me."

Lena responded with a low groan. "I don't want to wait, Karl. I'm cold now."

On cue, an elderly man came out of the busy restroom and headed for his RV. He looked to be about in his late fifties, a bit chunky with a belly that was resting on his large belt buckle. There was a slight limp coming from his left leg, probably a knee injury from high school football. Karl quickened his step as he approached the man. It was his intention to make any observer think he was already a passenger on the man's motor home. From inside of his shirt, Karl pulled out his pistol. This was going to have to work with absolute precision.

The man pressed his electronic opener, it chirped and the lights on the RV flashed a greeting. A set of stairs dropped down and the man reached up and took hold of the silver handle. Karl moved in as the door opened.

As casually as he could possible move, Karl stepped behind the man and softly shoved his pistol into the man's back. "HI! Don't move, mister. I have a gun angled to pass through every vital organ in your body." He paused to sense the tension in the man's body. "Look, I don't want to hurt you, but I got a problem that requires me to borrow your RV for a short while. So get inside and we'll work this out to where you don't get hurt and I can solve my emergency." Karl was proud of his little speech, a lie, but pretty well phrased if he said so himself; "Move. Please."

Looking back, over his shoulder, the old man attempted to get a look at the gun that was in his back. He moved his eyes up to meet Karl's. "Look, son, I got a feeling …if I step up there…" He nodded toward the steering wheel, "I probably won't walk out of this RV. Frankly, there ain't no car worth my life." He handed the keys to Karl, "Take her…have a nice trip."

Karl could feel the old man's fear. He may have sounded tough and relaxed, but he was afraid. Karl liked that. It was not even the first time someone had said that too him. He knew he could get tough with the old man, but he decided to try another way rather than risk shooting him in the parking lot. Karl refused the keys. "I meant what I said. My wife has just had a baby. It died. We're broke, but we need to make it to Memphis…we just need a lift."Karl laid a hand on the man's shoulder. "I'm sorry about the gun, but I didn't know what else to do."

Slowly, the man turned around. "I'm Charley Burly. I just picked up this rig last night. I'm on my way home. I live in Memphis…my wife and two little girls are expecting me." Charley studied the young man's face: it was soft, good looking, but his eyes were scary. "Take the damned thing, son. I can always get another RV."

The prey wanted to slip away. That's how Karl saw him. He had to admit the old man was standing tall, but that only excited Karl all the more. "I can't leave you here. You'll call the police before I'm out of the parking lot, and besides…I've never driven anything this big." That was a lie. Karl had driven lots of big-rigs.

Charley could see where this conversation was going. He could feel his blood pressure rising. His heart was pumping furiously. "Okay, son. I'll break you in on the RV, it's real easy to drive, and you let me out about fifty miles up the road." Charley started to extend his weathered hand, but thought better or it. "Deal?" He was feeling an urge to go to the bathroom.

"Can I trust you?" If he could just get the old man to get in the RV voluntarily, that would work. "I got to get my wife. Our car's broke." He did his best to sound poor and needy, which he actually was.

Charley Burly produced a grin of stained teeth badly in need of capping. "I don't see where you've got anything to loose. You can get to Memphis. Find your friends. Leave the RV, if you want to, and I'll pick it up later." He tried a chuckle, but it came out too forced; It embarrassed him. "Hell, it'll be a good story to tell my kids."

'Tell his kids', like Hell. He'd tell the cops and then they would know where they were. It was the wrong thing for Charley to say, but there was no way for Charley to know that. Not that it would have made any difference to Karl. He liked killing: it was exciting and gave him a God like feeling as he held the power of life and death in his hand. Karl covered his feelings with a laugh, "Yeah, it should make a great story." *But you haven't seen the ending, Charley.*

Karl watched as the man mounted the steps into the motor home. Charley winced as his knee complained about the pressure. He took the keys back from Karl and sat in the driver's seat. It was a sand colored leather seat that wrapped the driver like the hands of a loving mother. The passenger seat was a twin to the driver's chair. The inside was more like a model home than a motor home. Most of the features were shades of brown accented by gold colored appointments. The cabinets were done in cherry wood panels.

"Nice rig, Charley." Karl bobbed his head in a series of mini nods.

Charley beamed with pride. He seemed to forget the circumstances. "Yeah, Martha always wanted one of these things. You know how the ladies can be." He put the key in the ignition: the pusher diesel jumped to life with the sound of a huge feline purr. The power was exhilarating. "Well, son, let's get your wife. Where're ya parked?" He began swinging the super sized horizontal steering wheel with as little effort as turning a pizza. "Love this power steering!"

It was soon apparent Lena had been watching the transaction of events. She stepped out of the car. She was wearing an Indian blanket and shuffling toward the RV. They had left in such a hurry she still had on her cold Arizona hospital clothes. For warmth, she had put on an old coat which belonged to the deceased hospital male nurse. No doubt…she looked the part of a homeless child.

"She looks a mite miserable, son." He opened the door. The set of steps extended for her ease of entry.

Making a show as a loving husband, Karl went to the steps and helped Lena as she struggled up the metal rungs. "Charley, here, has agreed to give us a lift to Memphis." Karl seated her on a couch behind the driver's chair. "Wasn't that nice of him?" He nodded at Lena, hoping she would pick up his cue.

She looked around at the interior…obviously impressed. "Got any food, Charley?" She was starving. The wood covered refrigerator was calling to her, or at least she felt like it was. Right now, she couldn't care less about Charley.

Chapter 33

No matter how he arranged the data on his workbench, Rudy was bothered. Something strange was going on. None of his old friends at The Bureau would talk to him about the airport incident involving Ed and Julie. They had hinted there was a problem but no one would confide in him what the issue was.

He had built himself a beautiful mini bar. It was stocked with liquor, wine and beer, but it was mainly for show. Sitting in his office chair,Rudy pushed his feet against the hardwood floor and scooted to the bar: it was scotch time. It wasn't going to solve any problems, but he needed to clear his mind. What would an engineer at the Palo Verdi nuclear reactor be doing with anything sensitive in a laptop case? Sure he could have something of importance, but not something that would get him killed. After dribbling two inches of amber liquid into a shot glass, he turned out the light and sat in the darkness. The glass felt cool in his hand as he looked out of his picture window that faced his backyard of desert stone and citrus trees.

Rudy's stomach jumped. There was movement in the back yard. Coyotes? Burglars? He kept his eyes glued to the window as he pulled out a set of books from his office library. The surge of anxiety was coursing into his bloodstream slowed down as he wrapped his hand around his nine millimeter Glock. Struggling not to blink, he watched, but nothing more seemed to be going on.
There…behind the row of cedar hedges, something was moving. *A man, short, broad shouldered, five foot eight, maybe nine: about forty feet away.* The silhouette looked familiar…maybe.

An involuntary action is what it's called. Rudy whirled about and held his weapon in front of him. The room flooded with light. "Rudy? What are you doing sitting in the dark?" Kate still had her hand on the light switch: her eyes squinted together as if they were pained by the action. "What time is it?"

He controlled his temper. Not that he was angry with Kate; he was miffed because he knew the person in the back yard would be long gone. "Just thinking, Kate." He paused and held up his drink. "Care to join me?" With a playful smile he pleaded, "How about turning off the light…it hurts my eyes."

Again the room was plunged into darkness as Kate dropped her finger on the switch. "Fix me one, Rudy." She pulled her white silk robe about her and dropped into a high back stuffed chair. "What's bothering you?"

He felt like saying 'nothing', but changed his mind. "I know there are more reasons why The Bureau is hot on the trail of the death of the engineer who was killed at the airport." He handed her the drink, "Nobody will talk, Kate."

"You think Ed and Julie are in danger?" The sound of her ice clinking against the glass sounded louder than it should. "Is that what you're talking about?"

During a brief silence. Rudy studied the back yard: nothing happening. "That's part of it, Kate, but it's all the secrecy that's got me confused. Sure, I'm concerned for them, but about what…I don't know." Rudy pushed his chair closer to her.

"Sooo…what's your best guess, Sherlock?" Her giggle echoed in her glass.

Rudy sighed. "I think The Bureau is hiding something." He held up his hand, it was barely visible in the dark room lighted only by a distant streetlight. "You'd think I'd be used to it by now, but I'm not." He considered telling her about the man in the back yard, but thought it would only frighten her. After all, he didn't have any answers for her.

Kate was crunching her ice: a habit that bothered him. "Are you through with the Puppy Killer case? Since you returned from Boulder you haven't said very much."

"Yeah, well, we're not finished; it just seems they might have left the state. If they have, I've got some real mixed feelings. I wanted to be in on the capture of those sick kids, but since they escaped from the hospital, the Boulder case is the last we've seen of them." Her question got him thinking in a different direction. Did the two cases have anything to do with each other? Puppy killers and Sky Harbor killers, if there was a connection, it wasn't obvious. "Thy just seemed to have vanished into thin air, but they won't stay hidden very long. They're killers. They love to kill. They'll do it again."

Kate let out a long yawn; "Ready for bed?"

Rudy glanced out the back window; yeah, why not?"

Chapter 34

"I give up!" I wanted to throw my laptop across the room. My face was red with frustration and anger. My trembling hands were testimony to my aggravation. For at least four hours I had been trying to open the disc I found in my laptop case. Prior to this attempt, I was skeptical that the young men at Sky Harbor airport had placed the disc in my case. If he had slipped the disc into my case, well, what significance did it have?

Sometimes things happen in our life, things that defy all statistics. I would certainly rank the next event as one of those times. There was a knock at the door; it was a soft rap, almost like the scratching by a timid dog.

"Yeah? Come in." I moved back from the desk and walked to the door. Through the sheer drapes that covered the glass window at the top of the door, I could barely see a head, it was Janet's son "Hi, Roland. What's happening?"

Roland was still dripping from his time in the outside shower. His habits reminded one of a hummingbird diligently darting about for today's fresh nectar. All day he constantly darted from one activity to another. "I'm going to the beach. Want to come?" Just one look at Roland and you would know where he spent his time. He was light brown with short brown blond hair and the sparkling eyes of youth. A nice kid.

I smiled, but shook my head. "I'm sorry, Roland. I wouldn't be very good company." I glanced back at my laptop. "I've having a fight with a computer disc...I can't seem to get it open."

"Yeah?" Roland's eyes jumped to another level of interest. "What's the problem?" His head darted about in an effort to see my laptop. I had the impression he was like a seal that had just spotted a tasty fish.

I turned and walked over to my laptop. Displayed on the top of the small desk, it didn't seem like such a stubborn advisory. I wasn't sure what I should say to him. "I found a disc in my laptop case." I'm sure my face registered my frustration. "It wants a password, or something." Not being able to think of any other words I just shrugged.

"Mind if I give it a try?"

Roland sounded more like a kid asking to ride my horse. I wasn't sure I wanted some kid messing with my laptop: I had a lot of books stored in it. I tried for a polite refusal. "That's okay, Roland. I appreciate your offer, but it's not that important."

Roland folded his arms and looked up at me. An impish grin formed on his smiling face. "You just think I'm a kid who's going to screw up your computer. Don't you?"

He had caught me. That's exactly how I felt. "No...that's not it, Roland. I'm sure you know your way around computers. Most of you kids grew up with them." I was sure I had amply protected my computer.

The sun had moved to where it now shot into his eyes: he narrowed his eyes and placed his hand above his eyebrows. "ED!" He was smiling, but I could tell I had offended his self-esteem. "I do this kind of stuff…all the time." He stepped up, into our room. "I won't hurt your computer. Just let me try."

He was now standing over my computer, he didn't touch it, but he was almost salivating like a dog staring at a steak.

Overcome more by his confidence than anything else, I shrugged and pursed my lips into an upside-down grin. "Okay, Roland, but what makes you think you can break in?" I tried my best to not sound condescending.

His fingers had already started moving over the keys. I'm sure he decided to attack the problem before I stopped him. "Computer games." He spoke softly.

"Computer games?"

He paused: obviously thinking about his next move. "Yeah, Ed, it's not unusual for us to find computer games that are blocked by passwords, or access codes. We get a lot of practice." He stopped and turned to me. "Can you tell me anything about the person who wrote this disc…it's not commercial." He folded his arms, looking like an Arabian genie. "Where did you get it?"

He had asked the million-dollar question. 'Where did I get it?' Was it at the airport? Did Rudy put it into my case? Was it just something that I picked up at a store? I wasn't sure. Maybe I should ask Rudy. "I'm not really sure, Roland. A friend of mine told me that…it is possible…that a man at the Phoenix airport dropped it into my case.

"Why?"

"Good question. But I don't have a good answer…yet." *Call Rudy!* That's what kept going through my besieged mind. I needed help. On the other hand, I was concerned that Roland, a kid, would either mess up the disc or my computer: maybe both.

Roland tilted his head and examined my indecision. "What are you afraid of? Think I'll damage your disc? I won't, Ed…I do this all the time."

I needed help. Roland had the experience, I didn't. Maybe he could open the disc. If he did…I could give Rudy more information. "You're sure?"

"I'm sure, Mr. Malone."

In spite of the thoughts that were going through my head, I forced a reassuring smile.

"Is that the disc?" He nodded toward the desk where my impotent laptop lay.

"Yeah." I paused and sighed as an emphasis to my frustration. "I can't get it to open. It just keeps asking for authorization. I assume it wants a password or some account number." I gave him my most serious look. "I would like to look at the data…at least enough to tell a friend of mine about its contents." I must have moved every muscle in my face as I mumbled, "Okay. If you want to try take a crack at it, BUT be careful. I don't want to lose the data." After the word, 'okay', he moved into the room and sat at the chair before I had even finished my lecture.

"Thanks, Ed. I'll be careful."

I clenched my teeth as I watched his fingers fly over the keys of my laptop. Every cell in my body ached to cry out the magic words that would stop the child from violating the keys of my computer. If he should wipe out the information, well, I wouldn't know what to do. I got up and paced the room until I couldn't stand it any more. "I'm going outside, Roland. I'll be right back."

"Sure." responded the absentminded voice which sounded as if the words came out of the computer. "Wish I knew something about the guy who wrote this." Roland didn't seem to be speaking to me, but rather to the inanimate computer.

Outside, on the wooden deck, I was surrounded by a myriad of local green plants that shot six to ten feet into the air. I began pacing until I remembered that Jake had a bottle of my favorite Merlot wine stashed under his sink. God knew, I could use a drink…I was feeling stressed, hot, and flushed. I opened the door to the house just as I heard Roland's soft exclamation. The word was like a rush of pent up air from a diver who had just cleared the surface after a deep open ocean dive.

"Yes!"

I froze in midst stride. Conflicted, I wanted my drink, but I was overwhelmed by the possible implication of what had just happened. I was almost afraid to ask. Had he just wiped out the disc? Locked up the computer? Blown the hard drive? I squinted in fear of his reply. "What'cha got, Roland?"

By the way he was speaking I could tell he was still concentrating on the computer's screen. "I got something, Ed. It looked like…something like one of those programs that help you arranges a house." He sounded disappointed. "It could have been a game like Destroyer, or Combat, but there aren't any creatures or weapons.

I plucked open the screen door and strolled over to the screen. He was right. Just a floor layout like something you'd see at an open house or Home Depot. "Huh." I wasn't sure what else to say, but the more I looked at it, the more it looked like a blueprint. "Looks like a blueprint, but more like a warehouse."

"Yeah, lots of the games I have look just like this, but they are for finding your way to a treasure guarded by trolls, or mercenaries." He looked up at me, accentuating his disgust. "If this is a game, it'll never sell." He turned as if to better study my reaction. "Where did you say you got this?"

I wasn't sure what I should say. I really wasn't sure what the truth was. Maybe it was a disc that belonged to Christine or Dell and they didn't want to admit it. I doubted that it belonged to Joel, but it could have come from one of his friends. "I'm not sure, Roland. But I'm sure it's not one of mine."

Roland grunted and returned to the screen. Slowly he scrolled down the pages. At first he seemed expectant, but eventually he began faster scans. After a few seconds I began to recognize what I was seeing. "You know, Roland." I paused and placed my hand on his shoulder. I expected him to stop scrolling. He did. "I believe this is a blueprint of a factory. I don't know whose, but I think it's important."

"Really?" He sounded interested now…maybe he had done something important. "Is this spy stuff?"

I had to chuckle. "I don't know about that, but it could be important. I have a friend back in Phoenix that I need to talk to." Two sensations rushed through my body, one was fear, and the other was excitement. My natural curiosity triggered my imagination. This could make a great story: if I lived to tell it.

Chapter 35

Charlie Burly was thirsty. He moved his eyes about the small bathroom of his RV. Forcing himself to take slow deep breaths had kept the old man alive. The shower was smaller than he had remembered, but it beat being dead. Charlie was a tough coot who had survived several near death situations. When he was just a kid he had laid in the snow of Seattle, Washington for the better part of the night. His mother had dropped dead on her way home from one of her favorite bars. At fifteen years of age a mother bear that was protecting her cubs mauled him. Since his youth, he had survived a car wreck, a small plane crash and a bought with cancer.

The vibration of the motor home had lulled him to sleep, but he was awake again. His wrists, ankles and mouth were wrapped in silver Duct Tape: probably his own. Charlie had no way of knowing how long he had been stuffed in the shower, maybe four hours…maybe more. Time was running out. He could not think of one single reason to believe these kids were planning on leaving him alive to testify against them. He would have to get free if he ever hoped to live, and Charlie had plans to live a lot longer than just the few days he would get waiting for his captors.

The door to the bathroom opened. His heart jumped to his throat. Adrenalin shot through his veins and awakened every organ in his body. Fight or flight the books called it…he was ready for either, but he had to get loose first.

The lid on the toilet made a sound. "Now don't you peek, Charlie." Lena spoke as if addressing an old family friend.

Charlie stayed still. It was best if she thought he was still unconscious. He leaned his head against the wall and closed his eyes. 'Looking' at that degenerate girl was the last thing on his mind. Willing his breath to slow down he lay as still as a wounded possum. His nerves twitched at the sound of the metallic door lock clicking.

Lena squatted down and felt the pulse in the neck of the old man. "My, your heart's pumping ninety to nothing, Charlie." She produced a seductive tone, "Guess you still get going when a girl's around, huh, Charlie." She closed the door and chuckled as she left the bathroom.

Charlie figured he hadn't really fooled her, but he didn't have time to worry about that. He moved onto his back: pain shot though his artificial knee. Gritting his teeth, he began working his taped hands from behind him to the front of him. It was painful and more difficult than he had thought, mainly because he was at least ten pounds over weight. Martha had told him he looked fine, but right now he wished he had dropped the weight.

Lena stepped from side to side as she moved to the front of motor home. She thought about telling Karl about the old man 'faking it', but she was not only sure that Karl wouldn't believe her, but something inside of her told her that the longer Karl didn't think about Charlie, the long Charlie would be alive. She liked Charlie, so, for now, she would just keep her little secret.

"How's the old guy doing, Leah?" Karl's head and eyes were darting about as he maneuvered the motor home down the highway. His arms rested on the oversized steering wheel.

She looked out the side window as if she were enjoying the countryside. "Ah, he's okay." She gave a quick glance at Karl. "Sleeping...I guess." In spite of her self she asked, "Karl...you're not going to hurt that old man are you?" Lena still wanted to believe there was some good in Karl. If she didn't believe that she would have to fear for herself. She rationalized that Karl had come back to the hospital just for her.

With practiced ease he snorted. "Why would I hurt him? He's been nice to us, transportation." He banged on the steering wheel, "Plenty of food." Karl stretched across the huge space in between them. "Yeah, he's a good old guy. We'll just leave him tied up some place along the road where someone can find him after we've got some miles between us." Karl tipped his head toward Lena and rolled his eyes. "'Course, we'll have to get rid of this fine transportation...can't have old Charlie telling them where to find us." With a pained expression he pursed his lips, "Yep, have to leave these nice beds. Good food." He sucked his teeth. "Yep, too bad, but...easy come...easy go?"

Lena held her breath. She liked the way things were. This motor home was the closest thing she had had to a real home for a long time. Of course she liked Charlie, but...hadn't he lived a long time? And didn't they deserve some happiness too? Charlie…the motor home…? Lena turned her face to the countryside. It was whizzing past sooo fast, just like life. She couldn't help it, she just felt sorry for herself: a life of tough breaks. She knew some would call it bad choices, but…it wasn't her fault.

Karl knew he had lighted a fuse inside of Lena's soul. She was young; Idealistic, naive. He snickered with a sense of self-satisfaction. "Hey, let's stop for the night. Man, I'm beat." He knew that she was scared to death of driving the motor home. "There's got to be a place where we can pull off the road and watch a little TV and catch the news. Karl liked listening to stories about himself. It didn't matter that the material was negative: it was about HIM.

She stretched. Tired from the day, Lena reclined her chair and arched her back. "Can we park near one of those fun places? I'm bored!"

He knew what she meant. Lena liked the loud bars where the 'wanna be cowpokes' pranced about in their cowboy boots and howled like hungry coyotes. Lena would line dance until she dropped, or some cowboy offered to take her to his car for a slug of Jack Daniels.

"Sure thing, little lady; I could use a little fun time. Maybe I'll get lucky." He turned down the edges of his mouth and made a happy clown face. "'Sides, I could use a gulp of cold, draft beer."

Karl watched her light up like a summer theme park.

"OH! That would be great, Karl." She leaned across to him and gave his cheek an enthusiastic peck. "You're just as much fun as I thought you'd be." She was still smiling when she said, "Harold would love this." Lena blinked her eyes. Harold was dead. That dirty writer from Arizona had killed him. She knew she should feel sad, but it just wasn't in her. Her face seemed frozen in an expression of mystification. Why had she said that?

"Yep, Old Harold always liked a good time!" If there was anything that Karl didn't want, it was a melancholy Lena: she could be a real drag. "I remember a time when we were in Montana, just after the annual rodeo." Karl broke into a loud, uncontrolled laugh. "He...tried to steal...the prize...bull. That damned thing...almost killed him." He struggled to catch his breath; partly because he could still picture his drunk, staggering, sidekick, and partly because he had succeeded in coaxing Lena into an eye watering snort. "You should have seen the look on that bull's face when he slipped and reached out to stop his fall." He paused. "Harold grabbed the bull by his 'privates' he just missed kicking Harold right in the head."

"Yeah, we used to have some great times." Lena sighed in between her eye dobbing sobs.

"Don't worry there, Lena. We'll get that son of a bitch what murdered your poor defenseless brother." Karl hoped she never learned the truth.

Chapter 36

From the moment that the swinging doors flapped open, Lena felt as if she had soared to another heaven. The smells of stale beer and Jack Daniels shot through the air like laser guided missiles. Her feet moved as if they were being pumped by fresh blood. Her hand moved to her right ear and pushed back her hair. She pranced like a doe in heat. Her eyes shot about the room, hunting for that special male buck that appreciated her enough to die for the privilege of a few minutes with her.

"High there, sweet thing;" a voice somewhere in the crowd.

Swiftly her feet moved over the hardwood floor: heals clicking, toes springing. Lena moved up to the twenty-feet long bar. The wood was chipped and scared by years of fights and neglect. Behind the bar was the movie like mirror decorated with amateurish depictions of bear, deer and water foul. A young bartender was prancing her way. He had the look of a predator. She liked it.

"What can I get for you, mama? His accent was probably fake; He looked like a New Yorker. *Probably some college kid off for the summer.* He flashed a perfect set of white teeth. "Pardon the smoke, buttercup."

This bar keep was trying too hard. "Wild Turkey on the rocks, mister, and don't spare the bird." Karl had been quiet…maybe brooding, but she didn't care.

Karl moved up beside her and spoke in a menacing tone. "Don't attract too much attention, Lena. We can only be here for a short time." From the corner of his eyes he watched the young bar tender pour her drink: he was really slugging the whiskey. He was probably hoping to get lucky. Karl stiffened as he placed his hand on her arm. "We're here for fun, so don't plan on spending any time here."

With a sophisticated flourish, the bar tender placed her drink on a sparkling white coaster. "It's on the house, little lady." Ignoring Karl, he looked up and down the length of the bar. "What's your name, Missy?" He rattled off in a well-practiced John Wayne ersatz.

She could feel Karl bristle as she picked up her drink and coyly sipped from her glass as she eyed the young man. "Why…I'm Lena." She signaled a smile filled with feminine interest. Lena could almost feel the heat from Karl's body. "What's your handle, cowboy?" She elbowed Karl.

She watched his lips as the man's mouth moved beneath a set of soft lips that seemed fashioned from strawberry fluff. "I'm Nute, ma'am; mighty pleased to make your acquaintance." Responding to a signal from down the bar he shrugged and tipped his gray Stetson hat.

Feeling like a piece of invisible furniture, Karl nudged Lena. This is not what he had in mind. He had thought they would go over to the bar and she would have a few drinks and a couple of dances...with...HIM. It was bad enough the insolent twerp behind the bar had not even asked him what he wanted, but now...Lena was encouraging the phony son of a bitch. "Look, Lena. Let's dance. I'll get a beer at a table." Karl didn't wait for an answer. He grabbed her by the arm and pulled her off of the barstool.

With her left hand she snatched the drink from the bar: spilling some of it onto her fingers. She put them in her mouth and sucked the fluid like a desert-parched prospector. "Jesus, Karl. Take it easy. I'm just trying to have some fun...OKAY?"

The back of his head burned as if a ray of sunlight had just focused on him. He fought the instinct to flip his head around and see who was watching him. His body was already beginning to ache from having to control his feelings; As he sat down, he slowly...as casually as he could manage, lifted his head and moved his eyes about the bar room. There he was; at the bar, leaning against the far end, just where the bar curved toward the wall

a policeman, probably a highway patrolman. Karl
bristled as he moved his hand behind his coat: to
the center of his back. The Glock slipped neatly
into his hand, but so did a feeling of frustration. If
it were not for the crowd and the lack of a clear
shot, he would have shot the man before he drank
his beer, now…he would have to wait.

"I'm going to take a leak, Lena." He eyed the
cop and stood up. "Get me a draft." Karl waited
for her to respond. "Get me a big on, I'll be back."
He stood tall, snorted, and took off toward the sign
that read, "Cowpokes". Glancing over his shoulder
he looked at the officer. Karl wanted to kill him.
As he approached the door to the hallway, he
glanced back. The officer was moving away from
the bar. Karl smiled…he had baited his prey. His
pulse began to race as he anticipated what he
wanted to happen. Like a stalking lioness his body
was alert. His senses heightened.

Before Karl, was a wooden door that was once a
forest green with the logo of a bull rider seated on
the back of an airborne bull. The arched back of
the bull and the fearless rider, who now had his
hand held high-- the faded image, had suffered the
abuse of time. They were covered with layers of
hand dirt and countless strikes by indifferent men
who focused on three goals: finding a woman,
drinking their beer and getting to the bathroom
before they either threw up or wet their jeans.

Karl opened the door with his left hand and smacked the logo with his right: perhaps it would bring him good luck.

To any causal person entering the bathroom the smell would have scorched their nostrils like a dose of acid, but Karl had other things in mind. His head and eyes moved in a coordinated pattern, searching for a place of advantage. He turned to his right and moved into a nook where two urinals had been scrunched in order to meet the flexible codes of the city. His fingers were trembling, not from fear but from the excitement of the kill. He moved the pistol from the back of his jeans to the front. He heard the door begin to open. Karl forced himself to relax.

Bill Proudy looked down at his hand. It was a fine hand, he thought. Long ,strong hands that had made him the local pride of the Grizzly basketball team. During his junior year he had set a new school record for points scored in a game, but that was before he broke his knee at the local swimming hole. Everyone had told him the lake was too shallow for such a high dive, unfortunately, they were right. His dreams of basketball fame shattered, he now worked for his uncle, Bob Proudy, the local sheriff. His gate had a slight limp as he pushed open the bathroom door.

With all the congeniality of greeting an old friend, Karl looked up from the urinal and chuckled, "Great place to hang out, huh, deputy?" He laughed at his own joke.

Bill moved over to the end of the long, chipped Formica counter that had one plastic sink. Just the week before, the older porcelain sink had been shattered during a fight over the treatment of a man's dog. "Sure is." Bill paused in order to consider how to say his next words. ""You look familiar. Do I know you?" It was an honest question. Bill had never been too bright about high school tests or memorizing things. At this moment he could not remember the flyer that now lay on his desk: a photo that perfectly depicted the face of Karl Boss.

Karl could almost smell the uncertainty in the voice of the deputy. "Doubt it...but then, I have one of those faces. People just find me friendly." Karl made the pretense of zipping up his jeans; instead he reached for the Glock that was slanted in his waist.

"Yeah, I guess that's it."

He heard the door begin to open: Karl's hand froze.

Arm in arm; two of the locals burst through the door, almost knocking it off of its hinges. "Hi, B.P., how's it hanging?" The large man looked like the big guy who played in the television series, Bonanza. He was at least six foot six inches and was dragging a smaller man as if he were a blow-up doll. The little man was almost unconscious, the perfect picture of the town drunk.

Officer Proudy swished a black comb through his thinning hair. "Doing fine, C.C. Luke out of it so soon?"

"Yeah, he ain't had nothing to eat, B. P." C.C. dragged him over to the farthest stall. "I'm gonna leave him here until he sobers up." His voice was a mixture of pity and disgust.

With a sense of amusement, Karl watched the touching display of hometown care. "Friend of yours, deputy?" He didn't mean to put an edge into his voice, but the two intruders had complicated his entertainment. Wearily, he watched the large man maneuver his soused friend into the tight confines of the bathrooms stall. A smile seeped onto his face. Karl had a plan.

"Friend's a little strong, but yeah…kind of." Bill turned his head to look into the stall. Perhaps he was considering helping C.C.

Karl moved over, next to Bill Proudy, ostensibly, to get a better look at C.C.'s endeavor. Moving close to the deputy his heart was now racing with possibilities. Karl could kill the deputy and C.C. and frame the drunk. That would be neat. Karl's nostrils flared as his breathing became quick and labored. In one swift movement he pulled out his gun and placed it at the head of the young deputy: Proudy had not even expected it.

Bill put his hands behind his head; Karl was too close for him to reach for his own weapon. He glanced at C.C. and wondered what the big man would do when he realized what was going on.

Then a strange thing happened. He recognized the
face that that been on his desk for most of the day.
It was that killer from Arizona. For the first time in
his life, Bill Proudy was scared.

Chapter 37

The power was out. The whole house was like a
morose cave. It seemed cold because of the
rainstorm that was blanketing the valley. The
sound of water splashing on the back yard patio
dominated the air. Each flash of lightening trickled
into the room strange shapeless silhouettes that
ranged from black and white to gray and colorless
shapes that defied interpretation.

"Rudy, did you pay the bill?" It was a pointless
question, but then, Kate was just making nervous
small talk.

Without shifting his eyes from the back yard, he
uttered, "Of course, I did...look at the neighbor's
houses...no power." He shifted to the side of the
bay windows and shook his head. Experience had
taught him it was a perfect night for intruders: the
thunder and the rain blocked sound. If the rain
continued it could obliterate tracks; "How about a
pot of hot tea?"

Kate giggled, "Ah...the power is off, Rudy."
Silently she moved across the room and placed a
hand on his shoulder. It was a tender touch,

conveying love and understanding; "How about a drink instead?" She watched as his head nodded against the pulsing thrust of another flash of lightening that was accompanied by a heaving vibration of thunder.

Gently, he placed his hand on hers. "Yeah, that would be great." Rudy's mind was miles away and years back in time. He could still picture the night he was on a ship that was approaching the coast of England. He had been invited to the wheelhouse. His heart seemed to be jumping about as if it were seeking a place of security. Stepping into the room, all he could see was a wall of water. Waves towered about the small destroyer. They split into hundreds of waves that washed and assaulted the entire deck. The water ran down the windows, changing everything into a picture of ghoulish shapes.

Kate had seen this far away look before. She smiled as she moved closer to his side. It was a face filled with understanding of the many ghosts that often plagued Rudy's sleep. A soft clearing of her throat jolted him back to Arizona; "Scotch and water." She clinked glasses with him and then pulled her pink robe together against the inclement weather. "Are you just absorbing the weather, or are you looking for something?" Her tone was not reproachful, but rather one of understanding.

He delayed his answer as he swallowed a sip from his drink. "Honestly, I'm not sure, Kate." He turned to face her. "I keep thinking about Ed and his family." He paused for another wave of thunder to pass. "I think they're in trouble. Maybe more trouble than they even know." Moving to a nearby-overstuffed chair, pensively he lowered himself into the embracing arms of his favorite chair; he leaned forward. She had been with The Bureau and he was used to confiding in her. "I got a call today…from Phil."

"The bureau chief?"

"Yeah." Now he leaned back and rested his head against the high back. "You know that guy who was killed at the airport?" In the darkness he flipped up his eyebrows.

Kate waited for a few seconds. She blinked as if she had missed a point. "Sure…the guy that worked at the nuclear plant…Palo Verde." She sipped her drink and waited, but Rudy was just sitting as if he were in a trance. "What about him?"

"Phil said the dead guy he was working undercover."

"Doing what?"

"Selling blueprints to a band of terrorists" ; Rudy sighed as he made a reflective pause. "I think Ed has the plans."

Quickly, Kate jumped in. Her voice was almost trembling. "What plans, Rudy?"

Rudy shook his head. It was like a gesture of denial; "The layout of the plant…particularly the sensitive places for maximum effect to create a nuclear explosion."

"Phil told you that?" Kate leaned forward and touched Rudy's knee. She wanted his full attention. "Why?"

"He thinks someone in The Bureau might have tipped off the terrorists that their contact was with the FBI." In a movement of frustration, he looked up at the ceiling. "I think he believes that Ed was in on the deal. The dropping of the disc to Ed was done on purpose. Since Ed had the disc, they didn't need the agent, so they killed him."

"Ed's a terrorist?" Kate pulled back her head squishing her eyebrows together and pushed out an exaggerated snort. "Give me a break, Rudy! What's Phil been smoking?"

Rudy responded with a sheepish smile. "Phil didn't mean Ed told the terrorists the agent was undercover. He just wondered about the coincidence of Ed's arrival at the airport, his sitting next to the man, and the surveillance tape which seemed to show the agent passing something into Ed's laptop case." He shrugged his shoulders, "It just looks like the agent thought Ed was the drop."

Pursing her lips, Kate did a slow shake of her head and rolled her eyes in a mock gesture of consideration, "Naaa!"

Soft shades of lightening -white filled the room, bathing the mahogany bookshelf and spotlighting the bookends. Three seconds later a resonance of thunder slipped into the space, almost unnoticed.

Chapter 38

For the umpteenth time I pressed on the 'enter' button of my laptop and asked myself the same question, 'Why would anyone want this blueprint?' Roland thought it was a neat model that could be used for a video game…I just didn't know. Rudy seemed to think the man at Sky Harbor Airport was killed because of it. Julie just wished I would leave it alone. I couldn't seem to do that, even if I probably should have.

From the corner of the room, Julie stirred as she rolled over in her twin bed. "Are you still at that thing?" I could hear the mixture of disgust and mild irritation in her tone. "Just send the thing to Rudy and be done with it."

I just leaned back in the chair and replied, "He hasn't asked for it." I tucked my hands behind my head and formed a face that indicated the simplicity of my reasoning.

Julie propped herself up on one elbow and returned a 'snotty grin'. "And why do you think that he hasn't? Ed?" cat and the canary look.

Being a mature adult, I returned the 'snotty grin' and continued my display of superior logic. "Because he…" My voice trailed off as I finished my words, "He…doesn't care about it, or he thinks it has no value?" I could feel my face shifting into a mask of puzzlement.

Her eyebrows shot up, "Maybe he already has a copy…Ed." Sitting up, she fluffed her pillow, "Maybe even the original…Ed." Julie leaned back and crossed her arms over her chest.

Life's embarrassing moments. It had not even occurred to me to e-mail a copy to Rudy. There was no doubt but what he was interested, I could tell that by the conversation we had the other night. Thinking out loud, "Why would he have a copy? Where would he get it from?" I stroked my morning beard with my fingers, a habit I had when I was seeking inspiration.

"Rudy may not be FBI <u>active</u>, but he still spends a lot of time with his bureau friends." An unexpected shift occurred in her tone, serious, even accusatory. "If I were you, Dear, I'd be more concerned about those Puppy Killers that we left back in Phoenix. What does Rudy have to say about them?" Julie banged her pillows with her fist-an exclamation point.

Just the mention of the Puppy Killers sent an alarm with the impact of a Stun Gun. It bolted across my chest and dropped to my gut. While I was fooling around with the blueprint, I hadn't given Karl and Lena a thought. Since they had been reported at Las Vegas I just assumed they would head to the North West…probably Seattle.

"Rudy and I haven't talked about the Killers." I noticed my voice had a tremor in it. "I doubt they have any interest in us. By now they are probably enjoying the Seattle space needle, or fishing in

Oregon." There, that was better, my voice sounded more normal. I got up from my four-legged chair and walked to the bathroom. This was not my favorite topic. "Hell, Julie, they might even be in jail by now." I chuckled as if I really 'nailed it'.

Outside I could detect the steps of Roland, Janet and Jake moving about on the wooden deck. It was going to be a sunny day. We would probably go to the sandy beach on the east side of the island. Lately, I had begun to realize I had to sneak short stops to catch my breath; it didn't seem serious, just noticeable. I would pretend to pause to look at a fence, a plant, a house, or even a seashell. Who was I kidding?

"I'm going into the house. Want some tea?"

Julie's voice had caught me off guard, but it was a welcome break to my wandering introspections. "Sure. Be right out." I closed my eyes. *Relax.*

Chapter 39

If he didn't do something, he was going to die. Charlie Burly considered the thought, strangely enough he felt conflicted. Sure he wanted to live, who didn't, but maybe he was also willing to die. It was just Martha and him now...the kids were grown and living their own lives. Was it really worth it?

The door to the motor home banged as it closed. Who had come in? Charlie strained his ears: it was quiet. Maybe they had gone out. Another thought occurred to him, maybe they were just trying to trick him…or worse, tease him. His knee was killing him; the pain was something he decided to live with, just another 'settle for'.

Life was slipping by much differently than he had expected. Pains and loneliness were now his constant companions. It used to be that enthusiasm and hopeful anticipation were his watchwords, what had happened to him over the years? People were asking him, 'what's wrong, Charlie?' that never used to happen. He took several shuttered breaths and looked inwardly. Charlie Burly didn't like what he saw…he had become a complacent coward.

It had been painful, but he had slipped his wrist-taped hands from behind him to in front of his face. Behind the tape on his mouth he muttered, "Old Charlie Burly isn't done yet, by God!" He could feel the change, it was like one of those comic book characters that said a magic word and they changed into an invincible super hero. First his fingers gripped at the tape and began ripping it from his mouth. The air that rushed into his lungs felt vibrant and pure.

Outside the sky was turning to a dark shade of slate gray etched in grades of red. A storm was moving in from the east and the setting sun was acting like the spotlight on a Broadway play.

Charlie could hear the rattling sounds of thunder bouncing off of the tree-covered hills. He moved quickly now, full of determination to get free and escape from his misfortune. The pounding in his ears assured him his heart was a willing laborer in his frantic goal. He ignored the pain that knifed into his injured knee and swollen fingers. Martha would be proud of him…he was fighting back, he was holding on to life. His feet were untied, now he was chewing at the bindings on his wrists.

If he could get to the front door, perhaps he could block it from being opened. A chill flooded through his bowels as he pictured himself coming out of the bathroom only to find the two lunatic kids sitting and waiting for him. Would that be the way his life would end? Would Martha ever know what happened to him? He placed his hands on the door handle and slowly began to push it down, it moved faster than he had remembered. It seemed like years ago since he had last opened the door. Noiselessly, the door began to swing on its hinges. He could see all the way to the front of his motor home: no one was there. He moved forward and peeked around the side of the door: his wrists were still wrapped in tape. Fingers trembling; damn, he couldn't see into the back of the motor home, where the bedroom was: the door was slid shut. What if they were wallowing on the bed? A shiver went up his spine; he would have to take the risk.

Charlie had not intended to spend the night at the parking lot so he had not put out the levelers, he felt awkward as he moved like a drunken sailor on the deck of a pitching four master. There was a spare key in the glove compartment. The salesman had put it into a small manila envelope…just in case. They had joked about Charlie's lament that his wife, Martha, was always misplacing keys and papers: the remembrance brought a smile to his glue flavored lips, he almost teared up. *No time for that.* As he continued walking, he bit little chunks out of the tape on his wrists.

Sitting in the front passenger seat, he began to dig about in the glove box. *Where's the key?* Frantically he clawed at the inside of the glove box, spilling papers, paper clips and pens onto the brown-carpeted floor. His head and eyes moved about haphazardly: a swell of panic was rising into his throat. Where was the key?

There was movement. There…across the parking lot, coming out between two cars. It was a policeman. Charlie stood up. He would flag down the officer. He was safe. Martha. His nerves tingled as he headed for the door, but he stopped. He couldn't believe his eyes. Karl and Lena were behind the policeman and it looked like they were heading straight for the motor home. Charlie smiled. He must have misjudged them…could they have had a change of heart? Not likely. It was too much to hope for. His newfound optimism quickly turned to self-chastisement. *Why didn't I just get out of here? Now I wasted my best chance.* It only took Charlie a few seconds to glance about the interior as if he were looking for a place labeled, 'exit here if you want to live.' He would go out the driver's side.

They were coming close to a motor home. Bill Proudy walked as if he were in a stupor, he couldn't believe that C.C. was dead; his mind would not accept the horrible mess he had just seen; blood flowing... moving over the green concrete floor, finding its way to the stained metal drain cover. With one muffled shot behind the big man's ear, he had dropped to the floor like a dead bird. Luke lay passed out next to C.C. Guess you could say that it was Luke's lucky day. Bill wanted to talk, but he was ashamed ..his voice would crack from fear. What kind of people were these?

In a subdued tone, Lena spoke to Karl. "Karl, does this mean we can keep the motor home?" She read the confused look on his face and smiled, "I really like it, Karl."

Shaking his head in a gesture of disbelief he kept his eye on the deputy. He was sure the cop was going to piss his pants. "We'll see." Some times she could act so dumb he questioned if there were posts that dense. "Maybe the deputy has some ideas." Karl chided the panicked man, "What'cha think?"

Usually Bill did a lot of talking by moving his hands. He reminded himself he had been instructed to keep his hands in his pockets. "I wouldn't make a very good hostage." He let out a forced laugh, "Who would want me?" Bill had meant the words

173

as a way to deal with his tension, but it backfired: if he wasn't a good hostage…why keep him around? "My uncle is the Sheriff, maybe he could help." He had to stop talking, he was feeling ill.

All three of them stopped as they came up to the passenger side of the motor home. Karl handed the key to Lena. "Open it!" His words were excited as a kid ordering his favorite ice cream cone. He watched as Lena turned the silver key and the steps slid down under the door. "Give me the key, Lena."

Bill was moving his head, one might have thought he was at an intersection and was checking on the traffic to his left and to his right, but Bill Proudy was looking for help. He had a feeling that if he entered that 'bus' he would not come out alive: already he had witnessed a murder. This man was a cold-blooded killer, and he loved doing it.

Before she stepped into the motor home, Lena had a feeling something was wrong. Her eyes caught the glimpse of papers lying on the floor under the passenger's seat. She was only reasonably certain she had not dropped the papers. Her body responded with what felt like a surge of electricity. Karl would be mad.

Bill was behind Lena, he stopped his ascent when she stiffened and turned to a statue. Fearing something was about to happen, Karl stepped back and quickly spoke in words of alarm. "What's going on? What'd you stop?" Like the sound of a rattler's tail, the words had a fatal tone.

"She stopped!" Bill explained. For one flash of a second, he considered trying to kick Karl in the face, but one thought of missing stopped his twinge of bravery.

Lena fought for a delay. "I just lost my balance, Karl...and I was looking around." She plopped into the seat and quickly picked up the papers. "Sorry!"

Officer Proudy came into the 'bus' and sat at the kitchen table.

"Where's a good place for gas?" Karl jabbed the gun in Bill's direction. "And don't get any ideas. I'll let you go just as soon as I can. Karl often wondered if he really meant what he said when he said it. Probably not, but then he didn't believe he was all bad. When he told Charlie he was going to let him go...maybe he meant that. "Lena, check on Charlie. See if he needs anything?"

"Sure." For the first time it occurred to her Charlie could have made that mess in the front cab. Had he gotten out of the bathroom and been looking in the glove box? Lean slowed her gait. Where was he now? If he had gotten out; she paused and looked around.

"It's that way, dummy." Karl laughed as if he expected everyone to join in. "Jesus, Lena sometimes I wonder about you."

That was the same look he had before, she noted. "I know where the can is, Karl." Like typical teenage disgust, she wrinkled her face and spat out her words. Still, her steps were measured. She felt like a person digging the hole into which they were soon to be buried. "Honestly, Karl, you can be a real pain in the butt."

The atmosphere could have been humorous. It was like three people just hanging out. No threats; just relaxing fun. And who in the Hell was Charlie? Was he another one of this gang? How many were there? Bill wanted to laugh, but his mouth was dry. His teeth chattered. "Can I use the bathroom?"

Chapter 40

"It's the craziest thing I've ever heard, Ed. The state highway patrol picks up this old man, he's babbling about being held prisoner in a motor home. He looks like he just crawled out of one of the highway sewers. Captain Cateras was laughing himself sick until he heard it was two kids named", he made a dramatic pause which should have required a drum roll; "Karl and Lena."

I had felt the punch line coming, but the two off shore bank account numbers still made me fell a swarming pit of terror in my stomach. "Where did they find them?" I lacked Rudy's enjoyment of the story. "What city?"

He could tell I was not entering into the humor of the old man's plight. "Ah…close to, Memphis, Tennessee." Rudy sniffed as he adjusted his tone. "He said they kidnapped him at a truck stop just south of Memphis."

"So, they're headed my way, huh?" I had the distinct impression I had placed my hand over my mouth, almost wishing I had never said the words.

Rudy almost never lied, but this time he made an exception. "Not necessarily, Ed. They might just have gone that way to try to avoid the blood hounds." Switching to an attitude of encouragement, he added, "The authorities have been hot on their trail, Buddy."

Feeling the urge to be discouraged, I returned a forced chuckle. "Who do you think you're kidding, Rudy. They're coming after me…just 'cuz I was forced to kill that idiot brother of hers." I had pent up feelings I could not even reach. Lena's brother had been the epitome of low-life trash. The world was better off with out him. "You really think I don't know that?" I was getting angry; I wanted to yell until I broke the telephone into tiny pieces. "Jesus, Rudy!" I sucked in a mouthful of air…my heart was thumping like a trip on a Disney character theme ride.

Rudy glanced over at Kate; she had been listening and watching the whole thing. She knew Rudy meant well, but it was better to tell it like it was. Karl and Lena were tracking Ed and Julie just as certainly as a wild animal hunting its night

menu. "Tell him the truth, Rudy. You owe him
that."

"You're probably right, Ed...BUT, don't think
the police are taking these two lightly. They'll get
them before they get to you." Rudy glanced at
Kate: she shook her head. "Ed, are you armed?"

"Do I answer that over the phone, Rudy?" My
response was somewhere between a joke and five
pounds of irritation.

Rudy ignored my surly attitude. I could tell he
was making a pause in our talk. I was feeling tuned
into his predicament: he wanted to help, but there
were still too many unknowns. "When will you be
leaving...coming back?" Concern!

Looking at the wall calendar I studied the days.
If anything I ever did in my life was a pointless,
unnecessary gesture, it was staring at the calendar.
"Five days...Friday;" My mouth was moving, but
it was mostly prattle. Just a way to keep from
thinking about my family being tracked by two
homicidal maniacs, and we hadn't even talked
about the disc I had. My next words floated into
my hearing like they came from outer space.
"What about the disc, Rudy." I hesitated to ask the
next question. "Am I in danger about it, too?" I
waited, not really wanting to hear his answer... by
the pregnant pause I knew what it had to be.

"Maybe we should talk about the disc at another
time. We know there are...people who seem to be
interested in it, Ed." Rudy focused his stare on the
disapproving face of Kate. "Just a second, Ed."

Rudy put his hand over the mouthpiece of the phone. "What do you want me to say? He's already stressed out about the two Puppy Killer nuts." He shrugged.

"If he is in danger, Rudy"; she touched his arm: a gesture to reassure Rudy as well as calm him down. "At least make sure he knows to be on his guard. He'll get over it." Kate shifted her eyebrows shrugged, and pasted her face with a helpless grin.

Rudy's voice came through the line. It seemed so loud it made me jump, at least inside. "Kate says I should tell you to 'be on your guard'. I know you are already, Buddy, but until we can find out, for sure, why they want the blueprints of the Palo Verde plant, I'm not sure what to say." This time there was a 'birthing pangs' pause. "Have you noticed anything like, say, someone following you or anything else?"

"Do you count breaking into our room and ransacking our luggage?" I didn't wait for his reply. "A couple of nights ago, I thought two men were following us, but now, I'm not really sure. AND, I'm sure that both of us can think of why someone might want the blueprints of a nuclear facility. Can't we?"

"Yeah, I know what you mean." In an effort to leave with a positive note, Rudy lightened his tone. "Hey, Ed. Enjoy your vacation. I'll meet you at the airport."

"Sure thing, Rudy; give our love to Kate." I hung up the phone and sat down. If I thought it would have helped, I would have cried.

Chapter 41

The pistol was disassembled. Parts lay neatly arrayed on the comic section of a U.S.A. Today Sunday edition. Holding the barrel in his left hand, the man carefully examined the lands and grooves before he forced the metal brush inside. He squinted and made a face that would have given any casual observer the impression he was playing the part of a K.G. B. agent for some movie. "I think... Friday would be a good day, Bill."

A recording of the conversation between Ed and Rudy was still running. Bill nodded as he pressed the 'pause' button. "Let's get this Rudy while he is on the move."

"Not a bad idea, but we don't need him, just the disc which Ed has." Peter had finished his cleaning and began to reassemble his pistol. The parts looked like toys in his big hands. "We just need to take Rudy out of the equation while we get the disc."

Leaning forward, the smaller man rested his chin in his palms. "Okay, I'm game, but what do we do about this Karl and what's her name if they find him first. According to the Fed guy, Karl and this girl plan to kill Ed… maybe before we can get the disc from this Ed …and he is the only one who knows where it is."

"Who cares as long as we get the disc?"

The little man shook his head. "So we get the disc. If you ask me, I don't get the point. If the F.B. I. knows about the blueprints floating about…why bother?" He paused long enough for the TV set in the other room to draw his attention.

Peter snapped the slide on his pistol. It moved effortlessly. He smiled. "Off shore bank account numbers, Bill. Off shore bank account numbers! That disc has the off shore bank account numbers of some people they'd like to put behind bars." He slipped in a clip full of nine-millimeter hollow-points. "That dip at the airport made a point of asking for extra money because of that list. It's supposed to have the off shore bank account numbers of cops, and some politicians that are involved. And they, my friend, pay the bills." With a single smooth movement, Peter slid his polished pistol into a dark brown shoulder holster. "You do want the rest of our money, don't you?"

"Sure, but it just seems this whole thing is dragging along too slowly. You know, as well as I do, the longer the exposure…the more likely they are going to snag us."

Ignoring the words of his partner, the big man said, "We'll need a little diversion."

"Diversion?"

"Yeah; at the dock." Peter popped the ring on a can of beer. The sound reminded him of the release of a silencer. "Yeah...they will come down from that house. They'll probably use one of those wagons to take the luggage to the dock."

"What if he has the disc on him?"

"Huh! We kill him, I guess; sloppy job, Bill. Stealing back a disc is not such a big deal, but killing a writer who has friends with the F.BI.... not smart."

The room became so quiet that, for the first time, they became aware of the slapping of the waves against the nearby pier. A sailboat was cutting through the channel; it made a wake that glided silently until it reached the pilings of the pier.

Bill's shoulders sagged as he sighed. "Okay, Peter, but we're running out of time. IF we don't get that disc, someone will be coming after us...just for spite." He moved his hands together, placing his palms on each side of his nose. Speaking softly, he muttered. "We had better kill him. We can make it look accidental, if they don't autopsy the guy. During the confusion, we can mix up the baggage."

Peter grinned. "You may have something there. Even if they do find out he was murdered...for all they know, it was those other two. You know, Karl and the girl."

Bill pushed out his lips as if he had just eaten a sour persimmon. "Sure. Why not, but we better do a neater job than we did in Phoenix. It was messy and we botched getting the disc."

"How in the Hell were we supposed to know he had already passed it?"

"To tell you the truth, Peter, I couldn't care less. I didn't get in this life to make friends, or get a 'rep'. I want the money. If I got to snuff the whole family, I will." He pointed his finger at the little man. "But I can damned well guarantee you, if we don't get that disc, we are both dead men."

Peter jumped to his feet. His face was beet red with emotion. "Hey, calm down, Bill. We'll get the disc!" He faked a smile that was supposed to display confidence. "What ever it takes...okay?"

Chapter 42

The jail cell was much smaller than he thought. In the movies they seemed to be much wider. It seemed, as long as he could remember, the tall, ugly man just kept asking questions. Charlie's eyes were focused on the man's long mustache that seemed to cover his lower lip. Charlie wanted to sleep, but all the sheriff wanted to talk about was his missing nephew, Bill Proudy. Looking at the sheriff, Charlie could not recall ever seeing a man whose whole face seemed to be slanted.

Charlie rubbed his face, wishing the compulsion to close his eyes and sleep would go away. "For the tenth time, Sheriff Bob, I don't know anything else. I escaped using the driver's side door. After that, I ran like hell, out of the parking lot, across the highway and into the woods. I JUST WANTED TO GET AWAY!"

Hidden beneath the mustache a voice spoke. "Come on, Charlie. You must have seen my nephew. Is he okay?"

"Officer Proudy, if I had seen him, I would have told you." Charlie's voice was hoarse. His speech etched with irritation. "All I saw was your nephew walking in front of the two varmints that tied me up. That Karl and the girl called Lena. If that was him, that is all I saw of him."

Charlie leaned his head back against the cold, gray, concrete block that shaped out three walls. With only a thin mattress and two blankets on top of a concrete slab that bulged out from the wall, the room was anything but hospitable. Charlie was not looking forward to using the combination-exposed toilet-washbasin that protruded from the wall. When was this man going to let him sleep?

Bob Proudy was still not convinced Charlie was telling all of the truth. For all he knew, this man was involved in the capture of his nephew. From his experience, most people were liars. Of course they had sent out inquires about him. So far, Charlie, if that was his real name, had no record, but time would tell. "Okay…let's try it again. What were you doing at the commercial rest stop?"

The woods had done a real job on the side of the new motor home. The paint was scratched from the front end to the back. Long lines of jagged silver looking lines had made the outside look like a unit that was ten years older than it was. On each side of the scared motor home were brush and trees; underneath were bent and broken limbs and leaves.

"How do we get off the motor home, Karl…we're blocked in by these green things." Lena leaned across seats: her face against the windows her head moving from side to side.

Karl considered his situations. He could not risk going to the next service station and with Charlie out there somewhere; there was always the chance he had gone to the police. He had just pulled down a rural road and slipped off the narrow road and into a stand of brush and small trees. There was no way he could tell Lena how angry he was. Things were falling apart and now he had a law officer stashed in the same restroom where he once had a non-threatening old man. "Just open the door, Lena!" He closed his eyes in an expression of frustration.

She placed her hands on her hips. Looking like a lecturing mother, she made a quick sigh. "I tried that …Karl." Lena crossed her arms over her chest and gave them a solid bounce. "A tree is blocking the door."

"I don't need this crap, Lena." He turned in the driver's seat and faced her. "We are in deep crap , Lena. If that old man has told them about us, we can't keep this thing. We need fuel, but almost anyone could end up turning us in. Not to mention we've kidnapped a cop." He slipped his hands behind his head, "We've got to get rid of this thing and find a car, if we are going to New York. You still want to, don't you?"

Lena frowned, "I want that guy, Karl. Let's do it! Make it happen!" There was passion in her. She was committed to killing all of the Malone family.

He always prided himself on his creativity. Karl took on a serious face that tightened his forehead and his lips, but he had an idea that might solve his dilemma. "I know you're mad, Lena, but have you ever really killed someone?"

She scowled, "What do you mean?" Lena had been around Karl long enough to know he never asked questions like that without a reason.

Karl turned sidewise and threw his feet onto the dashboard. "It's not as easy as you think, girl. They plead...sometimes cry. You're going to feel guilty, Lena." Karl tilted his head and blinked his eyes. "I don't think you can do it, Le." He looked at the floor and slowly shook his head. "You're just too soft."

Lena felt her confidence begin to melt like snow on an Arizona desert. She began to feel weak, even guilty and she hadn't even done anything yet. How about her brother, Harold Pepper, did she not care? Was she just a coward? "I might be soft, Karl, BUT I loved my brother. He raised me, Karl...I owe him."

Karl broke in; there was a mocking laugh in his voice. "Sure, sure, but you'll fold when it really counts. You'll get all soft about his kids...his wife. You think you mean it, but you don't have what it takes to kill a living person." He shrugged, "It's okay. I know you want to stand up for your brother. I understand that, but you'll fink out when it counts. That's because you don't have what it takes to take a life." The bait was out, now he waited.

She slapped his leg: he was surprised, it hurt. "Listen, you bastard I'll show you. I can be tough when I have to."

"You can kill?" He moved his head toward her and narrowed his eyes while he waited.

She focused her eyes at his eyes. It was a challenge. "Damned right, Karl."

"All right, Little Lady." He nodded toward the back of the motor home. "Kill the cop!" His tone was not confrontational, it was flat. Karl looked at the floor, his eyes moved about as if looking for an answer from some unknown person.

Lena heard herself suck in a mouthful of air. The cab of the motor home was much more quiet than she had remembered. Suddenly, she could hear the sounds of trees moving about the metal frame.

Outside, birds were chatting to one another. Her head felt light. Was Karl right? Would she fail when the time came? Was he right? If she could kill the cop, would that mean that she could kill the book writer? She wondered. "What would that prove?"

"Forget it, Lena. I didn't think you could." Magically, Karl sounded sympathetic. "See what I mean?"

Lena opened her mouth. Words came out. Were they hers? "I'll do it."

"What?"

"I'll do it, Karl. Maybe it's the only way that I'll know I can stand up for Harold." The idea made her sick, but so what? If it made her sick…then she would just have to deal with it. "I'll do it."

He was amazed at how easily she had bought into his plan, but then she always was easy. Karl knew she could turn him in if she had no real crimes to her credit. The cop, Billy Proudy, had been a gift. IF she decided to turn on him, he would have a cop killing to trade for leniency. Karl handed her the officer's pistol. "Here!"

While examining the weapon, Lena twitched, she asked, "What do I do?"

"You know how to shoot the gun. The rest is simple." He nodded, "Take him outside and pull the trigger." He patted her leg. "We'll leave him in the woods. Then we'll go get a car and zip off to the north east." Sympathetically, he asked, "Want me to go with you?"

"Why not"; She didn't know why she said those words, but it seemed the right thing to say.

Karl had hoped for a clean kill. He didn't want to be an accessory to killing the cop. How could he hold the crime over her head if he were involved? It felt like one of those tic-tack-toe moves that makes you lose no matter what you do.

"Okay, but we had better wait for a better time."

"I'm ready now, Karl. You made a point, I agree. I need to get over my fear of ...shooting someone." She could not force herself to say 'kill'.

* * *

Bill Proudy could never have described his feelings. He was listening to a couple of kids chatting back and forth as if they were picking out a watermelon at the grocery store. They were talking about his life, not the tastiness of the fruit. He was scared, for good reason, it was like watching sands of grain dropping into the lower chamber: marking the final moments of his life. His thoughts turned to self-criticism. How did he ever allow himself to get trapped by two kids?

Chapter 43

Death seems to come in al kinds of sizes, shapes, and colors: at least it feels that way. According to Rudy, I had at least two different sets of people who were hunting me as if I were an Alaskan trophy bear. The third thing closing in on me could be my heart valve, but then it could be just my overactive imagination working against me.

The big day had finally arrived. We got up on a cool but sunny day in late June. The morning sea air was soft and refreshing: a perfect day for traveling. Before we realized it, our cloth sided bags were packed and sitting on the floor of our bungalow. About every ten minutes I had moved the computer disc to a different spot. As a plan of last resort, I put an empty disc in the outside pocket of my computer case and the actual disc in Julie's oversized purse: the disc was well protected in a plastic case. When we were in flight back to Arizona, I could put it back into my computer case.

The screen door to the main house snapped shut; I looked up and saw Julie turning toward our door. She looked as vivacious as ever; her brown, natural curls reflected the morning sun; "Ready to go?" She extended a cup of hot tea. "I thought we could stop at the deli before we head for the ferry. We could get a hot breakfast. Lord knows when we might be able to eat something."

I glanced at the bed where she had left her purse. I considered telling her where I had put the disc, but then- decided against it; "Sounds good to me." I was happy to be able to change the subject that was pulsing through my troubled brain. "Actually,

I could use a hefty sandwich." I made the effort of matching her enthusiastic tenor.

"Roland said he would stay here and watch the bags, he has a science project he wants to finish." She pushed her way out onto the wooden deck and did a little twirl as she examined the sky for weather. "Looks good, Ed. I think we'll have a smooth flight home."

"Rudy said he would meet is at the airport. He has some news he wants to go over with me." The words had just fallen out of my face. I knew I shouldn't have said them, but now it was too late. "Nothing crucial, but he has some stuff that would go well in my book." Now I had done it. Her face changed to a scowl.

"Are you hiding something from me?" Her eyes changed from a soft milky gray to gunmetal blue. Her lips shifted from a soft pout to a thin line of red; "What's he want to talk about, Ed?"

"Stuff...just stuff." I walked past her before I got trapped into confessing all of the fears and demons I had been conjuring up while I waited for her. How important the disc was, I did not know, but by now I suspected it was a blueprint of the nuclear plant. My latest guess was there were a couple of terrorists who were after it. As for the Puppy Killers, I was pretty sure they had not yet arrived at New York, much less located us. Now...I felt like a real shmuck lying to Julie. "It's just book stuff, Julie. Don't go making up something just to have something to worry about."

I could tell she was irritated by the guilt trip that I laid on her, but it worked.

After she snapped her purse from the bed, she moved up behind me. "Okay. Let's get something to eat." The only indication she was still miffed was when she let the screen door slam so hard it bounced against the door jam. I hoped the kids didn't hear the slam.

"I wonder if they can make a sandwich like an 'egg McMuffin'."

In the distance I could hear the sounds of the motor craft moving about in the bay between the island and the mainland. For a Friday morning it seemed particularly quiet, but then I had not really had that much experience at Fire Island. We walked in a kind of silence, each of us caught up in the privacy of our own thoughts and memories. We greeted the many people we met on the way. They were old and young and every age in between. Bicycles politely passed by us with no more interruption than the soft jingle from their silver ringer. The sound spoke of another time when we had our turn at being children.

I reached for Julie's hand. It was cool, as it always was. 'Cold hands, warm heart.' "So…have you had a good time?" I paused, "Did you enjoy seeing your brother?"

We moved to the side to avoid the two men. They looked a bit out of place because of their long faces and furtive stares, but then, maybe I was just being paranoid. They moved by us and headed in the direction from which we had just come.

Julie was saying something but my mind was focused on the two men who just passed by us. "…but I haven't seen Jake for almost twelve years. I think he's happy, except for the problems he's having at work." Julie paused and lowered her voice; "I used to worry a lot about Jake, so I guess I'm mainly happy that I got a chance to see how happy he is."

"It's never a good thing to spend too much time with relatives; usually three days is about all most people can take." I spotted the deli; it was just ahead and to our left. The store had been on Fire Island for ages, it was a combination grocery store and deli. I knew that my words were mostly automatic while my eyes moved about like some cartoon sleuth. "We'll have to eat fast if we are going to catch the next ferry."

Julie was munching on her hot ham and cheese sandwich. "You know, I just realized that we have barely seen the kids since we got here. Roland has kept them so busy they have been invisible." She shrugged with an impish, guilty grin. "Christine and Dell have practically lived at the beach."

"Thank God for Roland, otherwise Joel would have grafted himself to us instead of Roland." I had one of the best laughs I had had in days. "I think all of the kids are packed. As happy as they are here, they can hardly wait to get back home to their own beds, toys, and friends."

"I was the same way when I was their age." Julie smiled as she gently pounded the table top at the deli. "I feel that way now...still young!"

By the time we had finished saying good-bye to some of the people we had met, we were rushing to catch the local ferry. Roland had gotten us a large wooden sided wagon for taking our luggage to the dock. All of the children were already at the dock, leaving Julie and me to pull the entire luggage that was left. Julie had four pieces and I had two and my laptop. I can't say I was looking forward to pulling that wagon, but it was better than trying to carry the luggage.

Julie was feeling 'antsy'. "We're going to miss the ferry, Ed." She took off toward the wooden path to the water front.

It always reminded me of the scene from The Wizard of Oz and The Yellow Brick Road, only this was The Wooden Topped Sidewalk. "Okay, Julie...don't worry, we'll make it in time." I was speaking this just as I saw the ferry pulling up to the side of the dock: it was early.

"ED, the ferry's here." She picked up her pace.

I'm not sure how to describe what happened next. I wanted to move faster, I wanted to keep up with her, but it was like someone had put a plastic bag over my head. I was trying to do something I had done for a lot of years, but it just wasn't working. I kept thinking it was going to clear up and everything would be as it always was, but nothing good was happening. The only solution that was helping was when I would stop walking and suck in several quick breaths, in the mean time, Julie was getting closer to the dock and further from me.

"ED, the ferry's here. Hurry up; we're going to miss the boat!"

I managed to suck in enough wind to yell, "Go ahead. Tell them we're coming!"

"Okay!"

I felt an urge of resentment, as I wondered why she didn't help me pull this wagon, but there was no way she could tell I was laboring. Each step seemed like the last one I was going to take. The wagon didn't become heavier; it just refused to move fast enough to keep up with Julie. Taking a good breath was becoming more and more difficult. It was like trying to run up a hill that was making itself more steep every minute; an endless uphill escalator.

At right angles to a stretch of concrete walkway, the wooden part of the dock begins. The dock itself is shaped like an upside down letter 'L', jutting to the left at the small end. Julie met me at the point were the concrete just turned into the long wooden section. I had stopped to catch my breath.

The look of irritation was replaced by a look of concern as she dashed up to me. "What's wrong, Ed. We've got to hurry. The ferry's leaving." She tipped her head as she studied my face. "What can I do?"

"Help me…pull the wagon." I could see the people waiting at the short end of the 'L'. The friends that we met at the deli and the two men we saw on the road.

Julie grabbed the other side of the wagon handle. It felt great. We picked up the pace, but now I was moving so fast that I was really struggling to get my breath. Something was wrong, and it wasn't going to get better. I now had a chance to enter into a luxury I had to deny myself… fear. We were getting closer to the ferry, but I was beginning to feel weak. My mind was convincing me I was in real trouble. I sat down on a pile of wood; people were dashing about, some saying hello..I waved to them, and then I passed out!

Chapter 44

He was dead. No doubt about it, he looked strange. Like a rag doll, his legs and arms flopped like loose pieces of rubber. It was his eyes that surprised Lena: they looked large and glassy. A trickle of bright red blood, mixed with saliva, seeped from the corner of his mouth. She felt like a statue, or maybe a person watching a one-hour TV program where the dead man would soon get up and seek approvals for his performance. The pistol felt hot in the small hand of Lena Pepper.

Accentuated by a snort of disgust, Karl Boss pivoted and began walking back to the motor home. His muffled voice dripped with disapproval. "I told you, you weren't ready to shoot anybody. Jesus, Lena, you could barely shoot the guy in the shoulder." He stopped and looked down at her. "I had to finish that trooper off for you...I guess your little brother didn't mean that much to you."

Lena bent over and threw up what little food was in her stomach. She gagged as the contents quickly emptied. "It was...my first time ...Karl." Scenes of blood and flesh spattering against the foliage and trees kept zipping before her eyes. She wanted to yell at Karl, but she felt too weak to talk or walk any further. Using an aging stump as a stool, she sat down and put her head between her legs. "Aren't we going to bury him?"

For Karl it was a disappointing conclusion. He had planned to use the murder of Deputy Bill Proudy to blackmail her into doing more of his dirty work, at least the ones which didn't excite him. "Go ahead. Bury him, if you want to, but I'm for getting out of here."

"Where are we going?" She quickly forgot about her concern for burying the Deputy.

"We need a car...a real car. I think the motor home is too hot now." Karl was going through the officer's wallet. "Huh!" He smiled. "At least the cop had some dough on him, almost five hundred dollars...not bad."

Lena wanted to rip into him for his calloused attitude, but instead she found herself encouraged by their newfound wealth. "Wow! I could use some new clothes. I haven't had a change since we left the hospital."

"We need food, lame brain. And we need gas for our car." Karl bit back like a rabid dog. He was still seething about having to shot the cop.

She cast a girlish look at Karl, "Didn't he have a credit card?" Lena was impressed with her hard won brilliance.

"Daah;…if you want to be caught by the police and sent to the gas chamber."

"Huh?"

"For God's sake, Lena; don't you know nothing?" He flipped the empty wallet at her. It hit her in the face, almost cutting her cheek. "They track the credit cards by computers, dummy. As soon as they know he's gone…they'll flag his cards; they probably already have."

"They won't know until they find his body."

"Yeah, and then they will link us to the card we used and fry us." He turned and continued walking, his feet stamped in the field grass. "Besides…that Charlie fella has probably told them everything by now. He might have even seen us marching that cop out to the motor home."

Lena stood up and began to run after him. She wasn't too sure he wouldn't kill her…she was a witness. "Does this mean we won't go to New

York?" Right now, she wasn't sure just how she felt about continuing to chase the writer.

Karl considered the question. It had risks, but on the other hand, New York could be a good place to get lost. He could easily dump her, even kill her and leave her in some ally. Right now it was better for him to be traveling with a young girl, it made him look less dangerous. People were usually suckers when it came to dealing with a couple. If he were a single guy, they would always be a bit wary. "I think I owe it to your brother. Harold would want me to get even for him. That is, if you still don't have the stomach to pay them back for killing him."

"I just froze, Karl. I won't do it again. I'm all right now!" She grabbed at a broken stick and started swishing at the foliage and grass. Karl's words were beginning to hit their spot. The guilt, and the pity she had felt for Bill Proudy were almost gone, washed back out to sea like a wave on a sandy beach. "Hey, I have an idea."

"What?" He sneered with irritation.

Lena's ardor was dampened, but she was determined to make her repentance heard. "I'll do the next job, Karl. I know we need to stop for gas and cash. Just let me try. I need to get some experience. Isn't that what you were trying to say?"

"I wasn't *trying* to say anything. I *said* that you had no experience." There was no more discussion to be made. "Grab your stuff, we've got to get out of here and get us a ride."

She turned her head toward the spot where Bill Proudy had lost his life. The thought made her flash back to the birth of her daughter: one life into this miserable world and one more out. She wondered how her exit would be. There were parts of her thinking that seemed strange to her. Was this part of being a mother? She shrugged off the thoughts. "How far do we have to go?"

"Maybe a hundred twenty five miles…not too sure, but we've got to go through Virginia, Pen., and across New York." He stopped walking and stared at her, "Are you up for this? 'Cuz; if you're not we can just go to Canada or freeze our butts off in Montana."

"Sure…I'm ready, Karl. I'll be okay, just give me a chance."

"Well, we'll see." He took a long stride and headed for the motor home, "We got to the hustle if we're going to catch them before they leave New York."

Chapter 45

There was something they weren't telling him. He could sense it in his bones. It had happened before, but this time it really bothered him. Rudy

Sonfreg gripped his computer mouse and slid it about the flat screen monitor. He understood the need for security, but like any F.B.I. agents he didn't have to like it. As the images shifted, it became evident someone had every intention of blowing the Palo Verdi nuclear power plant to smithereens.

Kate slipped into the room, mindful of Rudy's ability to focus on his work. "I thought you were retired. When are you coming to bed?" Lightly she placed his small hand on his shoulder. "You've been at this for hours."

He stiffened, not from her touch, but from the surprise she was even in the room. "Ya, I think I've milked this thing for as much as I can get out of it…at least for tonight." Rudy started shutting down the computer. "I got to tell you, Kate…these guys are serious."

When the screen went black, she lowered her voice. "Why did you say that Ed might be in danger from these terrorists? I thought you were concerned about those Puppy Killer kids?"

Rudy gave a sardonic grunt. "Yeah, I think the copy of the blueprints might have a list of the people who are involved in this plan. If that is the case, The Agency thinks there might be some F.B.I. agents on that list." He looked about the room to make sure everything was in its place and none of the visual monitors were blocked. "If that is true, he will have people from both sides after that disc."

She looked puzzled, "How come the C.I.A. has their nose in this one? The Agency doesn't usually get that involved in domestic issues."

"Part of the new Homeland Security package. Besides...these guys have international ties." He couldn't hold back a soft sigh. "I'm afraid Ed might not live to write his book, Kate. I'm not sure anyone can keep him safe. The main problem is they want to catch these guys when they try to get the disc back from Ed, so they aren't doing anything to help him get rid of it."

"Well, no one can kill him until they have the disc in their hot little hands...can they?"

"That's right, Kate, but sometimes Ed can be pretty stubborn: he's just as likely to make them work for the disc. And they are damned well not going to take the risk that he has seen the list, or made a copy of it. They can't afford to let him live."

"So you're saying that, if the Puppy Killers don't get him...the terrorist will?" She looked at the floor as if she were hunting for some lost answer that could save their friends.

"They should be leaving today. I don't think those Puppy Killers are in New York, so they'll miss him. I think! But I also know the terrorists have people there now. Whether there are rouge agents there, I don't know."

The room seemed to fade into silence. A sense of pressure could be felt in the chest of the couple as they began to slowly make their way down the hallway to their bedroom.

"I hope the kids and Julie are safe." Kate issued a plaintive mumble.

"I wish I could guarantee that, Kate." Rudy gave her an affectionate kiss on the top of her head. He moved his head from side to side in a gesture of frustration, "This one is out of my hands. Right now...I wish we had left the Puppy Killers alone and the Malones had stayed at home."

Kate responded with a kiss to his cheek, "You know, Rudy, sometimes I can't help but believe that-- not much is really in our hands." She allowed a reflective pause, "When do you expect to hear from them?"

"Should be tomorrow, K; we've got some things to talk over. We're trying to track that Karl and Lena pair, but for now, they seemed to have disappeared again... somewhere around Roanoke, Virginia, or Harrisburg Pennsylvania. It's possible they have high jacked a car and dumped the motor home. The Virginia State Patrol is checking into it." Rudy yawned, "Boy, I'm beat!" He turned out the light, but wished he could have turned off the thoughts that were reaching through his mind. *How in the Hell were Ed, Julie, and the kids going to make it through all of this?* And what was it that The Bureau wasn't telling him?

Chapter 46

The crowd was gathering. People were stretching their necks, trying to get a better view at what was happening. There was a man lying on the dock, a man and a woman were performing TV class cardiac resuscitation. Every day they had watched this procedure performed on the TV show, ER, but today it looked different. The man looked peaked, just lying there like a Halloween straw-stuffed charioteer. One of the resuscitators was calling to the man, "Jack, Jack, Jack?"

Helplessly, Julie watched the scene. It did not seem real. Her mouth opened, "His name is Ed …not Jack!" She crossed her arms as if trying to protect the hurt that was surging in her heart. "He's my husband!" She fought back the urge to cry…Ed wouldn't like that. She felt helpless. Not that Ed would die, but how could she help? He was lying there, maybe dying, and she could do nothing.

A murmur drifted through the crowd as two Medical Technicians pushed their way through the growing watchers. They moved about with practiced and indifferent efficiency: placing their instruments about his body. One of the men spoke to Ed. "Ed, can you hear me?"

I opened my eyes and looked at the M.T. My eye lids floated up like the coverings on a mechanical headlight. "I'm okay." I watched as the technician busied himself reading the information that was

rolling out of a black box. "I'm okay." I reasserted.
Why didn't these people go away? I was all right.
So why weren't they leaving? I looked around and
felt hemmed in by the wave of bodies.

The technician did not shift his eyes from the
bewitching black box. "I don't like the readings we
have." Suddenly he turned his attention to the two
people who had been performing the CPR. "You
are both doctors?"

A uniform response came from the two. "Yes,
we are both cardiologists."

"These are the readings I'm getting." The
technician made a point of shielding the
information from me. "We need to transport him to
a hospital."

"He'll never make it" The male cardiologist said.
"Call in the 'chopper'."

I relaxed. This was out of my control. All I
could do was to lay there and let my body be
moved about as these people wanted. I didn't feel
that I felt that bad, they were probably just erring
on the side of caution. It was almost an 'out of
body experience' as they picked me up and carried
me to the waiting helicopter.

It was a confusing experience. It was my first
civilian helicopter ride, but I could have thought
of some better conditions under which to have
taken a ride. A smiling face plastered a breathing
mask that enveloped my nose and mouth. The
swish-swish of the rotor blades was all too
familiar: I had heard it in a million movies. I had

even thought about it …how it would have sounded had the Army sent me to Korea. A motion on the other side of the helicopter caught my attention. Julie was climbing into the 'coptor'. This was just like 'MASH'.

"Are you okay?" The smiling face finally spoke. The whirling of the rotor blades was beginning to pick up their tempo.

The EMT had placed a breathing mask over my face; I had to talk loudly to overcome the noise. "Yeah; I have a heart valve problem. I've known about it for the last twenty years, but they haven't wanted to replace it! I have no cholesterol problems and no heart damage!" I did my best to be under control. Somehow, I felt safe.

Julie was trying to give me an assuring smile, but it seemed to be coming through dripping eyes. I gave her an assuring wave, not just to be brave, but I actually felt fine…maybe I was in good hands. Time would tell, but for now, we were headed for a hospital in Stony Brook, New York.

The hospital had been a veteran's hospital at some time in the past, but now it was a university hospital bearing the name of Stony Brook State University Hospital. The next events came like a combination of the TV-E.R.series and a deployment of a Swat Team. The moves for handling 'trauma' cases was as well rehearsed as any Broadway play; everyone knew his, or her, job. Equipment was in place and questions were asked from a chart that looked more like something a commercial pilot would be using as a 'pre-flight' checklist. Members of the team moved about with a combination of efficiency and smiles of assurance that everything was going to be all right.

I wasn't that sure, but I felt a simple valve job would soon fix the problem. Maybe, if they hurried, I could still make my flight to Phoenix.

All the time, Julie was hovering some place in the immediate area. They asked me questions to ascertain my alertness (brain damage) and physical capabilities (stroke). I knew it sounds unsettling, maybe even scary, but, actually it was a welcomed relief from considering my death, or the death of my family at the hands of two kids or some terrorists. For the time being, I put all of those other fears far to the back of my mind. If they could find me, and I didn't think that would be easy, then I would deal with it.

I was settled in my space behind a sliding curtain. I couldn't help but wonder if I looked as badly as the other people I saw on the way to my space. I probably did!

"You're looking pretty good."

It was as if Julie had read my mind. The perfunctory lines delivered to those whom you know will probably not make it to the next morning. Was that the case? I was sure I was going to be fine, but then, I had been wrong before.

"I sent the kids on to Phoenix, they're going to stay with Kate and Rudy...it's a good thing that school is out." Julie smiled as if she addressing a tail wagging puppy.

Trying to sound as blasé as a husband sitting on the divan at home, I puffed out a few words, "So Rudy and Kate know about my problem." I still could not call it what everyone else was saying, 'a heart attack'.

Julie nodded. It was evident she didn't know what to say to her sensitive husband. "I called as soon as I could. There was no sense in keeping them here…there will be too much going on. Rudy and Kate said they would be glad to help out."

"It's nice to have friends." I rolled my head to the right and looked out of the window. My view consisted of concrete and a panoramic view of Long Island. It had not yet settled into my mind what Julie was going to do. Her brother and family were returning to Florida and the house would be rented out. That meant Julie would have to find a place to stay, close to the hospital, and yet something we could afford. Not wanting to burden me with her plight, she focused on getting me patched up.

"The hospital gave me a list of places to shop for bed and breakfast accommodations. Jake will help me house hunt before he has to go back to Florida." She made a pause as if to inform me we were not going to continue on this subject.

With things calming down, I began to consider I was now a real sitting target for any kooks wanting me dead. By now they were sticking things in my blood veins and hanging bags of God only knows what. It was now going to be my first night in a hospital: I did not know what to expect. Thoughts seemed to get jumbled. One minute I was coherent, next, I was thick tongued and seeing double. I felt helpless. Like a newborn baby, I was flat on my back and totally dependent upon the whims of the people around me. Frightening!

Julie was kissing my cheek; I hardly noticed what was going on…all I could tell was that I was getting real sleepy.

"I'll be back tomorrow morning. Tonight I am going back to The Island, but Jake will help me find a place tomorrow." All of her actions indicated she was not concerned, and I knew that, but as drugged up as they had me, I had no idea what she was feeling.

Night began to close in on me and I could hear the movement of nurses, doctors, and orderlies gliding about on their sneaker soled shoes. Two or three cubicles away from me I could hear a patient, an elderly lady, yelling at someone to send her home. I certainly sympathized with her. If ever a person were to feel vulnerable, it would be at a hospital: it is literally a matter of life or death. But then, even outside of the hospital, I had people who might take my life: two of them for fun, the others, for some cause.

Chapter 47

At six o'clock in the evening, June 30th, 2003, Karl and Lena entered a small independent convenience store on the outskirts of Oceanside, New York. The building was just before a small neighborhood and was probably once used as a home for a middle class family. The second floor level had just put on some lights. White curtains that covered the open window were wafting from the evening ocean breeze. The single gas pump that stood guard outside looked to be as old as the building.

"This looks like a good place. Out of the way, no police patrols, mom and pop operation. Hell, they probably don't even use a bank!" Karl laughed as he pulled out his pistol and checked to make sure the clip was full. Satisfied, he snapped the clip back into the pistol and primed a round. "Let's get gas and some munchies; we can use the time to check the place out for cameras or lurking customers."

Lena could fell a rush of excitement. *So this is why Harold liked it so much.* She studied Karl's emotions; they were like a raging tide that was bringing every facet of his emotion to the surface. His eyes were widened; his cheeks were tense with secret enjoyment that he was not yet sharing. Even his skin seemed to take on a new luster. "Now, Lena, you don't know these people, so it should be easier for you to deal with them." He gave himself a nod of agreement: his words were wise. "Okay?"

The trill was almost more than she could bear. The idea that she, little Lena Pepper, could be in charge: she would be <u>so</u> in charge. She could boss these people around…they would have to do what she said. Lena had never experienced such a rush of power. Yeah, she had the power! It was almost with a gesture of reverence that she took the pistol from Karl's hand. Then, like a bolt of neon light, a reality displayed itself in her mind. With this gun, even Karl would have to do what she said. She fell 'in love' with the gun. It was better than having a strong boyfriend. She was the boss of the gun and it would do what she told it to do. It would protect her, give her power and yet she was in charge of it. Flooded with the rush of ecstasy, she opened the car door and took a stance of one who feared nothing. "Hey? Are you coming, tough guy?"

While shaking his head, Karl laughed at the transformation he had seen in Lena. He had seen it before. The rush of power, the feeling that you were now invincible, he knew it all. He had learned that the gun was an evil genie, a deceptive master who soon possessed its possessor. "Just hold up, little lady. Calm down! Remember, to act normal and not like Ma Barker or like we are Bonny and Clyde."

She liked that. Bonny and Clyde, she wondered if Lena and Karl could ever be as big as they had been. "Don't worry about me, Karl. You just do your thing and I'll do mine."

"Okay, Bonny. But remember, what we want here is to get our gas, supplies, and THEN cash and no witnesses." He looked into her wild eyes. "Got it?"

Lena tested the weight of the pistol. It felt good, even comforting. "Got it, Clyde." She grinned, "Say, could you call me Bonny...just when we're doing the jobs." She blushed like a girl on her first prom date.

Karl chuckled. He had to laugh at her sudden transformation. On one side he was amused, but he also felt a little unnerved by her surge of independence and self confidence. He flashed her a wry look, "Anything you say...Bonny." He moved his head toward the entrance. "Now, let's go. Put that gun under your coat."

Doing their best to act like a young couple of vacationers, they strolled toward the bar covered glass door. The concrete driveway had been warped into a sort of odd mosaic, with random cracks that housed weeds and shredded grass. The door opened easily with only a slight creaking as the hanging cow bell over the door announced commerce was still alive.

From their left side came a foreign accented voice, "Haroo."

Karl and Lena returned a perfunctory nod and headed for the snack isle.

"We need some gas. Do we get it ourselves?" Karl was examining a package of potato chips, attempting to be as casual is possible.

The voce behind the counter was sitting on a high stool. "Got ownree legular;Lu glet, less?"

Karl snorted and then gave the old man an acknowledging wave. *When you come to this country, learn to speak English.;* "Sure thing, Jo." He glanced at Lena to check on her progress. "Hey, Lena, you done yet?"

"Yeah, I think so." Abruptly she began to prance her way to the front of the store. The old man behind the counter smiled at her.

"Plety lady." He put down a cigarette he was going to light.

Lena came back with a sarcastic mutter, "Think so, huh?" Her movements were so fast that Karl perceived a blur. The gun popped into her hand and then barked: it seemed muffled by the overstuffed store. Spatters of blood seemed to erupt from the chest of the man. He moved backward, his face a cacophony of expressions.

Overhead, in the house above the store, Karl and Lena could hear movement. Feet were stomping across the wooden floor and down a flight of stairs in the back of the store. Karl reached for his weapon…he had none. His head jerked from side to side as he first looked toward the stairs and then at Lena. Instinctively he charged toward the exit door, his arms and legs moved like a cartoon character trying to run under water.

Lena's voice came from somewhere behind a shelf displaying potato chips and Cheetoes. "Where're you going?" She was pointing the pistol in the direction of the thundering stairs.

The familiar sound of gun fire burst into the store. Canned goods and packaged items began to erupt like kernels of popcorn at a movie theater. Glass shattered and pieces of wood split. Karl felt the bite of what felt like a large bug. A spot in his lower back burst into hot, boiling pain. He was leaking something hot and sticky. He had been shot by one of those Oriental idiots. Damn Lena! He had told her to get the gas and stuff BEFORE she did any shooting. "Go...go...go!" He yelled at Lena as he limped out of the glass door. He could see the expression on her face...she was laughing as she exchanged gun fire with the men at the back of the store. She was going to get him killed if she didn't get out of there now.

Lena reached behind the counter and opened the cash register. With hands as steady as a diamond cutter, she harvested the green backs from the machine. Only once did she give the old man an indifferent look. She felt the power, and it was good. To some unknown place in the universe, her fear had vanished. She had never felt so alive. Below the cash register was an old thirty-eight caliber revolver; she snatched it up and tucked it in the elastic band of her pants. This was more exciting than any carnival ride, road race, or party. "Get in the car, Karl!" She walked out the front door, she didn't need to fear the bullets that were flying about…she was invincible.

Karl forced himself to move into the driver's seat. He reached to turn the ignition key, but his arm didn't move. A bolt of panic shot through his body as he looked at his hand, it was red with dripping blood. He had been shot in the right shoulder, he didn't even know it. He moved as in a dream. His left hand crossed over and turned the key, the engine responded with a weak roar. Of course he had been nicked before, but never really shot. He was scared. *Damned Lena, it was all her fault.*

Bullets ripped into the metal and glass of the car as they sped away into the night. Neither of them spoke. She was high on the adrenalin of crime, and he was numb by a prodding fear of dying. The irony could not escape him, he was the dispenser of pain, the injector of death…how had this happened?

At his first opportunity, Karl pushed the steering wheel into a right turn and went down a side street. He was talking, but his words sounded far away. "I need a doctor. I need a doctor." Under a streetlight he could see a reflection of his chalky face, "I'm hit, Lena. That damned Chink put a couple of bullets in me." He knew he was whining like a baby, but he didn't care. "I need a doctor!" He could feel his body turning weak; his strength was draining out of him like a punctured balloon. He pulled the car over to the curb and stopped. With the door open, he vomited into the street.

A voice was speaking to him, he knew it must be Lena, but he found it hard to focus on her words. He was losing blood fast.

"Look! Up there; one of them blue signs with the white 'H' in the middle. There's a hospital up there on that highway. Move over, Karl, I'll drive." She pranced around the car and mostly pushed him into the passenger seat. "What will I tell them? I can't tell them the truth." She had the car in motion. She was speaking quickly, but calmly.

It would not be much longer before he would be unconscious. His head bobbed around like a car doll. "Drive by. Tell them a drive by." He did not even know his body was now lying in a shapeless heap. He didn't even care; he was beyond caring, beyond any worries.

As if she didn't have a care in the world, Lena Pepper drove down the high- way in the direction indicated by the little blue sign. Her body still vibrated with the flashing scenes of the convenience store at Oceanside, New York. Fantastic!

Chapter 48

It wasn't a particularly brilliant plan, unless one considered the simplicity of the thinking. Peter and Bill had planned to retrieve the disc with as little notice as they could. They had ascertained when Ed Malone and his family would be leaving the island. If they could divert everyone's attention for just thirty little seconds, they could exchange the baggage and be on their way. Chances were Ed Malone would not even notice what had happened until he had returned to Phoenix, Arizona.

They watched as Ed pulled the wagon toward the dock: God he was slow! What didn't make sense was when his wife had to run over and assist him in getting the luggage to the wharf. With detached horror, they watched as Ed Malone sat down and then passed out. They could not have asked for a better distraction if they had planned it themselves. While everyone was hovering over Ed Malone, they were switching luggage, but they could not get to their prime objective, Ed's laptop: it was lying under his prostrated body.

Peter rolled his eyes at Bill as they stood at the back of the crowd, feeling totally impotent: what could they do?

Bill tipped his head to one side and wagged a movement of unbelief. "I don't believe this, Peter.

That damned disc is probably right there in that green computer case, and we can't touch it."

Peter struggled to be optimistic, "Maybe it's in the bags we exchanged." He winced in disbelief as he looked over his shoulder and saw a medi-copter hovering over the baseball field. "Can't anything be simple?"

Like watching a stage play from a set of uncomfortable metal chairs, Peter and Bill had watched the entire show of the Medical Technicians picking up Ed Malone and his elusive green bag. They were being wheeled over to the waiting helicopter.

With a forced surge of optimism, Peter looked up at the departing whirlybird and muttered, "Well, at least at the hospital it should be easy to find him and the green bag."

"Let's roll, Peter. Our time is running out. If they are going to be on schedule, they need these prints…and more importantly the assurance that no one knows their off shore bank account numbers. If anyone finds out who is behind the demolition of a nuclear power plant, we'll be lucky if they give our corpses a ride to the morgue." His voice was barely audible, but Peter got the point.

Together they rushed to the delayed ferry and jumped inside. The grinding and thudding of the diesel engines were prominent enough to drowned their thoughts. Everyone was occupied with the events of the dockside and the helicopter. It was almost like listening to a Las Vegas gaming conference. Would the man live, or was it too late? Who was he? What really happened?

Peter and Bill also wondered. Was it all an elaborate hoax to get Ed Malone and the disc off the island without incident? They would soon know…they hoped.

Finding the hospital was easier than they had thought. Stony Brook was a very well known hospital, and not really that far for them to travel. With any luck, if Ed Malone didn't die on them, they could get to the computer, get the disc and hot foot it to Phoenix.

Peter was unusually pensive; he hated hospitals ever since he accompanied his mother to an emergency ward just to see the last few moments of his father's life slip away because of an industrial accident. Times had been tough for the family, and his mother had been a real bitch from that moment on. It was at that point of his life everything had turned to crap. His mother had begun a program of drug abuse, and Peter was in and out of foster homes and jail. Peter blamed the hospital for letting his father die. "I don't like these places, Bill. Let's get in and out of here as fast as we can."

The emergency ward was humming as if it were a hive for retuning bees. People were dashing about trying to comfort the injured and placate the people who had arrived with them. Insults, threats, pleading, cries, wailing, and passive pain filled the polluted air.

"We better swipe some uniform and blend into this mess?"

Peter made a face. He just wanted to get out of this reminiscing chaos.

Bill stepped aside to allow a determined looking young girl hustling along side of her boyfriend. Her hand was placed upon the glistening stainless railing. As the gurney slid past them, Peter looked down at the scruffy face of the young man. Apparently the guy had been shot in the chest, maybe also in his arm, he looked bad…peaked. The scene was too reminiscent of the night his father's ashen face lay on one of these 'sliding coffins'. Quickly, he averted his eyes. He could hear the girl murmuring to the young man, "Stay with me, Karl; stay with me. Look at me."

"Over this way, Peter; I think this will take us to the staff locker rooms." Bill reached out and jerked on Peter's hairy elbow. "There should be some uniforms we can snag." Bill looked back, Peter's eyes looked glassy; "Hey, big guy. I need you to focus on this."

The hallway door pushed open with surprising ease. The smell of moist concrete mixed with antiseptic odors was floating up from the stairwell. To Peter it was like a graveyard crypt. "Down there?"

"Yeah; looks right, Peter;" Bill was enjoying the trepidation that Peter was experiencing. "Let's go!"

The big man baulked. "Look, Bill. You know I don't like these places. And besides, they are probably still running tests on Malone. He won't have a room for at least several hours." His large hand gripped the stained metal railing that had once been painted a soft green, now it looked like old dishwater frozen into one long Popsicle.

"Okay, you got it...we go slow, but the faster we get this job done, the sooner we can get out of this place. Okay?" Bill had seen Peter place explosives inside of schools and public malls; he was still surprised by his partner's panic. Maybe Peter had lost his nerve. There was growing distrust of this big man. Was there something he wasn't telling Bill, maybe there was a bomb in the building, or maybe Peter had spotted some kind of trouble? They were running late on this contract, perhaps Peter had been contracted to take out Bill...just as a gesture of trust.

At the step just above Bill, Peter stopped and looked down. Under ordinary circumstances he was a big man, but standing on the step above and looking down he was ominously imposing. "Why'd you stop, Bill?" Peter looked about the cavernous surroundings. "Hear something?" Peter put a hand to his ear.

If he was up to no good, I'd know it. Wouldn't I? "Ah, yeah, you're right. I thought I heard something." *God! I never thought I'd have to watch my back with Peter, but I better.* "I'd feel better if you would lead the way. You're big and

people don't like to ask you questions, buddy."
Bill felt stiff, tense. Scared!

Chapter 49

Rudy felt sick to his stomach. Where was this all
going to end? His eyes continued to float over the
words on the computer screen: they were words,
but the thoughts were flowing into one picture, the
Malones were in trouble. He leaned back in his big
leather office desk chair.

"You look awful, Rudy." Kate had just entered
the room, a plate of cookies and a hot cup of
steaming coffee. Not that Kate was a Nancy
Homemaker, but she could whip up Rudy's
favorites and she enjoyed doing it. She had just
returned for a quick trip to the local Trader Joe's.
Leaning over his shoulder she began reading the
screen. "Oh!"

Snatching a cookie off of the plate, he pushed it
into his mouth and mixed it with a cautious sip of
hot coffee. "I think they should have stayed here.
Why the hell did they have to go to New York at a
time like this?" Feeling speechless, he shook his
head and looked up at Kate.

She moved forward and read The Bureau report.
Except for an occasional gasp she was mute. When
she had finished, she understood why Rudy felt as
he did. "Is this possible?"

"Which part"

Kate dropped herself slowly as she sat in her office chair. "What happened to Ed? I didn't know he had a heart problem." She stopped to express her confusion. "He had heart surgery?"

"That's what it says. I don't know anything else." Actually he did. The Puppy Killers might have killed a convenient store guy, and the two killers which had been after the disc were probably in the New York area. They were probably the two who made the mess at Sky Harbor airport. They wanted that disc, maybe it was important. "Heart surgery is pretty much routine now a days, Kate. I don't think we need to worry about the surgery."

She bristled at his presumed indifference. "So there's no reason to care?"

"I didn't say that, Kate. I think the surgery is less of a threat to Ed than what someone could do to him while he is doped up recovering from surgery."

He turned his swivel chair so that he faced her. "I just finished a call from Julie. She wants to send the kids here until they can come home. She thinks it will be too tough on them to have to stay in New York while Ed is in the hospital."

Kate gave a sympathetic nod. "I hope you told her they would be okay." Her eyes moved about as she was thinking, "They can use the spare bedrooms...I'll have to wash the sheets." Standing, she began to pace the room. "Is Julie afraid that something is going to happen to the kids, or is she just being practical?"

"I think, just practical, but you have a point."

Kate stopped her pacing and looked out of the back window. She was deep in thought. They had never had any kids of their own, but she loved kids and was often accused of being a child in grown up cloths. "Actually, it will be nice having them around."

Rudy smiled; "Someone to play with?"

"Yeah; so, when do we pick them up?" Her mind was already racing about meals, TV programs, school, the back yard, and the safety of their swimming pool.

"Tomorrow…they're due in at four-forty-five, Delta 3749. I can pick them up." Rudy paused to let the information sink in. "Which room do you want to give to Christine and Dell? I think Joel can stay in the room next to us."

Kate was still deep in thought. "Ah…yeah; sounds great; I'll make up a batch of spaghetti. I think I remember they all liked it that last time. Have you checked the pool? Is the gate safe?" She wasn't really asking questions, but rather clicking off thoughts that were zapping through her lightening mind.

Were the children in danger? Rudy reflected on that thought. Would the terrorists want to hold the children as hostages if they didn't get the disc they were after? Then there was the possibility the Puppy Killers, Karl and Lena, might reverse course and return to Phoenix. "I'll make sure our surveillance equipment is operating." He bounced up from his office chair and started toward the back yard.

"Hold on, Rudy. Are you expecting trouble?" Her brow tightened as the smile left her lips.

Attempting to be as nonchalant as he could manage, "Not really, but it never hurts to be prepared." He made a slow shrug, "Ed and Julie would appreciate the extra caution."

"Okay, I'll get busy on the rooms." Kate muttered to herself as she walked out of the room, "What else could go wrong?" She had no ideas, but she was getting a bad feeling.

Chapter 50

In a small country town, Karl's bullet wounds might have been a cause for great concern, but on Long Island it was all too often as common as beer and a sports program on television. They were more concerned with saving his life and his arm. Of course reports would be filed, but, for now, they accepted Lena's story they had been shot at while heading for their car, a few shots might have been fired at them as they drove away. Lena was a practiced liar; she played the part of a frightened kid lost in the streets of New York. Just a case of random gunfire, she was garnering buckets of flowering compassion. The thugs had stolen their wallets and purses just before she and her brother had made a dash for their car.

The young doctor reminded Lena of one of the doctors on E.R., she couldn't remember the name, but he was a hot fox. Wide eyed, she studied his manly features as he removed his green head covering: he was still in surgical scrubs. "Well, Miss Riley, I think your brother will be all right." He flashed a smile filled with New England style large, white teeth. His bushy yellow-brown hair spread over his head like a field of cut wheat. She could have gazed at him all day.

"So, he's going to be okay?"

"I'm sure of it, but he could be in for a bit of a battle about that chest wound, and he might have some trouble before he gets the full use of that arm. Frankly, he is really lucky you got him here as quickly as you did. Fifteen minutes more and …" Feeling nervous, he said, "Well, later. You rest now."

She watched as he walked over to a nearby elevator. Lena loved the way he swaggered like some Montana bull rider who had just completed his mandatory eight seconds. Fifteen seconds after the elevator door closed Lena began to notice she was hungry. A rolling tug at her stomach reminded her she had not eaten since ten thirty that morning. Still thinking about the sophisticated doctor, she glanced overhead for a clue leading her to the hospital cafeteria.

It was the talk of the day. Some guy had been brought in from Fire Island, only the coincidence of two cardiologists being at the loading dock for the ferry had saved the guy. 'Talk about luck.' He had been rescued from dying by a miracle. He should have been dead, others said he had been dead, but was resuscitated.

The story was fascinating, maybe even like Karl's. Hadn't the doctor said she had saved his life by rushing him to the hospital? 'Fifteen more minutes and he might not have made it.' Isn't that what he said? She picked up a leg of fried chicken and sank into rapture at the though of biting into its succulent meat, but her movement stiffened as she heard the conversation at the next table.

"Sometimes you just have to believe in some kind of God. That Malone guy couldn't have been in E.R. more than an two hours, when they took him to his room, pretty as you please...like nothing had happened to him." The man spoke with an unmistakable accent, but Lena understood every word the man was saying. "He came in on the red copter, and now he's joking around with the staff. "They must make 'em different in Arizona." His speech was followed by a round of shaking heads and mumbled interjections.

She had lost her appetite. Just the thought of eating in the same building with her brother's killer caused her to feel weak and flushed with surges of heat. Having done the best she could do to calm her vibrating nerves, she turned toward the next table and addressed the narrator. "Are you sure that he is out of E. R.? From what I heard, he was almost dead, maybe really dead."

"Sure thing, Sugar; Up there in F3, just jabbering away like a new born robin." He glanced about the table as if gathering affirmations. "Saw him myself." He flicked up his curled eyebrows in a gesture of finality.

"You say he's from Arizona?"

"Yes, he is. Phoenix I believe; came up here to visit relative on Fire Island." He threw in a short smirk followed by hunched shoulders. "Guess it got too...friendly for him." The table burst out into a round of giggles, smirks, and chuckles as the man picked up his food tray and headed for the cafeteria's dishwashing machine.

She quivered. It must be the same guy. Maybe it was too coincidental. Did they know who she was, did they know about Karl? Lena tried to return to her eating, but she just couldn't find the will to enjoy anything but the cup of scalding, chicory laced coffee. Suddenly, all she could think about was finding Karl and talking to him about what she should do. He would know. *F-3, huh?* Out loud she mumbled, "Where's that F-3?"

* * *

Finding hospital uniforms was easier then Bill and Peter had thought. The employees had the practice of pitching their uniforms into a large laundry basket and plucking a replacement from a pile that was basically a grab-bag. Peter had to take a used uniform because none of the clean ones were large enough for his frame. The problem of snagging an identity badge was even more simple than the uniforms had been; several of the discarded uniforms still had badges on them.

"Hey, look, Bill. I'm Charlie Pierce, custodial engineer. Mom always wanted me to be an engineer." Peter chuckled.

Bill responded by shoving a four-wheeled yellow mop bucket at him. "Well, Charlie, what do you say we get to swabbing some floors? Did you get his cubical number?"

"F-wing, Bill... I think. But it could have been E-wing. I had to read from an upside down piece of paper." Peter sounded apologetic, it was typical of the way he lived his life...one big apology.

They moved toward the service elevator. Under their uniforms, strapped to their backs, were their weapons of choice. This was not the first time they had used this routine to get at one of their contracts. Peter scrunched his nose at the smell of antiseptics; he preferred the harsh odors of cleaners like bleach and ammonia. They had gone through the luggage they had 'exchanged' at the ferry dock, but found no disc. "You sure he has the disc here, Bill. I hate to go through all of this for nothing."

Bill did his best to sound positive; "The green laptop case must have gone on the chopper." His raised his voice in an effort to sound more authoritative. "He's got it alright; He better!"

Chapter 51

To anyone who has gone through surgery, there is a sudden awareness that, for some period of time, a doctor, hopefully a competent one, was poking about in your insides. Beyond that, there is the fact you were totally impotent; you were as helpless as a piece of meat in a butcher's locker.

I awakened to find myself in a standard metal gurney, wrapped in white blankets. My view should have reminded me of a baby's crib with all sorts of dangling apparatus: a pull up bar, and bags of differing colors adorned the perimeter. To my right was a view of Stony Brook, but I was in no real mood to appreciate it. At least I was alive. Somewhat bloated, groggy: anything but hungry. Beyond the partition that separated me from other patients, I could hear the nurses, and doctors making their rounds: I thought I heard Julie.

"Oh, he's awake." Now I did feel like a newborn. "Mrs. Malone, he's awake."

I was reasonably certain this was not the first time I had awakened, but I was too whipped to argue.

The concerned face of Julie appeared from behind the mobile curtain. She was smiling as if I were her favorite puppy that had just been treated by the local veterinarian. The obligatory words began to drop from her lips, "You look great, Ed." She gave my hand an affectionate pat and my cheek a cautious kiss. "The doctor said everything went well."

What didn't he tell her? I didn't want to smile. I didn't want to talk or ask about the latest baseball scores of the Arizona Diamondbacks. I was convinced any effort outside of allowing my body to repair itself would be totally counter productive. "Good." I managed a weak nod.

"I called Kate and Rudy. The kids are fine and miss you."

I could tell she still felt a bit nervous, after all I had dropped 'dead' right at her feet. But right now she was struggling for some words to say that might make the both of us feel better. Anybody observing her could tell she loved me and was both concerned and relieved I was still hanging around, but the day's events had forced a new awareness in to our lives. Invincible Edward, was not only defeat able, but mortal. Life's time bomb was still ticking.

Wanting to do something, anything, to help me, she reached for the water pitcher which was equipped with a flexible straw (everything first class). "The doctor said you should drink plenty of fluids."

Right now I could use a glass of Merlot ...make that a bottle. At this point the last thing I was thinking about was any attempts on my life. As far as I was concerned, there had been one, and I was surviving it.

Julie, guided the blue straw into my mouth and nodded with approval as I took a few pulls of water. For the second time I felt like that newborn infant getting his daily treat at suckling. "That's great, Ed. You're really looking good. How do you feel?"

Other than the fact that I have had some guy digging about inside my chest: ripping out my heart and patching in a new part. "FINE." Julie burst with a motherly smile as if I had just spoken my first word and it was 'mommy'.

I was beginning to drift in and out of sleep, somewhere, during one of my nods, Julie slipped away. I am sure it was only after planting a kiss on my bloated face. The first night passed rather uneventfully, and the next day was filled with follow up questions, tests, and visits by amazed people who had heard about my miraculous rescue at the ferry dock.

I was startled awake about, maybe eleven o'clock. I was in a strange place; it was like a warehouse of solid concrete. People were shouting, and crying. I could hear one poor soul pleading,

"Please…don't take my liver. I'll die." Shadows were casting strange images about the wall on the other side of my partition, they were moving about as if cast by an oscillating light bulb. My God, how did I get put in this place of horror? I was convinced that I was the victim of a fiendish plot to take my body parts. I had seen a movie about a place like this. A mad doctor would get these derelicts and remove their organs, selling them as donor parts. I couldn't believe it. Stony Brook had seemed so proper, like a regular hospital. Maybe this only happened at night. Yes, that would explain it. At night they would take patients to this place in the basement of the hospital. Later, they would tell Julie that I died of complications.

The shocks of fear coursed through my mind and rippled in every cell of my helpless body. When would they come for me? Would Julie ever know the truth? I don' dare fall asleep, but I was so sleepy. Maybe a quick nap would be safe if I tucked myself in so that I'll wake up if they try to get to me, but I could not sleep. It was like no fear I had ever experienced: a nightmare that would challenge the pen of Steven King.

Sometime during the night I must have drifted off to sleep, the ghouls of my nightmare must have returned me to my place upstairs. For a few minutes it was impossible to separate fantasy from reality. The morning nurse entered my space and began the morning routine as if nothing had happened to me. I wondered if she was in on the midnight trips to the basement, or if she was oblivious to what went on at night. I studied her with anxious eyes and a nervous mind.

"How did you sleep, Mr. Malone?" She was not looking at me, her eyes were trained on her ear thermometer and the morning orderly that was bringing my breakfast. They nodded at each other as if passing on some secret code.

Should I tell her, or should I play dumb, just in case. "I think I was awake most of the night…too much excitement I guess." *That should alert her and her minions that I was not a patient to be trifled with.*

After taking my blood pressure and temperature, she moved on to the next cubical, where an ailing elderly lady was recovering from a liver ailment. It occurred to me she might well have been a victim of the 'night raiders'.

Talk about relief! Julie waltzed in carrying a bundle of flowers and her equipment for passing the time while I slept. I could hardly wait to tell her about the horror chamber, in which I had spent the night, but I was concerned about being overheard, after all, it was rather a clandestine business they had going on in the basement. I ate my breakfast in silence while I waited for the right time to enlighten Julie. The time finally came.

"You're not going to believe what I am going to tell you, Julie." I spent the next fifteen minutes, or so, telling Julie about what was going on at the hospital. I told her how they took people to the basement and how they stole organs from the helpless patients. Her face was attentive, but wrinkled with disbelief.

"Oh, come on, Ed. I can't believe that this hospital steals organs from their patients. They'd get caught." She offered a sympathetic closed mouth grin. "You must have been dreaming. You know, you have been through a lot over the last few days." She patted my hand as if offering a compassionate touch to a nut case who might turn violent at any moment.

I responded with a disgusted glare and a sigh. "That's how they get by with it...nobody would believe that it was true." By now the food I had just eaten was beginning to take effect and I was getting sleepy. I decided, if I was going to stay awake all night tonight, I had better get some sleep now. "I told you... you wouldn't believe me."

Of course, as it turned out, it was the drugs that made me hallucinate. (At least that's what they told me.) I can joke about it now, but at the time, it was like living in the middle of a mid-evil horror film.

Chapter 52

Lena tensed as she listened to the doctor's words. He was trying to be nice, trying too hard to suit her.

"He's not doing well, Miss Pepper." The doctor curled his fingers and checked his finger nails.

Where did he get my real name? She wanted to ask him, but she chose to avoid an issue. "What do you mean?" She tensed, her face turned to a snarl. "You said he was going to be okay!"

Following a sympathetic nod, he stared through his eyebrows, but tipping his head and attempting to look pedantic. "His wounds were not *that* bad, but his health was. He has a rather severe case of untreated diabetes. He suffers from malnutrition and a very low white blood count, but I am not only concerned he cannot fight off the infections he has acquired." He raised his head and looked into her eyes. "Are you aware he is HIV positive?"

Lena almost jumped out of her chair. "Isn't that…AIDS?" Her mind did not even want to consider the possibilities. She had had sex with Karl, not often, but how often did it take to catch that horrible thing? "Are you telling me that he is going to die from aids?" She wondered if the doctor could tell she was shaking uncontrollably.

The doctor's lips sucked in and formed a straight line above his stubbled face. His narrowed eyes seem to indicate he was considering something.

"Miss, Pepper. Have you been sexually active with Mr. Boss?" He paused. "Have you been checked for AIDS?"

She knew he was speaking in a normal voice, but the word…the thought jumped out at her. No, she had not been checked. At least not to her knowledge, she wasn't sure that she wanted to be checked; it would be easier to just pretend she was safe from the dreaded disease. "There's been no reason to check me, doctor. Karl and I are just friends." Lena got up from her plastic seated metal chair; she wanted it understood there would be no more discussion about something as scary as aids. "When can I see Karl?"

He picked up a pen, tapped the end against his desk blotter and then pitched it as if tossing a pebble into a stagnant pond. His eyes flitted to a desk clock shaped like a baseball diamond. Standing up in the back of the ball field was a score board that was a clock. "He should be in his room by now. Listen to the nurse, she will tell you what precautions to take to avoid any of Mr. Boss's fluids." There was a distinct ring of disgust in his manner. "Just as a precaution, you'd better have yourself check as soon as possible."

Lena wanted to scream at him, to tell him to stop scaring her. Her mouth opened, but all she could manage was, "Thank you, doctor, for your concern, but I'm sure that I'm okay." Her trembling hand circled the doorknob. Her knees felt wobbly. She told herself all she had to do was to get away from this man and she would feel right as rain. After closing the door, she walked down the checkered hallway. Her steps were strange, like walking in surf water. "I don't have aids! He was just trying to scare me. I don't have aids." Her fingers slid through her locks of hair as she muttered the magic words that would keep her safe. It was like the incantation of Dorothy from The Wizard of Oz, "There's no place like home." All of a sudden she didn't want to see Karl; he had been nothing but a curse to her life ever since she first met him. She wasn't in New York to be with Karl, she was in New York to get even with that bastard of a writer who killed her brother.

"Are you here to see your brother?" The smiling nurse was holding a tray covered with a large white cloth. "He's resting right now, Miss Pepper."

Lena flinched. She had not even realized she had walked right to Karl's room. The nurse had asked her something, but…what had she asked? "I'm sorry, what did you say?"

Tilting her head the nurse stared at her. "Are you all right? You look a bit peaked, dear."

"Do I?" She could feel her body collapsing, but it was like watching someone else as they unfolded to the cold tile floor. "I don't have aids. I'm too young." The words formed at her lips, but aborted into the air as she lapsed into unconsciousness.

The three oriental young men that were following her stopped and pretended to be studying the selections available on the hallway vending machines, but in his mind's eye he was focused on the bloody scene at the family's convenient store. The girl had simply dropped to the floor. Had she seen them? In any case, they would have to wait for the girl to lead them to her boyfriend.

Out of the side of his mouth the largest of the three men asked, "Are you sure she's the one that shot Uncle Jimmy?"

His snarl flared his nostrils. "Damned right I'm sure. She's the one." He nodded toward Lena, his head moved so quickly that it gave the impression he was trying to break something. "You and Wong stay here. I'll get a line on the guy." He slipped a dollar bill in the machine and punched up a black coffee. "I told you that police scanner was right. They're here. Believe me now?" He snatched his coffee cup from the dispenser and took a cautious sip. "Don't loose her."

"Sure thing, Zip!" Chu snapped into his best tough guy pose as he watched his hero swagger down the hallway.

Wong talked into the air. "I still don't get it. Why shoot old Jimmy? He never hurt anyone."

"Yeah." Chu fixed his eyes down the corridor. The girl was being revived by a group of medical people, most of which had just been passing by. "They didn't even get that much money." He tilted his handsome mixed oriental and Caucasian face, his brindle eyes blinked. "Sure it couldn't have been a hit by those Korean pukes?"

"Hell, no! If it had been those guys we wouldn't be here." Wong used the back of his hand to rub off a piece of chocolate. "Besides, they don't use girls." He leaned to the side so he could hear one of the nurses talking to the girl.

"How do you feel, Lena?" There was an expected sense of urgency in her tone.

So, that's her name.

"I'm okay." Lena sighed. She was embarrassed, but mostly just mad for having shown so much weakness. Her mother used to cuff her for being such a worrywart softy. "Really, I'm okay. I just have had a couple of hard days."

Yeah, like killing my uncle...lady. Wong riveted his eyes on Lena as he spoke to Chu. "When we find the guy let's do the two of them so they can see each other die."

"Works for me, Wong; Zip will agree!"

Chapter 53

With a full moon riding high in the after midnight sky, the two men moved about the hospital ward as if they were a well trained cleaning crew. Bill was emptying the waste cans and checking for engorged catheters. Peter used his mop handle to move his yellow bucket smoothly about the tiled floor. The ironic thing was it was

240

the way they had met when they were serving time in Florence prison.

Nurses and volunteers darted about in their starched looking colored uniforms: pink, green, blue, and white were the favorite colors. A nurse wearing a smock covered in cartoon characters was working the wing where Malone was recuperating. If he didn't have the disc here, well, he must know where it is: at least that was the wishful thinking of the two mercenaries. Killing Edward Malone was not the objective of their employer, but they would if they had to.

"She should be done any minute now. Start working toward the last bed in the wing...next to the window; just as soon as she's out of there." Peter was speaking out of the side of his mouth, he felt foolish but he convinced himself it was safer. "I'll stay back and block anyone trying to get into the wing."

"What if it's not here?"

Peter flinched. Sometimes Bill could really be a candy-ass, a pain in the butt. "Just check everything; his bags first and then his clothes. Just be quick about it!" He squeezed out another batch of water from his mop. The liquid sound of the cotton head slapped to the floor as if he were smacking Bill for asking stupid questions.

The men worked rhythmically. Bill faked emptying trash cans while Peter moved his mop over the same spots until he thought he might go through the floor. At last the nurse was adjusting the cubical patricians as she headed out of the wing. Peter reached for his yellow marker that read 'caution, floor wet'. He placed it on the floor much like an interior decorator placing an indoor fichus plant: searching for the precise spot for the exact effect. "Okay, Bill. Start at the locker."

Bill moved his thin frame as if he were going to tiptoe across the room. When he got to the wall where the lockers were he hesitated. Moving his head from side to side he studied the metal lockers. At first they just reminded him of High School, an act that sent him into countless images during a particularly difficult time of his life. At just the age of seventeen he had gotten into a fight with the school basketball coach. The coach made the mistake of not only ridiculing Bill, but kicking him off the team because he was often drunk or getting into fights. Bill killed the coach. The court said it was the fault of his alcoholic father and neglectful mother. Bill knew it was because he hated the coach. That was good enough for Bill. "Which one is it?" He spoke in a loud whisper; his voice emitted a slight crack.

Peter stopped swinging his mop. "Jesus, Bill. How am I supposed to know? "With a shake of his head he resumed mopping. "Open them and look." Peter had an idea. "He's a writer. He probably has his computer here...look for the green case."

By the time Bill had opened and closed the third locker his reminiscing about High School was ended. There, lying on the bottom of the lower half was a green laptop case. As quickly as he could, he opened the case and examined the discs inside. There were at least ten discs; most of them did not have any kind of understandable label. He decided to take them all. Gleefully he hunched his back and smirked as he closed the locker door. *Peter's going to like this...first time, I got it!* Using great care, like placing eggs in the bottom of a glass dish, he put the treasures into a plastic trash bag. "Got it!" He shout-whispered to Peter.

With a smiling nod of approval, Peter gave him a 'thumbs up' and began backing up and out of the wing. "Watch the floor, it's wet!" He was smiling so hard it was causing his cheeks to ache.

Chapter 54

Talk about a horrible night! I could hardly wait for Julie to arrive for her morning visit. Every few minutes I would lean forward and peek around the hanging partition. I looked at my breakfast tray, it was empty, but I could not even recall eating it.

I had fallen asleep (darned medications). Opening my eyes I saw Julie sitting in the hospital imitation of an easy chair, she was reading a novel written by one of her favorite lady authors. I knew I wanted to say something to her, something specific, but I was having trouble recalling the subject. "I must have dozed off."

"I guess, I've been here for almost an hour. How're you doing? She marked her book and closed the paperback pages.

How come everybody asks that question? Do they really want to know, or is it just polite chatter to a hospital patient? "I'm great, but these darned medications make my mouth dry and I can't remember the name for some things. I had a horrible time remembering what to call peanut butter."

Julie gave me a sympathetic smile; it seemed a lot of people were doing that. "Well, at least you didn't have to fight off a band of organ stealers."

We had a good laugh about my bout of paranoia, but it also triggered my handicapped memory. I think I was a bit animated as I began to tell Julie about my latest hospital adventure. "You're going to get a kick out of this one." I leaned a little closer to her, it was not meant to be a conversation for the general population, and believe me I could hear everything that my roommates were gossiping about. "I think that someone was in my cubical last night."

She tilted her head, "Of course there was. There are night nurses, cleaning people and even priests making their rounds." Her tone was as if she were trying to explain about the Easter Bunny to a three year old child.

"Okay, wise guy. I know that! I'm not talking about those guys." My face was wrinkled up into an expression usually reserved for disgusted puppets. "Some one was going through those lockers." I gestured with my head indicating the bank of mushroom brown metal cages that held our worldly treasures. "I think they were looking for something."

"OH! They were probably only making sure they were clean, or had the wrong locker the first time." She patted my hand, "I'm sure it's nothing for you to be concerned about, Dear."

Whenever Julie pats my hand or calls me 'Dear', I know the school teacher in her has taken over and she is trying to either instruct or dissuade a childish fear. "Check my locker then. See if anything is missing." I was curt, maybe even defiant. "You'll see. It's not my imagination…this time it really happened." I didn't actually KNOW there was something amiss, but, actually, I was not completely convinced the dream about the organ stealers was actually a nightmare. "You'll see!"

With the reluctance reminiscent of a convict being called to the death chamber, Julie struggled up from her 'comfortable' chair. "Okay! Okay! I'll check." As she did the dead-man shuffle toward my locker, she asked, "Just what do you want me to do?" Her arm was limp as she reached for the handle.

"Come on, Julie. Humor me! Just see if anything is missing." I rolled my eyes and bounced my head about my shoulders, a universal display of impatience.

The locker door opened, vibrating like the wing of crashing airplane. Reluctantly, Julie looked over the contents of the locker. I might just as well have asked 'the convict' to examine the electric chair before it was used on him (or her). "Everything's here, Ed!"

How did she do that? She mixed her words so they sounded both like degust and an 'I told you so' sermon. "Is my laptop there?" I craned forward to see for myself.

"Yep, it's still here." She bent over and picked up the case by its brown leather handle. "See?"

Even from across the room I could see that several pockets were unzipped. I tensed and looked around to see if we were being observed. "Bring me the case, Julie."

She gave me the look of a disapproving teenage girl. "It's here, Ed!"

I wanted to have her check my coat where I had put the Palo Verdi disc, but, if anyone were watching they might know where I had hidden it. And maybe the organ stealers weren't just a figment after all.

It was well after eight o'clock before Julie left the hospital. For hours I had agonized over asking Julie to check my coat and see if the disc were there, maybe it was gone: if it were, what was I going to do?

I slid myself over to the edge of the bed and lowered my feet to the floor (real fun). The pain was not as bad as I had expected, but it was there. After pulling the back of my hospital gown to where I was no longer exposed. Dragging my four wheeled liquid medicine tower, I shuffled to my locker. Before opening the locker and putting my hand in the inside pocket of my coat, I made sure no one was watching. I reacted with a shameless smile when I felt the square plastic case which held the disc. I had the disc. My elation was short lived when I realized my green laptop case had been unzipped, but then, maybe Julie had done that.

"Mr. Malone, I see you're up. How are you feeling?"

Same old questions, but the nurse caught me off guard: I almost jumped out of my skin, right through my nine inch incision. "Doing great; Just getting some exercise."

"Don't lift that laptop…remember, nothing too heavy. Want some help?"

"Na, I was just looking for something." I bent down and stuck my hand into the unzipped openings. All of my discs were gone, the copies of my new book, some financial stuff, all gone, but I had the original on my hard drive. For a brief moment I considered telling the nurse. I glanced at the way she was busily making my bed and dumping out chunks of paper and food tray items. There would be no point of telling her…I doubted that she was part of the vast conspiracy to obtain the disc. BUT, I was convinced that I had been visited. Organ thieves or just disc robbers?

"Your bed is ready" She whisked out of the wing as if she were a puff of smoke.

It was realization time. If they didn't get what they came for, and they didn't, they would be back, or worse yet, they would want to search the rental home where Julie was staying. Now, I was really worried. Julie is a bit feisty; she might actually confront the disc robbers. It would be dark in a few hours, but she wouldn't be home, she would be at the Fourth of July fireworks display with two of the nurses from the hospital. My other problem was that the medications were affecting my memory and I couldn't remember her local phone number or where I had put it. The waves of depression were causing me to feel tired, even sleepy. I decided to catch a little sleep before calling her. Before I went to sleep, I put the disc inside of my middle pillow, inside of the pillow case.

Chapter 55

I was awakened to a flurry of voices. It seemed as if the very walls were alive with voices of varying pitches, volumes, and health. After struggling to focus on one voice, I managed to sort out the reason for all the chattering. It seemed, last night, two men were apprehended, right in our wing. They had dressed themselves as janitors, but they didn't fool my elderly neighbor, Mrs. Hollingsworth. At three o'clock in the morning, she became suspicious and rang her medical bell. She whispered to the nurse, the nurse called security. It took security just a few seconds to see the two men had phony identifications. They were ushered away by four very angry looking, very large guards probably on vacation from the defensive front line of the New England Patriots.

I didn't know, but I hoped they were the men who had rifled my locker…the ones that Julie said had not been touched. My eyelids flipped up, I had forgotten to call her. I had slept clear through the night, missed the fireworks. As if by a stroke of magic, I saw Julie coming through the door at the middle of the corridor. She was moving quickly, but appeared unharmed: apparently my imagination had gotten the better of me.

"You won't believe what happened to me." Julie was out of breath, her face was beet red.

I was certain she was going to tell me about all of the fireworks she had seen the previous evening (Julie loves fireworks), but instead she plopped into my imitation padded chair and began chattering like the proverbial magpie.

"Someone broke into the home where I was staying." She took a deep breath and corrected herself; "Well, they didn't really BREAK IN; they got into the house while I was at the fireworks." Her face lit up, "Oh, Ed, you should have seen the fireworks. Some of them went off in front of the Statue of Liberty…it was absolutely inspiring…"

I held up my hand, "Julie, you were telling me about the break in." I held up my hands as a gesture of confusion. "Did they take anything? Are you all right?"

For the next hour I listened to Julie switch from the fireworks, to the 'break in', to the climate, to the hospital service, and back to the fireworks. Finally she told me the doctor said we could <u>not</u> go home by ground transportation or by airplane until ten days after my operation: they were concerned about the cabin pressure on my chest. We had about five days to go. "Okay, let's move the departure day to five days from now."

Blithely she said, "Okay!" Then she continued talking about how close she had been to the overhead fireworks.

<u>Chapter 56</u>

Karl was dead. The doctors had thought he was in bad shape, but had not expected him to die of a sudden heart attack. The attack had happened just after Lena had gone into Karl's room. He was resting peacefully so she sat down in one of the hospital pretend chairs. She looked up when the oriental attendant came into the room and injected some pain killer into his intervenes tube. He gave her a congenial nod as he left. Ten minutes later, Karl went into convulsions: he never recovered.

"Ms. Pepper. How are you doing?" The doctor was playing with his pen by flipping it between his fingers like the actor in the movie <u>Top Gun.</u>

Lena had just lost her brother, Harold when he had helped Karl break into the Malone home, now she had lost Karl. Karl was not a particularly nice person, but he was someone she was used to, and she worried now that she was alone. "I'll be all right, doc." She dabbed at her eyes and sniffled into her tissue. "I just want to get back home; to Arizona."

"Yes." He hesitated as he cleared his throat. "There is going to be an autopsy, Ms. Pepper. It seems…"

Her head snapped up as she studied him with her red rimmed eyes. "An autopsy;" She struggled for words, "I thought you said he died of natural causes…a heart attack?" Her eyes were blinking rapidly.

The doctor pursed his lips, stopped his pen trick as his eyes moved about the room. "Yes, well, it seems that he might have been murdered." He studied her reaction. "It appears to have happened while you were in the room with your brother." He leaned forward over his desk, "The police are concerned that it might be homicide."

Lena's eyes opened as she understood the implication. "They think...I murdered my brother?"

"Come now, Ms. Pepper. We both know he was not your brother." He paused; "As a matter of fact... both of you are wanted for questioning in at least three states, including New York."

"What!!" She did the best she could to look both shocked and indignant. "I don't know what you're talking about. My brother dies in this crummy hospital, and now you want to blame me." She shot to her feet. Her mind whirled. How would Karl have handled this? "I don't know who you think we are, but you have us confused with somebody else!" She moved forward and placed her hands on the desk top. "Go ahead and have your stupid autopsy...I don't care. I didn't do anything to Karl. You screwed up and now you're trying to blame me. Well, go to hell!"

Fearing for his life, the doctor moved his chair back from the desk. He eyed his desk drawer; did he dare reach for his pistol that he kept in his desk? This was the kind of thing for which he kept it. "Maybe the police have made some kind of mistake. It happens, "Ms. Pepper; his voice was trembling with fear. It seemed ridiculous he should be afraid of this young girl...but he was. There was something about the dark fire that seemed to move about in her squinting eyes.

"Your damned right they made a mistake. And so have you. I don't have to take this crap from you!" For a split second she paused as if she were trying to decide something, then she turned and strode toward the door. She wondered if the police would be on the other side of the door. She would have to risk it. With utter abandon, she pulled open the door and marched through it. She had pulled it off. Karl would have been proud of her. No police! Yet!

* * *

Chu watched as Lena left the doctor's office. While keeping an eye on her, he picked up his phone and punched in his speed dial. The other two men from the convenience store robbery answered. "She just left. She's walking fast, headed for the lobby."

"Do we stop her, or follow, Zip?" Wong's voice sounded irritated, if he had his way, the girl and that brother of hers would both be dead. When he shot the air into Karl's drip line, it was all he could do to keep himself from killing Lena who had murdered his beloved uncle, Jimmy: instead he had smiled at her.

The response was low and soft, Zip knew how Wong felt, but he had other plans for the insolent girl. "We will follow her. She might have some more friends or family. I want her to suffer." He paused while he reflected on the thought. "Don't lose her." A wave of sadness shuttered thru his strong frame.

* * *

The man behind her looked familiar, but then she had never been able to tell one oriental from the other. Lena was walking as fast as her little legs could carry her. If the police started looking into her background (maybe they already had). No, if they had, she would be in custody. Without stopping, she looked into her purse and placed her hand around the airline ticket that Karl had bought for her…she would be traveling alone. She glanced behind her, now there were two oriental men following her. Could they be police?

Deftly, she exited the hospital and walked out to the curb: an elderly couple had just gotten out of a cab. With a solid bang on the side of the cab, she managed to get the operator to stop. "Take me to J.F.K.!"

"You look a little young, girl. You got the fare?" The dreadlocked Jamaican tipped his head down as if he were studying her.

"You drive! I'll pay!" The voice sounded authoritive for the size of the girl, money was money.

The driver rolled his ample lips into a pooched upside down smile. "Okay, girl; no need to get mean." As the car moved away from the curb, she watched as the two men were joined by a third:

they were running toward the parking lot as the taxi finished the circle at the front of the hospital entrance. Lena leaned back in the vinyl seat and contemplated her next move. What was going on? Who were these guys? She began to nibble at her already abused fingernails.

"Where're you from?" The cabby's jovial voice sounded like a commercial for 'the island'. "You're not from here", he declared.

She barked back. If there was anything she hated it was a chatty cab driver. Lena knew that he was either really bored, or he was trying to smooze her in order to get a fat tip. "Hey! Just drive the friggen cab, will ya?" Her brain was whirling. Images were starting to click into place…it was like seeing every third frame of a motion picture. Suddenly, it clicked. Her insides turned to slush; she felt a slow rise of bile into her warm throat. They were from that convenience store they robbed: she killed that old man behind the counter. Oh, God. She had to loose them. If only Karl were here to help here, but he was dead. She swallowed as she bent over and clutched her stomach. They had killed Karl! Oh, God, she was in trouble. What was she going to do?

The voice from the front of the car startled her, "You okay? You don't look so good, girl." The man's voice changed pitches as he turned his head to look at her. "Don't barf back there, girl." Sympathy was not in his words.

"Go to Hell!" She meant to be more forceful, but her anger was lost in the fabric of the floor mat. Lena felt like throwing up. She wanted to disappear. She managed to raise her head and look behind the cab, but all she could see was a mass of cars, but she knew they were back there. She was being hunted...hunted, like some animal. She wasn't an animal, she had killed that old man because she had to prove herself to Karl...anyone could understand that. It wasn't her fault.

Lena began sliding to the side of the seat; the cab had made a sudden swerve toward the right. "Ah, Jesus, girl. I ask you not to barf. Why you go and do dat, girl? Ahhh..."

The car had stopped and the man was pulling at her arm, she could feel it, but was helpless to respond. Like a rag doll her body slipped across the seat. Her butt was now on the cold concrete. She watched as the cab driver searched her purse.

"This all you got, girl?" Disgust accentuated every word. "I take this...for de mess." He threw the purse at her as if it were a piece of rotten fruit. She was positive that she had never felt as sick as she did now. From her sitting fetal position, she watched as the cab pulled from the curb and faded into the surrounding traffic. Lena was alone, sick and frightened so badly she was shaking. Reaching into her inner strength, she struggled to get back to her feet. It wouldn't be too long before the guys in the car following the cabby realized she was no longer in the cab: maybe they knew it already. Her shaking fingers slid through her stringy hair. *I've got to get to the airport.* It was as simple as that, she had to get to Phoenix, Arizona. There were things hidden about the cabin site that she would need in order to kill the writer and his family. *All this happened because of that nosy bastard!*

Chapter 57

It seemed the day for us to leave New York would never come. Not that the hospital had not been competent or nice to us, but enough is enough. I wanted to get back to my bed and my house and our familiar things...especially our schnauzers: and of course some of our friends. By now, I was beyond caring about organ stealers, or locker thieves. I hadn't even thought about those kooky kids and the men after the computer disc...I just wanted to go home. My thoughts were interrupted by Julie, she was all smiles.

Her voice was coated with enthusiasm, "Well...I just signed the last of the papers. Let's get on that plane!" With that announcement, she stood next to the orderly that was to push my wheelchair down to the parking lot. A nurse who had befriended us was waiting to take us to the airport.

For the next hour and a half, I tried to lower my anxiety by cracking jokes about anything that came to my mind. I was going home, and that was all that mattered. Then the weirdest thing happened. I began to think about Rudy, Kate, our kids. Sure I was going home, but what about the disc? Involuntarily I touched my chest where the disc was secreted in my inner pocket. "Are the kids okay?"

"Ed!" Julie's tone was chiding. "I just gave you a five minute report about their time swimming in Kate's pool. Of course they're all right. Honestly, you don't seem to be listening to a word I'm saying."

The most eventful thing about the trip home was a wheelchair ride between terminals. It beat walking. I had always wondered about other people I had seen being pushed about the terminals…now I knew.

We bumped our way onto the Sky Harbor runway and I got another ride to the baggage claim area where we were greeted by Christen, Dell, and Joel. Rudy and Kate stood to the back until we had finished being surprised by the mobbing we received. It had been a month since we had seen the kids, but they looked like they had aged at least a year, maybe more.

"How was the flight, wonder boy?" Rudy slapped his hand into mine and gave me a hand squeeze befitting an injured combat soldier.

I nudged Joel's head to one side, "I'm better than new, Rudy. Have they been good?" I gave Joel's hair a tussle. "And how was this guy?"

Rudy glanced over at Kate. He tipped his head as he watched the children squirm. "They were good as gold."

Not wanting to press the issue, Julie paid the skycap. Kate and Julie grabbed our baggage cart. The ladies marched ahead with the children close behind them. As I had anticipated, Rudy spoke to me in a low voice as he pushed my wheelchair.

"Have you got the disc?"

"Sure, in my pocket. Is it still important?" I craned my neck around to try and read his face. He looked straight ahead.

"The car is just over there." He seemed more relaxed now that I had told him I had the disc. I gathered he had been getting some grief at the office.

We were pulling up next to his SUV when I asked, "So…why is the disc so important? I thought you had one just like it."

"Not just like it, Ed." He moved the chair around so I would be closer to the back door of the car. He helped me out of the chair. "You'll have to sit in the back…can't have that airbag slamming into your chest."

"What's the difference, Rudy? Not about my chest, but about the disc."

He did a mystery movie look about. "We believe there might be a list of terrorist operatives, possibly some of their finances on your disc. Just a rumor, but if we are right, you just stumbled into a nest of mad hornets.

"Exciting, huh?" I was feeling pretty good now that I was back in my home town. The near tragedy I almost suffered was left back in New York; I was miles away from that near death experience. That was then…this was now.

Rudy shifted the conversation. It was his typical way of centering on what he felt was 'real life'. "The Pepper girl has disappeared in New York; at least The Bureau can't seem to find her.

My response was off hand, perhaps flippant. "Maybe she just lost interest in us. Best I can tell…if I hadn't 'died' on the dock at Fire Island, I would probably have been killed by her or those idiots after the disc." I didn't give him a chance to respond, Rudy closed the back door on the SUV and I settled back into the warm seat: it felt good to be home…it felt good to be alive!

Chapter 58

Typically, the room was dark. The moving strains of a country western song were coloring the walls with images of unrequited love and betrayed loyalties. As the song moved into an instrumental bridge, Rudy looked over at Kate. He was feeling particularly grateful for the many years she had been by his side. "Strange isn't it."

She knew what he meant. For Kate it was easy to read Rudy's thoughts. "Yeah, I miss the kids too, but…I also am enjoying the silence." She had never had any children. At one point of her life it was a career decision, but now she was medically at risk to have any children. She loved kids, she was kind of a kid herself, but she was realistic: she would never have any children of her own. She would never be a mother, involuntarily, a few tears slid down her cheeks. "Any regrets, Rudy?"

"Regrets?" He knew what she was thinking, but saying the words was something he just couldn't do.

Kate took a deep breath, a silent sniffle escaped from her throat. "That we decided not to have kids?" She paused as the music disc changed to a new song. "Sometimes I do, Rudy. I just wonder what it would have been like to have little Rudy's running about the house."

A reflective chuckle greeted her comments. "Or little Kates playing with Barbie dolls; would you have been willing to share your dolls?" He leaned his head back and looked through to darkness. "If we really feel the need to have kids, we can always borrow Ed and Julie's." He gave a few snorts in an effort to lighten up the conversation. "I don't know, Kate. I think we would have done a great job, but I know what you mean."

The words had been said, she felt better for having said them. "Now that Ed and Julie are back home, are they going to be safe? Can Ed survive all of the tension that goes with wondering if someone is trying to kill him or his family? "

"I think they'll be okay. I have the disc. I made a copy." He clicked his tongue against his teeth while he gathered his thoughts. "I don't think anyone knows where Lena Pepper is, they lost track of her when she was in New York." Rudy paused, "You know her brother died in Ed's house, and then her boyfriend was shot and died in New York. The three of them were responsible for that Puppy Killer spree. You won't get any sympathy from me. I'm glad that she's alone."

"So, you think she is harmless?"

"Well, I wouldn't say 'harmless', but I think she is less likely to come all the way to Phoenix just to track down Ed."

Kate leaned forward; her face was lighted by the outside lights which were scattered about the garden. "Okay, but what about the disc? Just because you have the disc, does that mean no one will go after him? What if they think he has read the disc or copied some of the information?"

* * *

The big man squirmed as he tried to get comfortable in the high-backed seat. He tugged fiercely at the seatbelt; it barely reached across his large stomach. Wrinkling up his nose, he arose, he snarled at the man seated next to him, "Jesus, Bill, why didn't you get first class seats? This damned thing is like a baby's highchair."

"You're the one that wanted to get out of town as fast as we could. These seats were all that were available for Phoenix, or did you want to go to Alaska instead?" He chuckled while his partner struggled to be comfortable; it served him right for the mess he made of the New York job: no disc, no success! No success, and we had better disappear, Peter. We're just lucky all they did to us was throw us out of the hospital."

Bill raised his upper lip as he snarled, "If those damned cops hadn't held us up, we could have had the disc, now that writer fella has probably given the thing to his FBI buddy."

His finger pushed on the recliner button and the seat top moved back three inches, "Like you said...we had better consider a long vacation in South America." Peter moved his head to the side so he could speak toward Bill's ear; it was difficult because the rest of his body was wedged between the two armrests. He pulled up Peter's armrest and sighed. "That's better." He took a deep breath and whispered, "If that disc is already in the hands of the cops, I only hope we can get away...much less stay hidden." He put his hands together so they looked as if he were praying. Even he could not escape the irony.

The drone of the airplane was as indifferent to the life of the two killers as the woman who was waiting for them at the airport. To any casual person passing by, she looked like any other customer waiting to be called to her flight. She was dressed as a business woman who had a briefcase containing precious documents. Her lightweight business suit was fitted, but styled so as to not be memorable. After glancing at her watch, she returned to rifling the pages of her copy of USA Today: they would arrive in thirty minutes.

"Bill?"

"Yeah?"

"I've been thinking."

"Boy, are we in trouble." The thin man chuckled.

"I don't think they intended to let us get out of this alive." He was sweating from the confined area: he wiped his brow.

Bill wrinkled his forehead, his eyes shifted about as if looking for the answer, "Why'd you say that?" He felt a wave of nausea move up from his stomach.

"Think about it!" Peter used a hash whisper. "If we had found the disc…we would have had to verify it was the right one, wouldn't we?"

"Sure."

"Well, we would have seen the list of off shore bank account numbers, Bill." He paused to let the thought settle in. "For all they know, we have seen the disc, we know the off shore bank account numbers, and we are holding out to blackmail them." He tried to calm down, but instead he ended up talking faster. "Either way, they're not going to take the risk that we might have a duplicate disc, wrote them down, or plan to bargain with the cops, or draw out some money" He turned his head and looked out the window as the plan banked and he could see the water towers at the east edge of Phoenix. "Peter, we're dead meat, buddy."

As the reality of Peter's words sank in, Bill began to tear up. He wasn't ready to die...he was still a young man; he had a lot of plans. He fought to convince himself his paranoid friend was wrong, but the more he thought about it, the more sense it made. Why would they trust that kind of information to a couple of nobodies? The answer was...they wouldn't. Large tears began to work their way out of his puffy eyes.

Chapter 59

By now, there was a good chance the police had put out an APB for Lena. The All Points Bulletin would make air travel really risky, then how could she get all the way from New York to Phoenix all by herself? Lena ordered another cup of disgusting coffee and swept the airport lobby for some sort of inspiration. Was she still being followed, she didn't think so. Lena missed Karl; he would know what to do. Her mind worked frantically as she studied the other passengers who were moving about, sitting down, but particularly as they went in and out of the bathrooms.

Had she looked more carefully, she would have seen each of her exits now had someone watching her. Zip was only ten feet behind her, casually eating a bag of potato chips and thinking of how he could make her suffer as his family was. Uncle Jimmy had not been involved in the gang stuff that the younger family members were enjoying. He was a peaceful man, and yet this heartless thing had killed his beloved uncle as if he were a cockroach under her shoe. Zip was not even sure that Uncle Jimmy would approve of him getting even, but he didn't care. He crunched up his empty plastic bag and imagined he was wringing her neck. Zip stiffened his body as he watched Lena stand up and slip the strap of a large white canvas bag over her shoulder as she gripped a purse that was black with silver studs that formed small triangles.

Lena walked past Zip and went to the opposite side of the food court. He could watch her as she went through the line and came out with a small bag. For a few minutes she sat at a high stool and munched on her meal. His eyes were riveted at her every move, even as she pitched her rumpled up sack into the nearby trash container. Now, she moved back across the court and walked to a water fountain that separated the two restrooms. The men's was on the left and the women's was on the right. She bent over the fountain and studied the movements of the people going in and out of the bathrooms.

Zip couldn't help it! The loud cries and activity caused him to look away from Lena. He wasn't dumb; immediately he knew what happened. Some numb scull, probably Lena, had started a fire in the trash can at the place where she had just eaten breakfast. Faster than his head had moved to the right, it moved back to the water fountain…she was gone. He stood up and scanned the hordes of traffic, she had disappeared. Had she gone into the crowd, or had she gone into the bathroom, either was possible. Zip's face turned a dark red as the anger rippled through his body. He had lost her…a stupid girl. He had lost her! His only conciliation was he believed he knew where she was going.

* * *

Lena had been with Karl and her brother, Harold, when they had done the same thing in a convenient store. Everyone rushed to the smoking bathrooms and the boys had rushed to the cash register. It had worked like a charm.

She moved about in the restroom, no one paid attention to her; they were all rushing to the exit to see what was going on in the lobby. Grabbing the first empty stall she could find, she went inside and began her quick change routine. It took her less than three minutes to complete her transformation.

She wasn't sure if anyone was still following her, but she bet on it. She also certain they could not recognize her now.

She looked just like a million other people coming out of the restroom; her Mets baseball cap covered her hair while her jean jacket covered her small breasts. She looked just like any other young boy exiting the men's restroom. Her purse and bag had been dumped into the bathroom garbage can. She would have to avoid the airlines, but she had hitch-hiked before, she could do it again. Chances were pretty good, by the time she arrived at her destination, she would be driving her own car. Maybe she had an even better idea! Lena broke into a wide smile as she lowered her head and walked toward the airport exit; that would take her to the long term parking lot shuttle.

Lena had been wandering the parking lot for fifteen minutes before she spotted her prey; an elderly woman pulling a heavy luggage cart, she looked tired. Lena lowered her voice, "Lady, can I help you? That looks pretty heavy." She nodded toward a far row of parked cars, "My mom says you looked like you could use a hand."

Returning a suspicious look, the lady considered the young boy. He looked innocent enough, maybe even a little effeminate, but this was New York and a dangerous place. "Thank you, son, but I'll be fine." She took a deep breath and started to continue her chore. She was tired and her car was way down at the end of the row. If only she had gotten out of the shuttle at the right level, she would have been right at her car.

Lena shrugged. "I told mom you would tell me to go away." She threw open her hands, "I don't blame you. You're in New York, and I'm a stranger, but Mom insisted." Lena turned and started walking toward the fictitious car. "Sorry to have bothered you, Maim."

The old lady stopped. What could it hurt? A young boy and his mother just over there, after all, she was from the mid-west where people trusted people. "I'm sorry, young man. I guess it would be all right." She moved her cart so that it was in an upright position. "Actually, I think I could use a little help." She smiled; her eyes twinkled with a light mist as she thought about her grandchildren. "There are not very many children willing to help an old lady. I'm sure your mother must be proud of you." She watched as Lena grabbed the handle of the cart, the boy's hands were so small. "You remind me of my grandson, William. He's fifteen."

Lena interrupted. "Which one is yours?" She raised her head and craned her neck as she looked down the endless row of cars.

"The white Ford on the end;" Something made her feel unsettled;. but what? The grandmother picked up her pace as she struggled to bring forward the feeling she was experiencing.

Lena pulled the cart; it was heavier than she had thought it would be. "Wow, Lady, you're a lot stronger than you look." She tried for a joking tone that might relax the old lady. Lena had always prided herself on being able to sense things, and especially the feelings coming from people: this lady was becoming nervous.

There were just a few feet to go when the old lady turned her head and looked at Lena. "How old are you, son?"

A little short of breath, Lena looked at the old woman who was just a few inches taller than herself. "Like you said, I'm about the same age as your grandson." She pulled the cart up to the trunk of the Ford. "I'm a little short for my age."

"I want to thank you and your mother for helping me. I don't know what I would have done without your help." She reached into her cloth covered purse and pulled out a wallet.

Lena waved her hand, "You're welcome, Lady. I don't need anything, and Mom would get all over me if I took any money."

The old lady nodded and pressed the remote button to open her trunk. "Could you put those bags in the trunk for me?" She knew what had bothered her, but she could not bring herself to confront the person in front of her. She opened her car door.

"I think you have a problem back here, Lady." Lena pointed down at the gray concrete. "Your tire's really low."

Her concern overcame her caution. With quick steps, she walked around the back of the car. The lighting was poor and her car was close to the curb. "Is it serious?" She leaned over to get a better look at the defective tire.

With the speed of a desert snake, Lena checked her periphery and grabbed the tire iron out of the trunk. She wanted the car. She needed the car and this old lady was in her way. The black tire iron seemed to move through the air like a hawk diving on a field mouse.

With a sudden realization, the old lady could see there was nothing wrong with the tire. The boy had no Adam's apple. The tire was not defective. What was going on? She felt, rather than heard, the loud crushing thud as the tire iron bit into her silver strands of hair. There was no pain, just a feeling of floating into a pool of black.

Furtively, Lena looked in all directions. She was convinced she had not been seen. Quickly she used the grandmother's dress to wipe the blood off of the tire iron. The wound was oozing rather than gushing, Lean wondered what that meant. She threw the purse into the front seat, and then she looked at the unconscious woman: Lena didn't think she had killed the old lady, but either way she could not take the risk of someone finding her and reporting the stolen car. With every ounce of strength she could muster, Lena pulled, dragged, and tugged until the woman was in the trunk.

"Where did she put the parking ticket?" Lena's little fingers searched the purse until she found the yellow stub in a side pocket; she pulled it to her lips and kissed it as if it were a winning lottery ticket. Now it was time to count the cash, four hundred and fifty dollars: it was more than the haul at the convenient store. She would have to remember airport parking lots...they were great.

For a weekend, the highway was not very crowded. Lena had a full tank of gas and an open road to Arizona. It would be a long time before the police put out a search for the Ford, but she would keep her ear to the radio. Being careful to obey all of the traffic laws, she relaxed as she slipped the car into 'cruse control' and put the events of the last few days someplace where she would not be bothered by them. Right now, she had one lose end and that was the old lady in the trunk, what a stroke of luck. She had been looking for a car to break into and now she had a free ride. Malone would not even suspect she was on her way to kill him.

Lena's thoughts were interrupted by an SUV that was pulling up along side her; it was positioning itself to pass her. She glanced over and found herself looking into the eyes of a row of kids that were staring at her. *They must really be bored.* She considered sticking out her tongue, but decided to remain anonymous. Her mind began to drift, way back in time; she could remember traveling with her brother, Harold. He was always a brat, but he was her brother and everyone feared Harold Pepper: it made her feel safe. Maybe she didn't love him the way other girls loved their brothers, but he protected her, even if she feared him too.

The SUV pulled away and began fading out of sight. She would always remember the thought; it was as the sun was setting. Malone has kids!

Chapter 60

His head was moving so fast that he was feeling light headed. Where had she gone? He felt stupid, he had fallen for one of the oldest tricks in the book: distracted by a small fire. Zip tried to console himself with the thought she could still be in one of the restrooms, but he didn't dare go into either one of them: she could get past him if she were in either one.

"Where is she?"

Zip looked at Wong and Chu; they were gawking about the waiting area.

"Well, where is she?" Chu repeated himself as he continued looking.

Zip took a deep breath, "I think she's in one of the restrooms...but I don't know for sure.' He tensed as he anticipated the next words.

Wong moved in close to Zip's face. "What do you mean, 'you don't know'?" He poked a finger in the Zip's chest, "What happened?"

"There was a fire..." He pointed across to the **food** court. "...at the other side." Zip tried to stand up straight, "I turned when I heard the noise and…she was at that water fountain, but when I looked back, she was gone."

"You were suckered?" Chu slapped his leg as he bent over in mock laughter.

Zip's face turned red, "She might have gotten away, but I know where she's going."

"You mean Phoenix, don't you?" Wong interjected.

"Yeah; " Zip answered defiantly.

Chu snarled, "We already knew that, wise guy. If we had wanted to chase her to Arizona we would have done that."

"So, what do we do now?"

"Wong, I first want to check to see if she is in one of those bathrooms."

Wong emitted a low sigh, "Okay, Chu, you take the men's room. Zip, you check the girl's room. I'll watch to see she doesn't sneak out while you two are searching." He gave a smug chuckle.

Chu swaggered toward the men's room, but Zip waited. "Look, Wong, I know I screwed up… and I'll check the girl's room, but if we don't find her, I'm willing to go to Phoenix." Wong said nothing so he continued, "For Uncle Jimmy."

Chu was already coming out of the men's room. He was shaking his head.

"We'll see, Zip." Wong nodded at the women's restroom. "Check it."

Zip did not swagger to the ladies rest room; he strolled to the entrance and stopped a woman who was coming out. She went inside the restroom area and soon returned. Zip shook his head as he walked back to joint Wong and Chu. "She's not in there…I guess she got away."

"She didn't take the airplane, I'm sure of that. The police scanner had an APB on her. They would have alerted the airport."

"Then why was she here, Chu?"

"You got me, even if she disguised herself she couldn't get out of here unless she had a plane ticket under a different name."

"Maybe she used her brother's ticket, Chu"

Wong held up his hand, "They didn't come into New York by plane, so they probably didn't expect to leave by plane…too easy to trace them." He made a fist, "What else does an airport have lots of besides planes?"

Chu and Zip looked at each other. They didn't catch his meaning. Restaurants? Luggage? People?

With an inscrutable smile, Wong announced, "Cars. Lots and lots of cars."

Chu cut in, "She couldn't rent a car, Wong. She would need a credit card, and ID."

Zip nodded, "Yeah, but she could steal one."

"Sure she could, but someone would miss it sooner or later, and she would need a ticket to get out of a rental area." Chu was still not convinced.

"If I am right, there will be a report of a stolen car. We'll take turns on the police scanner, and I'll check in with Ralph."

"You mean the maintenance guy that works for Avis?"

"Yeah, they hear things." Wong was deep in thought. "Maybe he knows one of the security people who check the rental level video tapes. He could give us a 'heads up'."

"You mean tell us before the police?" Zip wrinkled his forehead. "Aren't we putting a lot of eggs in one basket?"

Wong expanded his narrowed eyes, "We wouldn't have to, but we don't have a lot of choices, do we, Zip?" He finished with a dramatically forced grin.

"I see where this is going, Wong, but I think you're forgetting something." Zip moved closer to Chu; it was a move designed to make him feel as if Chu were on his side. "I know where she's going."

"Yeah, we all know that, Zip, but did she fly or is she driving?"

Chu spoke up; he was clearly tired of all the wrangling. "Come on, Wong, it doesn't matter...she's gone. If she drives, flies, who cares..."

"I'll fly!" Zip pulled out a wad of cash that looked like it came from a 1930's gangster movie. "I got money...I'll find her." His two friends just exchanged looks. "You think I lost her, so I'll find her."

Chapter 61

Having the kids back at home was great. I was still a little weak from the surgery and drugs I was taking, but no pain pills. I moved into a spare bedroom where I would not be keeping the family awake when I needed to get up, which seemed rather often. Since five a.m., I had been tossing and turning like the proverbial teapot in a tempest: I just could not find a comfortable position. Julie came into the room and gave me one of those concerned frowns.

"How did you sleep?"

I leaned forward and, while adjusting my pillow, "Mostly on my back." It was my usual reply to a generic question.

She ignored my cavalier response and handed me a cup of hot tea. "Kate and Rudy would like to come by this morning, if you feel up to it." Julie plopped down at the foot of the bed and began sipping her tea from a cup that advertised a bank. The touted branch bank probably had one location and was hidden in the foothills of Montana: a garage sale item, no doubt. "How do ya feel?"

Immediately, I started into a tirade about the 'drugs' they were making me take; nothing serious; mostly some mild blood pressure pills and a beta-blocker, but they were meant to give my organ a rest from having to pump blood through such a narrow opening. "Damned drugs, they make me sleepy, and then they make me forget words."

She laughed because I had always been able to brag about my memory: one has to have good recall to be able to write stories. Writing fiction is like putting together four hundred pages of lies and you have to remember every one of them. "Welcome to our world, Ed." My patient wife took one more sip and said, "You sound fine, I'll tell them to come over at ten."

I snapped back, "Okay, but don't expect me to stay up for a long time…damned drugs make me sleepy."

"Okay, Grumpy, I'll tell the other dwarfs to be on their best behavior." Julie was leaving, but stopped and made a dramatic twirl. "Maybe I can find 'Happy'" Her giggle finally faded as she pranced down the hallway.

Her subtle reference to <u>Snow White and the Seven Dwarfs</u> was not lost on me: she was probably right. "Very funny. Very funny." But it made me laugh. Laughing is not really a fun thing when you are recovering from a nine inch slice down the middle of your chest.(well, maybe it is more like seven inches, but nine probably gets more sympathy.) "Don't make me laugh!"

She chuckled as she closed my bedroom door, "Get up. Get some sunshine, the kids want you to play linebacker with their lawn baseball game." (She is a bit confused about serious professional activities) Last thing she did was to stick her head back in the room, "Get dressed or I'll make you laugh again."

That one hurt, she could be really funny when she was in that mood. I got dressed, ate a hearty breakfast and finished just in time to welcome Kate and Rudy into our disheveled living room: the kids were still on summer vacation from school. The talk was light, mostly about my operation, the miracles that had rescued me from death and all of the antics our children had pulled while staying with Kate. Almost abruptly, the room became quiet.

"We need to talk to you about some things." Rudy's voice was almost ominous. He began fidgeting with his glass of water. "Lena has escaped from New York. At least, at this time, the police haven't a clue as to where she is." He paused, "They felt it was best that you be…cautioned about her disappearance."

Julie was quick to jump in. "Are you saying they think she might come here…" She gave me a chilling glance, "…after Ed?" Her eyes were moving in a blinking pattern, she was trying to hold back her tears, "Good God, haven't we had enough problems?" She had reached her limit. Like a well worn rubber band, her nerves were frayed and poised to snap. She cried!

I knew it was just a matter of minutes before she switched from victim to huntress: no one was going to threaten her family without paying a high price. The truth was, I was feeling much better than I had felt before my Fire Island flop on the dock, but my endurance still had a long way to go. I did what I could; I reached over and pulled her into a tight hug. At the same time I asked Rudy, "What do they have that could be of use to us?"

Rudy looked apologetic, "I wish I could tell you something useful. I'm sorry, Julie, for making you worry, but, Ed, we just don't have a lot to go on except she blames you for her brother's death and even for what happened to Karl."

Julie sucked in several sobby breaths and dabbed at her eyes: she was coming around. "I thought Margarita said Lena was the soft one. She didn't think she would kill anyone."

With the understanding only one woman has toward another, Kate's soft voice spread a balm of serenity into the room. "That was when Lena had her as a prisoner in the cabin, and before her brother died trying to kill you two. She's changed. I suppose she's more like a fiery lioness than the passive caretaker she used to be."

Writing books gives a person a chance to consider alternative actions characters might take, I now had a thought, but, considering Julie's mental state, I hesitated to bring it up. Julie was ahead of me. As if reading my thoughts, she looked at me and asked, "What about the kids, Ed?" She asked me the question, but then she looked at Rudy and Kate.

I wanted to lie to her, but it would have been pointless. "I don't know, Hon, but we had better keep then close to home until she is caught."

"Good idea." Rudy echoed.

"We'll help, if you'll let us." Kate knew how Julie and I were such 'do it your selfers'.

They meant well, but I couldn't see putting them in that kind of danger. "Maybe you could just beef up our security system, Rudy...that would be enough. No need for you two to get into Lena's path."

Kate chuckled, "We already are, Ed. She knows we're your friends. Hell, she might decide to come after us just to get even."

Julie blanched, she hadn't thought about that one, but she was smoldering with anger. "If that little bitch (she looked around to see if any of our kids heard her) thinks she is going to hurt any of us, she has another think coming; I'm not going to cower. She had better hope she doesn't come around here. I'll blow her damned head off." With a curt nod of her head, she settled back and snorted like a mother rhino.

Chapter 62

He had spent the entire day at the library. Zip researched the Republic's news accounts that referenced Karl Pepper and his sister, Lena. Before he had left New York, his buddy, Ralph, who worked for the Avis Car Rental service, had told him about the video tape showing the theft of the white Ford from the parking garage. Ralph's police friends also told him about the links between Edward Malone, the writer, and the Puppy Killers. Lena's dead brother, Harold, had been killed at the Malone house. The Phoenix police were looking for her to show up, any day now. Lena was also wanted in the disappearance of Grace Ember, the owner of the white Ford.

The cops ought to give me a medal for killing this wild woman. Zip was a criminal, but this lady was a full fledged killer. He was still having a problem sorting out the information about the cabin. He wondered who the kids were Leah was guarding, or watching, were they her kids?"

After stealing a car that was parked on downtown Seventh Street, Zip switched license plates with a similar car and then began getting familiar with the street layouts and the homes of Malone and Tracker, the ex-FBI guy. Lena, according to his information, would be stalking one or both of these people.

When he pulled onto the street where the Malone's lived, he could see a patrol car which was positioned just down the street: evidently they were prepared to welcome Lena back in town. Zip would have to get to her before the police got her or his debt to Uncle Jimmy would be really complicated. He cruised the block, all the time he was well aware he was using a stolen vehicle: what a blast!

Phoenix seemed like a nice town, lots of sunshine. Maybe he should move here and go to school. Zip responded with a silent chuckle at the thought. *Fat chance.* The cops have the right idea, cruise the neighborhood and wait for Lena to show up…if she was going to show up. It was a long shot, but not without high probability. At the end of the block he took a left and headed for the 101 Loop: he would come back at night.

Chapter 63

She could hear them, but she couldn't see them. The Malone's backyard was just on the other side of the gray block wall fence. Perhaps it was hunger, or a case of nerves, but her stomach was giving her fits, it growled and spasmed as she paced up and down the length of the wall. What she couldn't see, she imagined. The kids were splashing about in the family swimming pool: it was a nice day to be swimming. She wondered if her life would have been any different if she had been born into a nice family, but the illusion was as fleeting as drops of water falling on the hot concrete that surrounded the pool.

Lena could picture the squeals and shouts of the girls as they taunted their little brother, Joel. *At least they had a brother.* She was feeling both envy and hate for the Malone family, they had killed her brother. Lena didn't even know why she felt she should extract revenge, but somewhere inside of her she felt she would feel better when she had taken lives away from them. The imaginary scenes flashed through her tortured mind as she listened to the joy the kids were having. Confusing was the best way to describe it, she was excited by the fun they were having, but angered by the sounds of love and closeness they were experiencing: ENVY, was that enough reason to kill someone?

With some difficulty and a few scrapes, she worked herself high into a Russian olive tree that overlooked the Malone's back yard. There they were, playing! Through the window she could see the Malones had company, but the reflecting sunlight made it difficult to make out any faces. Much faster than she had intended, she slid down the tree and was rewarded by a long slice on the inside of her leg. From her backpack she pulled out a scented handkerchief and wrapped her slight wound. Tending to her wound, she thought back to the old lady she had left in the trunk of the Ford she had stolen at the Kennedy airport. Old Gracie had seemed like a nice lady, she wondered if anyone had found her. For a millisecond, she felt a nudge from her conscience. Why had she been hurting so many nice people who had done nothing to her? The thought moved away and she found herself filled with rage at the way life had treated her: it wasn't her fault; people just seemed to get in her way.

The wound was closed and she believed no one had seen her. Tomorrow she would find out what the children did during the day, she was sure she could snatch them with the old Puppy Killer trick of looking for her lost dog. It always worked. If she took the kids to her cabin, then the Malones would have to come to claim them, then she could kill Mr. Writer and his wife, she couldn't decide what to do with the kids. She paused to savor the thought, but there was nothing. Maybe she could make it across the border and live in Mexico; she had heard it was cheap to live there. She could start a new life, too bad she wouldn't have Harold or Karl to take care of her. She was alone.

* * *

"Did you hear that?" Rudy stopped with his glass of water only a few inches away from his lips. He cocked his ear toward my office. "You hear that, Ed?"

"Hear what?" I looked about the room wondering if Julie or Kate had said something from the kitchen, then a piecing fear shoot through my body; "The kids?"

Rudy stood up and motioned for me to follow him. He moved like a man with a mission: long swift strides I had only seen him use the night Farley was shot at the department store. "I think one of my sensors got tripped."

"You're kidding! There are all kinds of noises from the kids."

"I have some motion sensors out there, Ed" Rudy sounded brusque. "Not just audio."

Feeling my family was in imminent danger was the last thing I wanted to hear. "Maybe it was just a squirrel?" I wanted the creepy sensation to go away. "I've seen a lot of them in that vacant lot."

Rudy was already walking out the back door, "Jesus, Ed, give me some credit. My equipment isn't set that sensitive, maybe a dog or a coyote, but not some ground squirrel."

Our fence is too high for anyone to see over it unless they are a circus clown on stilts. Rudy paced back and forth, not wanting to go to the other side and risk scratching up his exposed legs, he just snorted, "Well, what ever it was…it probably is gone by now."

I found myself staring at him, "She couldn't be here already, Rudy. She had to drive the entire distance."

"How about the guys who are after the disc, they don't know you gave it to me." Then he turned his full front to face me, "Didn't you tell me you and Julie drove from Montana, thirty-one hours straight, to Phoenix?" He almost jabbed at my chest and then remembered about my incision, "So could she, she's young and she's mad."

Knowing that it was concern for me and my family, I backed off and conceded his point, "You might be right, at least it makes sense to be cautious." Slowly his countenance began to relax.

"Ed, I want you to understand something. Security systems are only as good as the people paying attention to them: they do no good if you don't trust them."

"Okay, okay, I get the point. Now, can we go back in the house and talk over a glass of iced tea?" Rudy was right, but I was in no mood to hear it.

Chapter 64

Things could not have worked out better. They moved about the house as if they had rented it for the summer. Peter looked strange in his blue jeans shorts and Diamondbacks tee shirt; his large frame accentuated his size. "Bill, I think I found the disc, it's right here by this laptop."

In two quick bounds, Bill was in front of the IBM laptop. His bony fingers clasped the disc and turned it over and over. "Yeah, I think you're right." He turned on the laptop and pushed the disc into the side drawer. The two men could hardly tolerate the wait as the computer went through its paces. Finally, the screen jumped to life and there it was asking for the password. "This is it, Peter. This is it! I recognize the logo."

"Get the damned thing and let's get out of here, those FBI'ers could come back from that writer fellow's place at any time."

Bill released a long sigh as he punched the button that ejected the disc. "Guess that FBI guy isn't as smart as we thought he was."

With a broad smile on his face, Peter looked like a famous fat comedian. "Yeah, well, this whole thing would have been a lot easier if we had just knocked off that writer and snatched the disc."

Slipping the disc into his pocket, Bill replied, "How in the Hell were we supposed to know he would drop dead on the dock." He chuckled, "If he hadn't dropped dead, we would have killed him…permanently." The two men were still laughing as they exited by the back door.

Rudy's motion activated camera returned to 'pause'.

The car radio was belting out a list of the latest top ten country western hits as their car glided down Scottsdale Drive. The Sun would soon hit its zenith: it felt good to be basking in hot rays. "You know, Peter, now we won't have to disappear to South America."

"That's good, 'cuz I was always bad at other languages." Peter slapped the top of the convertible's door and looked around: enjoying the view, enjoying life. "You know, this is really living; cursing down Scottsdale Road with the top down. The sun is shinning, and we're going to be rich, at least for a while."

"What you think? Do we still have to worry about them thinking we got a look at the list in that disc?" Bill's voice sounded a bit tense. He was a chronic worrier, and he knew it, but this time...it could be true.

Leaning back in the leather seat, Peter closed his eyes and waxed philosophical. "You worry too much, Pal. They know we don't have the password."

Bill didn't reply, he was watching the car that was behind them. "Peter, did you tell anyone we were going over to get the disc?"

"Huh?" With eyelids closed to the warm sun, Peter was almost asleep. The warming rays felt so relaxing.

"We're being followed."

In one movement, Peter moved his large frame from slouch to bolt upright. He whipped his body around before Bill had a chance to stop him.

"Who's following us?" His tone was not only questioning, but suspicious.

Two cars back now, but, for God's sake don't turn around. "You didn't answer my question. Did you tell anyone we were going to the FBI guys place?"

"I talked to Marla, but I never told her nothing."

"Jesus, Peter, she has the biggest mouth in Arizona. What did you tell her?" Bill had his eyes glued to the rearview mirror. His body was as stiff as the steering column. He raised his voice, "What did you tell her?"

"She wouldn't say anything, Bill?"

In disbelief, Bill moved his head from side to side. "You told her something, didn't you?"

Peter was watching the side mirror and acting unconcerned. "I don't think that car is following us, he's just going the same way."

"Did you tell her we were going to get the disc?"

"Yeah, okay, I suppose I did, but Marla's a good kid, she wouldn't talk to no one." He turned his face to look at Bill, "Honestly!"

"I'm gonna lose these guys." Bill pushed down on the accelerator and began heading south toward Highway Ten. "If they follow us…we know she talked to someone. The car surged as if it had been kicked in the butt by some invisible giant.

Peter turned around, "I don't see them. See, I told you, they weren't dogging us."

Bill kept his eye on the rearview mirror, but he could not see any sign of the car that had caused him to worry for the last fifteen minutes. He swerved west, and then south again: gradually working his way toward the highway. He couldn't see the car, but he had a feeling they were still on his tail. Was it the FBI that was following him or maybe the guys who hired the two of them…maybe he was wrong? Bill was beginning to drive like some drunken fool: no regard for his own safety or anyone else's.

"Hey, Bill, take it easy; you almost sideswiped that guy!" Peter tightened his seatbelt and swallowed.

With a sharp right turn, Bill shot up the ramp and started heading west, toward California.

"Isn't this the way toward that Palo Verde nuclear plant?" The car was going at least seventy-five miles an hour, but at least they weren't dodging in and out of local traffic.

Keeping his eyes fixed on the road ahead, Bill muttered, "I guess so." The wind was sweeping his words into the air as if they were caught in a fan. He tried to reason things out, if they were going to kill Peter and him, they could not do it until they knew the status of the disc. They could not let the police get a hold of the disc. *Yeah, that was it…just keep moving.*

"I think you got a bad case of the jitters, Bill. You better slow down or some cop is going to pull us over." Peter's hair was whipping around and his nerves were beginning to upset his large stomach. "We're not being followed, Bill. Can't we stop and get something to eat?"

In spite of himself, Bill broke into a laugh. It was hard to believe that, at a time like this, Peter was thinking about his stomach. But he had a point. If they stopped at the truck stop near Tonopah, he could either change cars, or find out if they were being tracked. "Yeah, sure, Peter. Good idea!" He tapped his left elbow against the pistol that was shoulder harnessed there.

"I could call Marla and see if she can meet us somewhere." Peter reached for his cellular phone. His pudgy fingers began punching as his nervous hand almost vibrated. "Marla? Peter…Bill and me, we're stopping at that truck stop near Tonopah; Yeah, the big on." He looked over at Bill, but there was no response from him. "See you there in a half hour…okay?" He closed the cell and laid it on the car seat; "Told you she's a nice kid."

They speeded along in silence until they finally came to the exit. Bill pulled up the exit ramp, but took the road to the right instead of the left. "Let's just make sure we're not being followed."

"Sure thing, Bill;" again, Peter looked out the back of the car. "Not a bad idea, but let's get over to the restaurant pretty soon, I got to take a leak."

Bill pulled up next to an abounded parking garage; it had gone out of business years ago when the freeway was installed. "Take you're leak now. There, next to the garage." He watched as Peter dutifully sulked off. Then, he picked up Peter's cell phone and punched, 'redial'. Nervously, he watched Peter and listened as the phone began to chirp. For sometime now, Bill had been suspicious of a number of coincident that were taking place. It was apparent someone was keeping track of them, and he didn't like it.

His thoughts were interrupted by a soft voice that whispered, "Roadrunner Realty". The voice that answered was a woman's, but it was not Marla's Texas twang. Bill wanted to hear her talk some more, maybe she had learned how to change her accent. "Can you tell me where you're located?"

In a very officious voice the lady answered, "Certainly, sir." She gave him the address, but he had no interest in writing it down. "We're in Scottsdale, sir. Just ask for Tracy and I'll connect you to one of our agents."

"Oh, I'm sorry, Tracy, but I was wondering if Marla was available." Bill caught his breath as he watched Peter zip up his trousers and turn to walk back to the car.

The polite voice resumed, "I'm sorry, sir, but no one by that name works here. We are a small office and I know everyone that works for Mr. Shaddock." She paused, "Perhaps you have the name wrong."

Bill slid the phone back on the car seat. Now he was worried, he knew who Shaddock was: he was the man who was acting as the go-between for the disc. Peter had just talked to that number and told them to meet us at the truck stop diner. Peter moved to the door of the car. Bill reached for Peter's phone, "Hey, Peter, what was that number for that guy, Shaddock? Maybe we should tell him we have the disc." How Peter answered would determine what Bill would do.

Peter pushed out his lower lip and thrust his double chinned face forward. "Darned if I know; he works at some real-estate company, but I think I have his number in my bag. I'll get it…it's in the trunk." With great ease he opened the long passenger door. "Pop the truck, Bill."

Without hesitation, Bill reached under the dashboard and pushed the trunk release. Peter must have known what Bill had done, it was out in the open now and Bill had only a few seconds to make his decision. Peter was a large man, but, when he needed to, he could move fast.

The move that Peter was making was designed to get behind Bill and eliminate him as easily as possible. Peter wasn't as scared as he thought he would be. Bill and Peter had been together for a long time, but Marla had thought it was time Peter should go out on his own and not have to always divide up the money: Shaddock had agreed, but he had cautioned Peter to wait until they had the disc. Putting on a show, Peter began moving the luggage bags about. "This trunk's a mess." He paused as he looked about the landscape to see if there were any observers. It would be too messy to kill Bill inside the car. "Hey, Pal, give me a hand here, will ya?" He patted his left arm to make sure his knife was accessible.

"Jesus, Peter, you can't find nothing." Sensing what was coming; Bill slowly opened the driver's side door and used the angle of the trunk cover to pull out his back up revolver, a thirty-two caliber Smith and Wesson short barrel. The thirty two was unregistered and totally 'clean'. "Why did you lie to me?" It was a foolish question to ask, he knew why. It had been touchy ever since Peter had been chummy with Marla.

Acting surprised, Peter straightened up and took on an indignant tone, "Hey, Bill…what're you doing?" He knew there was no turning back from the hole in which he put himself. Marla and Shaddock both had expectations of him. He moved his hands as if putting them up in the air, but in one swift movement, Peter gripped the blade of his concealed knife and propelled it at Bill's throat.

It felt like a bee sting as the thin blade entered to the right side of his wind pipe. Bill had meant to fire his gun, but his hand went to his neck instead. With each pump of his heart, warm blood was squirting out of his neck. His vision was bleared and he could no longer stand up. Something had gone wrong, and Peter had disappeared. Grasping his sticky throat, he fell to his knees and then rolled gently to his side. There was no pain, just a growing darkness.

After releasing the knife, Peter had ducked behind the side of the car and pulled out his pistol.

He had killed lots of people, but none he had known as well as Bill. Even as he watched Bill fighting to stay alive, he waited for a feeling of guilt or remorse to settle into his mind, but no such thing happened. *I must be further gone than I thought.* It had been a clean shot, the result of years of practice. Anyway, it didn't matter what Bill thought, Peter would soon have his money and Marla would be pleased.

When there was a lull in the highway traffic, Peter dragged Bills body over behind the old garage. He rolled the body of his 'friend' so as to remove his clothes and jewelry; it was his attempt to make it look like a roadside robbery. After the police had run his fingerprints, they would assume it was a business deal gone bad, which was exactly what it was. Then they would run a list of known associates: he could expect a visit, but Marla would be his cover, at least he hoped she would.

Chapter 65

So many things had been happening we had not, yet, had a chance to go out for a good restaurant meal, but, at last, the night had arrived. Rudy and Kate arrived at our house at six o'clock, their niece, Heather, was loaded down with her favorite music and movies: babysitter's standard equipment. Heather was a five year veteran with the Phoenix police. She was not a field agent yet, but it was her ambition, for now she was a 'probationary' with the violent crimes division: a records keeper. A pretty girl, at five foot eleven, she is a striking example of Germanic breeding.

I never cease to be amazed at the boundless energy of our children. When Julie yelled down the hallway that Heather had arrived, Joel, Dell and Christine dashed into the hallway as if they were practicing a fire drill. The screams and shouts of joy were only excelled by those reserved for Christmas morning.

Ever the vigilant father, I raised my voice and shouted a pointless warning, "Hey, you guys, slow down!" Christine responded by executing a short jump and planting a disarming kiss on my cheek: all without loosing her place in the race.

With the agility of a young gazelle, Heather dodged right and left and managed to make the kids snatch an armful of air. With one easy vault, she moved from the front of the couch to the back of the couch. She dropped on all fours and allowed herself to be mobbed by the advancing horde of three. When I looked behind the couch they reminded me of a pile of frolicking puppies.

"Easy on her;" there was no real danger, but it seemed the fatherly thing to say. "You okay, Heather?"

She dodged a grab by Joel, "Sure thing, Mr. M. No problem" Adroitly she pinned Christine into a tickle hold. "You guys have a nice time."

I was moved from my position as the grand protector and referee when Julie grabbed my arm and jerked me toward the door. "Come with me, Noble Protector, the kids will be fine." She interjected a phrase that brought out the words of Peter Pan and jolted me back to reality. "We want to get back before it's too dark, Ed."

After checking all of the doors and windows, I did a quick audit of Rudy's audio and motions detectors, they answered to their electronic testing: all lights were a solid Christmas light green. We exited by the front door, which I checked at least four times. Rudy and Kate were waiting in their idling four door passenger Dodge pickup truck: Rudy's favorite toy.

We didn't do a lot of talking. The truth was, we were all a bit nervous about leaving the kids at home...even with Heather there. The other side of the situation was we didn't want to expose Heather to possible danger. By now we were well aware Lena Pepper was someplace in the Phoenix area, at least there were a couple of alert businesses which identified her from the distributed fliers. All of these thoughts were weighing heavily on our guilt ridden minds, but it was obvious we could not be hovering over the kids every minute of the day, and besides, we were not even going far from home.

Rudy tilted his head to the side, but continued to look out the front windshield, "Ed?"

"Yeah?"

"Nothing new with the Pepper girl; A few of the agents think she might have gone south to Mexico." Rudy's hand moved and the sound of the turn signal thumped in the cab. "I think it's too soon to assume that, but it would make sense."

I nodded and looked longingly out of the back window: I wanted to be back at the house where I could protect my babies. I knew Julie felt the same way, but I also knew we were going to be on each other's nerves if we didn't get out for a short time. Most of the cars I saw at the curb were ones I recognized.

Julie moved closer to me, I suppose I was still vulnerable from my touch with death, but I appreciated her attempt to comfort me. "They'll be all right, Ed...you'll see."

* * *

Lena considered her problem: she wanted to get to the children, but they were not alone. Stroking the cream colored dog that was seated next to her, she decided the best way was to go right up to the front door, it was a small risk, but she had seen Karl or Harold do the pitch. It only took her a few seconds to slip a collar on the young Border collie. She would have to move quickly now: the fewer the number of people that saw her, the better.

With all of the tussling going on, it was difficult to hear the doorbell as it chimed. "Hey, you guys, knock it off. Someone's at the front door." Heather held up her hand as if she were doing vehicular traffic control. "You guys stay here. Christine…you're in charge." Sporting a broad smile, Heather moved across the floor, sliding her white socked feet like a cross country skier.

On the other side of the door, Lena squatted down and petted the panting dog. She looked just like a million other people who could be taking their dog for a neighbor hood walk, but inside her stomach was churning with fear and excitement. She hopped Karl would be proud of her: if he were still alive, which he wasn't. She tensed even harder, if that were possible, as the door began to open. The tall woman standing at the door was not Kate Sonfrig. From her squatting position, the woman looked huge, but she was smiling.

Heather was still catching her breath as she asked, "May I help you?"

Lena stayed down low, less threatening. "I'm sorry to bother you, but I was walking my aunt's dogs, and one of them who looks just like this one, got away from me."

Compassion formed on Heather's face: she loved dogs. "Oh, I'm so sorry."

What's she sorry about? Lena nodded, "Yeah, Aunty is worried sick." She stroked the dog, "I'm going from door to door hoping someone has seen Mate: that's the other dog's name." She looked up and gave a pleading look, "They're Australian sheep dogs."

Bending down to stroke the little Coolie, Heather spoke in a pained tone, "I'm sorry, but I haven't seen your dog." She straightened up and shook her head, "I certainly hope you find her, it, soon."

"Mate's a he." Lena's sorrowful face looked up at Heather, "Is there anyone else who might have seen little Mate?" She was proud of her selection of the words, 'little mate', it seemed so helpless. "Poor Aunty is so worried…and so am I. Mate doesn't know this neighborhood, he's probably frightened to death." She clasped her hand over her mouth, "Horrible choice of words."

Tipping her head to one side, Heather said, "Sure, I'm not sure that the kids can help you, but we can ask. Come on inside." Heather turned around and began to lead the way into the house, "Kids, have you seen a stray dog?" She shouted before she had even taken two steps.

Like a Jaguar pouncing from a tree, Lena got to her feet and stepped inside. She closed the door with one movement and pulled a small piece of metal pipe from her beltline. In one swift half circle, she hit Heather on the back of her head. The big woman stumbled, like she had just tripped over the edge of a scatted carpet. She buckled to her knees and then her face made a sound like a watermelon dropping to the wooden floor. Lena was about to hit the lady again when she heard the kids thumping their way toward the front door. She rolled the pipe under a nearby recliner chair. "Your mother tripped over the carpet. I guess it knocked her out."

Christine was in the lead with Dell and Joel close behind her. Dropping to her knees, she looked at Lena, "Who are you?"

"I've lost a dog. I was asking her for help." Lena hadn't really thought her plan through. There were three kids and only one of her, she also was afraid they had heard about the Puppy Killers and how they used animals as bait. She shifted the subject, "Help me put her on the couch...have you got a cold compress?" Lena would try to keep them busy until she could come up with a good plan. Her heart was beating like a baby thumping on a kitchen cooking pan.

Dell and Joel were staring at the small straw colored collie, they seemed frozen in time. Their young eyes moved from watching the strange lady and Christine move Heather to the couch and the panting tongue that looked like the mouth of a circus clown. The dog's eyes sparkled like the glass beads of a stuffed animal. Cautiously they crept over to the dog and began to pet the stationary canine that lapped them with an appreciating volley of wet slurps.

"Shouldn't I call 911?" Christine spoke as she looked at the wound on the back of Heather's head. "I think she's going to need a doctor."

"A good idea, ah…sorry, I don't know your name." That wasn't true, but it was no time for honesty.

"Christine."

"I have a better idea." Lena became animated as she paced about the area by the doorway. "Christine?"

Christine snapped her head up.

"We'll put Heather in my car and drive her to the hospital…it will save lots of time." Lena didn't wait for an answer, but bent over the motionless body of their babysitter. "Grab her feet! Kids, open the door." She was stunned by the unquestioning compliance of the children. "We'll have her there before the ambulance would have left the hospital." Furiously, she was deciding how to subdue the children once she had them in her car.

Dell opened the door while Joel grabbed the leash of the dog. Dell stood like a diminutive statue, "Maybe we should call dad's cell."

Lena tightened her grip on Heather's ankles. "Good idea, but let's wait until we get her to the hospital…we don't want them to get too worried. We can always call them from the hospital and give them the latest updates." Lena recalled her objective of keeping the kids busy. "I'll leave them a note, just in case they come here first or the cell phone isn't working."

As the door closed behind them, Lena's organized crew moved down the driveway and across the street to Lena's car. With any luck, she could be at the old cabin within forty minutes.

Chapter 66

I pulled out my cell phone. The meal was going great, but I had a creepy feeling: I needed to call the children. The seating was tight, so I leaned to my right to pull the phone from my pocket.

"What are you doing, Ed?" Julie gave me a disapproving glace from the corner of her eye.

"I'm going to check on the kids." I began punching in the auto call for our home.

Gently, Julie grabbed my wrist, "Honestly, Ed, you are such a worry-wort. Heather has them under control." She chuckled. "If anyone needs checking on, it's that poor girl."

Everyone laughed, even I. It was a bit over the top to be that concerned when they were being watched by an experienced police woman. A picture of the family wrestling with her flashed through my head, as usual, Julie was probably right. Sheepishly, I glanced around the table, but no one was really paying attention to my antics: they were all checking the dessert menu.

"Besides, Ed, they are probably all in the pool by now." Rudy had his eyes fixed on a gooey chocolate fudge treat. "I'm sure they are all right, worry wort." It was the second time I had been labeled with that appellation.

Responding with a good natured grin, I put the phone back in my pocket. "You're probably right. If I interrupt their swimming, I'll get razzed about it for the rest of the night." But, you know that feeling you get when your insides are churning about and your brain is whirring like a jet in a crash dive, well, I just couldn't leave the phone in my pocket. "I know I'm being foolish, BUT I just have to call. I punched the button and waited. Like a little kid caught with his fingers in a cookie jar, I grinned as I listened to each buzz of the electronic caller. After the fifth ring, I said, "I guess you are right, they must be in the pool."

Julie gave me a peculiar look. "I'm sure I put the outside ringer on when you went outside this morning, Ed. They should hear the phone." Her face contorted into a mask of concern. She studied me as I continued to listen for a response. "Ed...I think we should leave! Rudy?"

Moving as if we were all legs of a giant centipede, we got up from the table and headed for the door. I shoved a one hundred dollar bill in the hand of our waiter and mumbled, "That should take care of it!" I didn't slow down or wait for any pleasantries. By now, all of us were synergistically feeling a tsunami of alarm, maybe nothing was wrong, but, we just simply could not sit in the restaurant and ignore the surging pressures of fear.

"Rudy? Should we call for the police to meet us there?"

Rudy put the truck in reverse, his eyes danced as he considered my question. "Let's, I don't like the feeling of this whole thing." He nodded at Kate.

Like an old time gunfighter, Kate snatched the truck mounted phone from the dashboard and punched in 911. She gave her badge number and call for 'back up'. As if in slow motion, she returned the phone to its cradle.

I studied her movements: something was wrong. The dilemma was, if I asked, and there was something serious, I didn't want Julie to hear about it before we could do anything about it. I leaned close to Kate, "What's the problem?"

It was like she was reading my mind. She whispered, "Two cars are already headed to your house. Gun shots have been reported." Out loud she said, "The backup cars are on their way." She glanced at Julie, but it was plain to see she was staring out the car window.

We were gliding in and out of traffic. It gave me the feeling the truck was on auto-control and we were cartoon figures from a children's Saturday morning adventure show. No doubt we all had concerns, questions, and fears, but if we spoke of them, they might materialize. I knew Julie was mentally beating herself for taking the time to go out to the restaurant; it would pass in a few days. I just wanted to get there and protect my kids: know that they were all right. The time seemed to be slowing down and, just when we seemed to be moving a bit faster, Rudy put on the breaks.

"There's a fatal accident up ahead, at least that's what it looks like." Rudy craned his neck, looking for an opening where he could get a better look. If he had looked to his right, he would have enjoyed the glare that Kate was giving him for scaring everyone.

I turned to Julie, "It's not the kids, Julie!" I held her hand, "If it were the kids, we would have felt it." I watched her feeble nod, probably as much for my sake as for hers.

The cartoon became more real. I imagined what we all must look like from the air: cars haphazardly strewn about on a ribbon of asphalt. Like stick figures drawn by a fourth grade student, we all had 'unhappy' faces sketched into our oval faces. We were at a dead stop!

Chapter 67

Zip had watched as Lena walked up to the entrance of the Malone home. He was having a difficult time figuring out what Lena was doing, what was her interest in this place? He had planned to settle in for a long wait, when, seemingly out of nowhere, Lena came out of the house, a tall woman was being carried by her and some children: a little boy was pulling the leash of a reluctant dog. He wanted to blink away the images that were in front of him, but it began to make sense. Lena was a killer; he knew that from the way she had shot his Uncle Jimmy. The question now, was has she killed this woman and these kids were helping her get rid of the body…right in broad daylight?

They're sisters and a little brother. Now the weird screen was clear. She had killed this woman and they were helping her, and they were going to get away with it. Quickly he opened his car door and pulled out his pistol. He aimed for the back tire, but he heard an approaching car and he hit the license plate instead. The report startled Zip as well as several neighbors. *She's getting away!*

Swiftly, Lena pulled her car away from the curb and headed for Highway 17 and the cabin outside of Prescott, Arizona. She had just rounded the corner and disappeared from sight when Zip's police scanner alerted him patrol cars had been displaced as a result of the shot he fired. Jumping inside, he punched the accelerator and raced after Lena and the car full of conspirators.

Heather was stretched across Christine's lap and Dell's bony knees. "Miss… that man shot at us!" Christine was almost screaming, but out of concern for Heather, it was more like a subdued hiss. "He could have killed someone."

Lena knew who it was that shot at the car; it was that crazy Oriental from New York. Why didn't he just go home and leave her alone? She was furious;

he might just mess up everything. "I don't know!" She shot back in a loud voice, "Why?" Her mind was racing, "Maybe he is part of a gang and he was supposed to do a random shooting...how am I supposed to know?" Maybe she could use this to divert to the cabin instead of going to a hospital. She picked up her cell phone and punched in a group of numbers, the phone responded with a hissing hum. "Hello?" She looked knowingly in the rear view mirror and caught Christine's eye. She began a fake conversation with her phone. "I'm going to need medical assistance. Yes, I'll hold."

"What are you doing, Miss?" Dell blinked, expressing her confusion.

"I'm going to have a medical emergency team meet us at a place where that madman behind us can't shoot at us. It's a bit out of the way, but it will be safer for your friend and for us. I don't know why he is shooting at us, but I think it is better to be safe than sorry."

"My dad always says that." Joel philosophically nodded.

It was Showtime. "Hello." She paused as if listening to someone speaking to her. "I need a team of EMT's to meet me at 4454 North Summit Drive...that's close to Prescott." She paused. "Okay, I'll see you there." She tilted her head and yelled, "Okay, they'll have an ambulance for us." Inside, she smiled. The kids were too trusting to doubt her. Lena glanced in her rearview mirror and tried to scan for the oriental that had fired a shot at them, but in the confusion, she could not remember what the car looked like.

"Heather doesn't look so good, Miss." Dell's voice came across more as a whine than as a genuine concern.

Christine leaned as far forward as she could, "Maybe if they knew she was a policewoman they would get there faster."

Blinking her eyes in disbelief, Lena said, "I doubt they could get there any sooner. We'll get there just as soon as we can; it's just that we have to be clear of that maniac that is following us." *A policewoman, that's all I needed.* Responding to Christine's words, Lena pushed down on the accelerator, but the car did not pick up much speed: they were going up hill and with a heavy load. *Damn, this isn't how I planned it. I just wanted to get even with that creep writer.*

* * *

Not wanting to create another incident, Zip moved his car in and out of traffic using the greatest caution. He had her in sight and his ear to the police scanner in his car. Lena was not moving fast and he had lots of slow moving cars he could hide behind. With all this idle time on his hands, he busied himself thinking of what he was going to do to avenge his Uncle Jimmy. Would he kill her first or let the cops catch her with the body?

Maybe he could kill that brat brother of hers and the sisters before he did her. He didn't like killing kids, but if it made her suffer, then, for Jimmy, he could do it.

Ahead Zip watched as Lena went down an exit ramp and went west, the sign said, 'Prescott'. "What's she doing here?" He muttered out loud. A thought jumped into his mind, at the library, he had read an article about a cabin where she and two men had been staying: the Puppy Killer Gang they had called it. Zip wondered if the gang was as big as his New York one was. Maybe he should stop her now...before she met up with her 'Hood'. He began to accelerate, but she pulled off of the main road and started over a narrow off the trail path. He pulled back and tried to stay hidden, with a quick glace, he looked at the passenger seat and comforted himself that the pistol was resting comfortably on the seat. "It won't be long now, Unc." The smiling face of his departed Uncle appeared from his memory. Ironically, Jimmy had never approved of Zip's gang life.

Lena's car pulled behind a stand of bushes which partially concealed a wooden cabin; it looked like it belonged to a 1920's sharecropper

. Zip's hand made a sweeping movement as he jerked the car under a set of pine trees. Tenderly he held the pistol in his hand as he waited for the car to empty. He checked the clip and resolutely snapped it back into the butt of the pistol. Zip felt a sense of calm as he recalled the motto of his gang,

"Leave no witnesses". That had been the mistake that Lena had made…he wouldn't make the same mistake. *The kids will be first…the bitch will watch while I show her what it feels like.*

Noiselessly, the door of his rental car opened.

Chapter 68

Rudy's tires squealed as he rounded the corner to the Malone's street. At first glance the street looked like a local circus had come to town. Lights of white, red, blue were flashing from white patrol cars that were parked at angles blocking off the street. The neighborhood lawns of grass or crushed stones were dotted with adults and children who had come out of their homes in order to get a closer look at the entertainment.

Pulling the truck up to a patrol car caused a flurry of reactions. Officers moved their hands close to their weapons; others took up positions behind cruisers. Rudy rolled down his window and displayed his 'retirement badge' from the FBI. Slowly an officer approached the truck.

"You FBI?" The officer recognized the shape of the badge.

Rudy looked at me, "This man lives at that house." He gestured with his chin, "I'm retired

FBI. We called in the request for backup, that is, my wife did." Rudy paused, "Anything you can tell us?"

The officer pursed his lips, he was considering something;"How about you guys come with me." He pointed at me and nodded toward Rudy. "You ladies stay here."

Next to me I heard the sharp words, "Like Hell we will. I'm the mother, and she's a trained FBI agent." Julie was hopping mad, she moved to the door and opened it. "We're coming with you."

To my surprise, the police officer acted relieved. "Sure...why not." The four of us and the policeman began making our way toward the house: he started talking, "We found some blood on the floor, just inside the front door. There is also a thin trail that goes down the driveway and to the curb...probably a car. Our CSI team, thinks the blood came from someone tall, probably a woman, the hair was chemically lightened...dyed."

Julie gulped out her question, "Any sign of our three kids?" Her breathing quickened;"Two girls and a boy, thirteen, ten and eight."

The officer did a great job of answering. "We have no reason to believe they have met with foul play, Mrs. Malone."

With the cool voice of a competent surgeon, Kate interjected. "The woman is my husbands niece, she's a police officer...she was babysitting the kids."

The officer stopped, almost mid-stride.;"Does she work in Phoenix?"

Rudy seemed to know what was coming next. "Yes, she's working downtown." He began nodding his head. "She has her weapon on her and a locator…she's required to have them with her at all times. Am I right?"

With a reassuring smile the officer leaned toward his communicator. "What's her name?"

"Heather Larson." Kate responded in an officious tone.

The officer turned his head as he began mumbling into his communicator. "Yeah, she's on file." He turned back to his shoulder mike. "She was due for some night training, but they haven't heard from her. They are doing a locator search and hospital check."

I watched as Kate moved closer to Rudy, a nice comforting gesture. He was trying to take the whole thing as well as he could. Julie and I were feeling guilty for having dragged Heather into our mess.

"Does she know someone in Prescott?"

"Not that I know of; Maybe she met someone at work." Rudy's voice displayed cracking tones.

I couldn't believe it, I knew what was going on, not how she had managed it, but I was certain Harold Pepper's sister, Lena, was behind this whole thing. "I think I know where she is!" I could have been Euripides declaring, 'I found it!'

"They're at the cabin, Rudy...the one where we caught her with the little girl, Margarita."

"That's it, Officer. Ask the trace lab if she is on the west side of a bypass road." I was guessing their equipment wasn't that advanced, but it wouldn't hurt to ask.

"We can track her by her cell-phone and by the chip conceals on her person, but our equipment isn't state of the art...at least not for six more months." He shrugged, "Sorry."

I grabbed Rudy's arm, "Is your surveillance equipment still in place around that cabin?"

He shook his head, "Took it out last week." Rudy turned and began fast-walking toward his truck. "We're wasting time here. We know where she is...let's go!"

I could see the helpless look on Julie's face. No one had said anything more about the children, we didn't even know if they were lying in some ditch by the side of the road, or buried in our backyard. Maybe they were where Heather was, but then, maybe they weren't. We could end up losing valuable time if we went running off to Prescott and it turned out all that was there were Heather's clothes. "I think you're right, Rudy, but we don't have anything to indicate the kids are there. Maybe we should look around here first."

The police officer was engrossed in a conversation with one of the patrolmen. We had all stopped in our tracks. If we went up north and it proved the kids weren't there, it might turn out to be a serious mistake, but if we didn't go and our help was needed…well, that might be even worse.

Call it a sign from God, or just plain luck, but the officer rushed back to us. "Your kids went in a car that was parked right here. The neighbors said, 'they went voluntarily'. I don't know what that could mean, do you have any idea?" He shrugged, "Could they have gone someplace to take your cousin to the hospital, or just home?"

"But she isn't at home, is she, Officer? I know you must have checked by now." Rudy turned to me and held me by the shoulders, "You know this woman Lena and her Puppy Killer tactics; willing victims. It fits, Ed."

It was true. It fit. "Julie, hold the fort here. I'll go with Rudy." We sprinted to Rudy's truck. One of the patrol cars pulled up behind us. My heart felt like it was in my throat, it was the first time since my operation I had really felt stressed. The kids were in serious danger if they were with Lena. There was no telling what she might do. Her brother, Harold, was a killer, her boy friend, Karl, was a killer, and we had every reason to believe she was just as dangerous.

My hands were feeling hot and twitchy. "Rudy, I'm really scared. If the kids are with her…well, I even hate to think of what Lena is capable of.

"I know what you mean, Ed, I'm worried sick about Heather too. If Lena finds out she is a cop, there's no telling which way she will play that if she feels threatened."

Rudy's voice was about as unsteady as I had ever heard it. I felt rotten I had not even mentioned Heather; all I could think about was our three kids.

We talked to the trailing patrol car officer. It would be at least forty minutes before we could get within range of the cabin… if that was where she had taken them. "Can you have the local patrol check on the cabin; they can get there before we can."

The voice that responded was calm and sounded mature, "Roger. We have already requested a no sirens check on the cabin. They will only move in if they can see eminent danger."

I would have liked to feel assured, but I knew how 'high profile' cases often cause smart people to do dumb things. The most important thing for now was to find out if the kids, and Heather, were being held at the cabin. "Thanks."

Normally, Rudy and I would be talking strategies or small talk, but the truck cab was quiet as each of us was wrestling with our own fantasies and demons. The traffic was sparse, thank God. We seemed to be crawling while Time was racing at a full gallop.

Chapter 69

Christine was feeling nervous, not just because she was being held against her will, but she had carried Heather's feet when they brought her into the cabin and had flopped her on a dilapidated, dusty couch. She was sitting beside Heather and trying to comfort her as she moaned and moved her head from side to side. What was bothering Christine was, while she was carrying Heather in, she could see up the opening in Heather's culets and she spotted a pistol strapped high on her thigh: did she dare to reach for it? What if Lena caught her? Lena might kill all of them.

"What's on your mind, Missy?" Lena was snarling as she looked down at Christine.

"I'm concerned about my friend." She had spoken more forcefully and loudly than she had intended. Fearing reprisals, she looked over at Dell and Joel who were sitting on a pile of wood next to the stone hearth. "She needs a doctor, you know."

Lena snorted as she made a mock laugh. "If I was you, girl…I'd be more thinking about myself." She turned her back to Christine and strolled over to look out the window. "I reckon one of them smart cops will figure you're here." She waved the pistol in her hand, "I'm ready for them. You know, I want your daddy to be here when they try to rescue you. I've a score to settle with him." She turned and narrowed her eyes to narrow slits, "He killed my brother." The words were not just words, they meant something else to this crazed person, but Christine didn't want to think about what she was planning for her and her brother and sister.

The noise was more than unexpected; it was like a meteorite crashing through the roof. A flurry of shots sounded from outside of the cabin, the impact of the bullets was a series of soft echoes in the roof about Christine and the children. Four shots…four slugs in the ceiling.

"What the Hell!" Lena crouched down to the floor. "Where did those come from?" She turned toward Christine and formed a venomous face. "Who did that?"

Was she really waiting for an answer? Christine had no idea what had just happened. All she could think to do was to shrink in a gesture of humility and shake her head.

Lena moved over to a spot just behind the couch: she was using Christine and Heather as a shield. Two more shots came through the thin boards that made up the door to the cabin. Christine's teeth began to chatter in spite of herself. She dropped her hand down to where Heather's pistol was strapped. Fear gripped her as she asked herself, "Was it time to risk seizing Heather's gun? What if it wasn't loaded?"

The air was filled with a haze of dust and floating pieces waltzing in random patterns, appearing and disappearing as they moved in and out of a stream of light which created a slanting shaft of light. From the corner, near the fireplace a soft, guttural moan seeped into the abrupt hush.

"Joel's been hit!" It was Dell forcing out a string of words that sounded like a child telling her partner not to speak too loudly while playing hide and seek. She flapped her arms, looking like a bird preparing for flight. "He's bleeding."

With the speed of a pouncing cheetah, Christine left the couch and ran in a crouch to examine Joel's wound. "Are you okay?" It was a stupid question, but she felt she had to say something to relieve her anxiety. "Where were you hit?" Another dumb question, she could see a stream of blood flowing from the back of the calf of his left leg. Although she could tell it was probably a ricocheted wound, and not life threatening, she still reacted with a piercing clutch in her stomach.

In the most calm and innocent voice, Joel asked, "Am I going to die like the squirrel?" Joel had seen his friend use his pellet gun to kill a squirrel by shooting the animal off of the side of a tree. The two boys rushed up to inspect their kill, but they were not prepared to see the little creature twitching as it lay bleeding and dying on the lawn in their back yard.

"Don't be silly." Christine glanced over at the frightened figure of her sister, Dell. "You're going to be fine, Joel." She gave both of them a reassuring smile, "You'll just have a bragging scar, but we've got to stop the bleeding." She ripped off the belt from her Jean's shorts. "There… that should do…"

A loud cracking of wood announced the forced entry of Zip. He burst through the door while waving his pistol in all directions. The quick charge he made had caught everyone off guard, even Lena. "Don't anyone try anything! I got you covered!" His eyes were focused on Lena who had just stood up from behind the couch; she had been going to go to the window to see what was happening outside. "All of you get over by the fireplace! DO IT! NOW!"

Like frightened quail, they all scampered to the corner.

"What's wrong with her?" He gestured at Heather.

A flurry of voices responded.

"She hit her."

"She fell and hurt her head!"

"She needs a doctor."

Zip got the picture. He glared at Lena. "So, you're trying to kill someone else, HUH?" He jabbed his gun toward the cowering children. "Who are these guys?"

Christine took a mini-step forward, "She tricked us. She told us we were taking Heather to the hospital, but she took us here instead." Christine sneered at Lena, "And I don't think she called for an ambulance."

At the thought someone was coming, Zip's body instantly stiffened. "You're expecting an ambulance?" That meant police; they frequently traveled with an emergency call. His olive shaped eyes narrowed to a slit so small his dark pupils seemed to disappear. Thrusting his chin at Lena, he didn't wait for her lying answer.

Outside of the cabin the sound of approaching vehicles crunching gravel caught everyone's attention. The kids couldn't believe she had called for emergency help. Zip was thinking as fast as he could, he had just broken into a cabin and there were four witnesses. Lena knew it must be some kind of a swat team coming to rescue the kids.

"So you did call for help?" Zip was confused. "All right, it really doesn't matter...out the door."

"My brother has been shot." Christine asserted. "He would just slow us down." She had heard Rudy use those lines when he was talking about some of the cases he had been on.

By now Zip just wanted out of the cabin. "Leave her!" He pointed at Heather. "And him." He backed up and indicated the door. "Now get moving." For the first time since he found himself in this mess, he was clear. He would kill the bitch that murdered his Uncle Jimmy, and then he would use the kids to bargain his way out of the state. He didn't want to hurt the kids, but he was clear about one point: he was not going back to jail. He would rather die than go back to that place of Hell on earth.

"You'll be alright, Joel. Look after Heather. We'll be okay...don't worry." Christine grabbed Dell's hand and led the way out of the room.

Joel balled his fist and rubbed his eyes. "Don't you hurt my sisters; my dad and Uncle Rudy will get you if you do." The little eight year old sounded like he was six foot four and two hundred pounds of scrapping prize fighter.

Zip's mouth moved into an admiring smile. "You got spunk, kid." Lena was taking up the rear of the three hostages, he jabbed her in the back; "Move!"

Chapter 70

My heart was really getting a workout. It seemed impossible to believe it had only been a short while ago a doctor had been digging around inside my chest. I was exchanging words with Rudy, but none of them had any purpose other than warding off the darts of fear that were flooding into my mind. I knew we were traveling at a rate of speed that was somewhere between reckless and dangerous: I was thankful Rudy had some of the best high-speed training that was available, but my insides didn't know that.

The truck began to slow as we dipped down to make a left under the overpass of Highway 17. "You okay, Ed?" Rudy had glanced at me and my white knuckles.

"Sure, I always wanted to ride a death-defying rollercoaster." I hadn't meant to come out with a joke, but it was the best I could do to relieve my jitters. I even managed a tight smile. I can display outward self control when it's needed, and, boy, did I need it now. The speed of the drive was harrowing but the anxiety of knowing my kids were at the mercy of a crazy woman was enough to put anyone over the top. "I can see the patrol cars...over there, behind those bushes."

Without comment, Rudy guided the truck to a smooth spot just forty feet short of the cabin. He popped out of the driver's door and hit the ground running. He had not yet pulled his weapon, just in case the patrolmen thought he was one of the bad guys. He held his badge high and announced, "FBI, FBI, FBI.", until we were acknowledged. "Stay close to me, Ed."

I didn't respond, my mind was on other things. "There are some officers in the cabin." I wasn't sure I wanted to go on. If the kids had been murdered, I didn't want to see it. Maybe, in some insane way, if I didn't see them dead, I could go on believing they were alive. "I got to get in there, Rudy."

"Stay close to me." He repeated his caution. Was he trying to protect me, or did he just want to keep me from seeing the worst?

To the left of the cabin a group of five officers were looking up the hill and were obviously engaged in a heated discussion, I closed my eyes and hoped it wasn't 'who was going to tell us about our kids.'. I halted; fearing what I might find in the cabin had nailed my feet to the ground.

"Hey, Dreamer, get up here. Joel's fine." Rudy was standing on the porch and waving his arm at me.

But what about my girls? It wasn't that I cared more about the girls...I just wanted to know ALL of the kids were safe. It was good news, and I rushed up to the cabin: happy to see Joel and fearful of what I might hear about the girls. I didn't realize I had tears streaming down my face until Joel leaned his head back and asked, "Dad, why are you crying?" I could only respond by tightening my 'bear hug' on his precious body.

A familiar voice broke the sweet tension. Rudy knew what was going through my mind. "Joel says some oriental guy named Zip took that Lena Pepper and the girls up the hillside."

I loosened my grip on Joel and turned toward Rudy. He was kneeling next to his niece, Heather was being checked out by an EMT .

"Zip? Who the Hell is Zip?" Joel looked shocked at my use of the place of fire (Hell).

"I don't know, Dad. He just came barging through the door. He was shooting all over the place...that's how I got this wound." With pride Joel pointed at the bandaged wrapped spot on his leg: I hadn't even noticed it.

I looked at the snow white wrapping and then at his calm face. "Are you okay? Do you need to go to the hospital?" I sounded like a mother at soccer practice.

Joel produced an assuring grin, "The medics said it was just a flesh wound, I'll be fine."

I had turned my head to ask more questions about the girls. Joel tugged at my arm, "That's why that Zip guy didn't take me when they left."

A cursory nod and a smile were my best response, plus a ruffling of his tussled hair. "What about the girls?"

"They have a team tracking them down. Two snipers have joined them up the hill. I think we can tail along behind them, but they won't want us to get in their way. They have no idea who Zip is...he's a loose cannon."

"Joel, stay here." I pointed to the officer next to us. "Stay with him. We'll be back when we get your sisters." I grabbed his face and kissed his forehead. A short distance away, I could hear Heather responding to the 'smelling salts' of ammonia, she was mumbling some unintelligible words.

Rudy moved his ear closer to Heather's dry lips, "What is it, Sweetie? I can't understand you."

Heather tried to move her head forward as she felt the inside of her thigh; "Gone!"

Embarrassed, Rudy looked around the room; he motioned to a female EMT. "I think she thinks she has been raped, just do a quick check of her...ah, underwear. Please."

Rolling her head from side to side, Heather said, "Gun...gone."

The lady EMT checked for a thigh holster, and reacted by searching around Heather. "The holster's empty." She met Rudy's eyes, "I don't think it's here."

"Question is who has it?" Rudy's words caused us all to look around the room, as if we would suddenly find the weapon lying in plain sight.

Everyone looked at Joel, he responded with a shoulder shrug. "Search me; I don't know who has it."

Chapter 71

Zip was acting out the natural instinct of animal escape: head upward. He had no real idea where he was going, and he also assumed Lena was very knowledgeable of the area. Lena was a few feet in front of him, Dell was next, and Christine was leading the way. In his belt he had tucked the gun Lena had been waving at him; in his hand he had his own weapon. Even with two guns, he was feeling like a fox in a British foxhunt. So far as he knew, the local police had nothing against him except for the taking of the three girls, and one of them was a murderess.

Zip shoved the muzzle of his pistol in Lena's back. "Where does this trail take us?" He backed off a bit while he waited for her answer.

As blithely as a person giving street directions, she pointed with her chin. "That way leads to a tourist viewing spot. It has a few park benches and a rotunda with a barbeque grill." She looked over her shoulder, "Nice view."

Christine chimed in, "Our dad took us up there last winter: it was real cold."

Dell felt obliged to add her impressions, "We couldn't see down the valley because the cliff was too scary."

"Shut up!" Zip was feeling the pressure. Behind him there were police hunting him and Lena, but their main concern would be to rescue the two girls which he had thought were pals of Lena. Zip was really surprised when he realized Lena had intended to kill the kids in front of their father. She had told him it was to avenge her brother's death, but after the way she had just killed his uncle, he doubted her reasons: she was a cold killer. What was he? "Okay, we'll take that path to the barbeque."

Ignoring Zip's outburst, Christine spoke in the most innocent voice she could manage, "Why don't you just let me and my sister go, we don't have anything to do with this?" She was not sure of his motives, and he was a man who had captured three girls. Did he intend to rape them?

He snapped back. "I told you to 'shut up'. I need you guys for insurance. They won't bother us as long as we have you two." He was beginning to spend a lot of time looking over his shoulder. How close were his pursuers? "Now, behave yourselves and nothing bad will happen to you…okay?"

It wasn't 'okay' with Christine, but there was nothing she could do about it. Maybe she and Dell could escape once they stopped at the scenic view spot. With a mixture of fear and anger surging into her veins, she picked up the pace "Okay!"

A plan was beginning to form in Zip's mind. His anger was growing as he realized what Lena had gotten him into. She had killed his Uncle Jimmy, and now he was the hunted one. If he caused her to have an 'accident' at the cliff, maybe he could bargain his way out using the girls as his chips. He could give them the little one and keep the big one until he was safely out of the state, besides…she's kind of cute.

They were making good time now. A sign on the trail said there was a Scenic View just one quarter of a mile ahead. The four of them made crunching noises as they walked on layers of evergreen needles and pine cones. Squirrels darted along the ground and chanted a warning that invaders were coming into their homeland. Lena was nervously plotting her escape and time was running out.

At the crest of the trail there was a large clearing, it showed all of the usual signs of being a tourist stop. A few scattered beer cans and a clear glass whiskey bottle completed the picture; there were also signs it was a spot for young 'love'. Even at dusk, the view was much better than the kids had described. The bluff overlooked a small rivulet which was a good sixty feet from the crest of the picnic area. Nature had provided an array of sharp rocks and evergreens looking more like stakes strategically placed to defend a medieval castle.

Under his breath, Zip muttered, "Perfect." He looked around at the rotunda and a makeshift outhouse: this wasn't the work of the Forest Service. "Who built this?" He sounded like a typical sightseer.

In a detached voice, Dell said, "Some rich guy…not that many people know about it. My dad used this place in one of his stories; he liked it so he brought us here." She had been clinical, like she was giving a school book report. "I still think it's scary." She moved closer to Christine.

Moving her body into a typical teenage slump, Christine dropped her head to the side and addressed Zip. "My sister and I have got to go to the bathroom."

Lena jumped in; maybe it was an opportunity for an escape. "So do I. Please."

It should have been an easy decision, but Zip was conflicted. On one hand his mother had raised him to respect women, but he also knew the risks of letting them out of his sight. Gesturing at Dell and Christine, he said, "Okay, you two go into that outhouse…and don't try anything…I'll be watching you. Well, not…watching you, but watching the door. "Go!"

"It's yucky, Chris", Dell was pleading. "It stinks."

Christine grabbed her arm, "Never mind that, Miss Prissy. Would you rather wet yourself?"

Dell considered announcing she didn't really need to 'go' that badly, but Christine tightened her grip and jerked her toward the outhouse. "Ow!"

In spite of the situation, Zip found himself being reminded of his little sister. He missed her antics and strong will; more than once she had kicked him in the shins when he refused to let her have her own way. Like a trapped badger, she could bite and scratch if she didn't want to help to clear the after dinner dishes. Then sometimes, she would sit next to him and cuddle up and tell him how much she loved him.

Chapter 72

"What you grinning about?" Lena was posed with her arms crossed. Her face was serious and she looked much older.

He curled his lip and glared at Lena. Not only did he hate her, but she had just interrupted the first good thought he had in days; "None of your business!" Keeping her at a distance, he watched as the sisters closed the door to the old wooden outhouse. "I suppose you want to go next."

Lena shrugged, "Na, I don't need no outhouse, I just need a big bush." She reasoned if she could split his attention long enough for her to get a jump, she would disappear into the woods. He couldn't go in two directions at the same time, so she needed to run in the opposite direction from the outhouse. "How about over there?"

It was a golden opportunity. The sisters weren't watching, and Lena wanted a bush. "NO! Go over there, by the bluff, I don't trust you." From there he could keep an eye on the outhouse and Lena, he could also push her over the side and say she had an accident. No witnesses...the code of the gang.

It wasn't what she had in mind, but it could work...maybe. "Sure, I'm not that fussy. Just do me the courtesy of not gawking at me." She paused to study his face, "Hey, Zip?" He didn't trust her, but she didn't trust him either. She glanced at the bluff, and for the first time, began to consider Zip's motives. She could not survive a direct drop, but maybe she could climb down. "Better keep an eye on those girls, they're smarter than you think."

"Don't worry about them." Now he had the opportunity to work out his plan, the reason he had come to Phoenix, he was experiencing a rush of nerves. "Get moving!" He would have to be fast, before the sisters came out of the outhouse.

Feeling this could be her last chance, Lena held up her hands and nodded, "Sure thing. I have to move a bit slow, there is quite a drop over this edge and some of the edges are covered by brush."

* * *

Dell watched her sister. Christine was fumbling around under her over blouse shirt. Dell gasped, "Where did you get that?" She moved closer, "It's a real gun." Dell looked up and narrowed her eyes, "Does Dad know you have that?" Placing her hands on her hips she whispered, "You're so busted, girl."

"Hold it down, little sister." Softly, Christine put her hand over Dell's mouth. "I got it from Heather. It's for protection...I don't intend to shoot anyone, but we've got to get out of here before this guy and that crazy woman feel trapped."

With a quick jerk of Christine's hand, Dell faced toward the wooden door. "Okay, smarty, how do you plan to do that?"

Her father had shown her how to shoot a gun; he had also shown ten year old Dell. Christine checked the clip and sighed, the clip was empty. Her face turned a soft red and she began to tear up. "It's...empty, Dell. Useless!"

With a shrug and a thrust of her chin, Dell said, "They don't know that." Suddenly her tone was no long accusatory or condemning, she sounded supportive.

Christine retorted with a sniffle, "Yea, but I know it." Despair was bulging from her eyes.

Dell took a deep breath and reasserted, "But they don't know it." She patted her sister on the forearm, "You can act, can't you?" Then Dell gave out a little chuckle, "I know you can lie."

From outside Zip yelled at the sisters. "Hey, what's taking you so long? Don't be hatching any stupid plots. I don't want any trouble." His voice faded away as if he wasn't sure about his last statement. Having failed to push Lena over the cliff, he was berating himself …it had been a perfect opportunity, but she had decided to wait until the sisters finished using the outhouse.

Christine raised her voice and tucked away the small pistol. After she smoothed down her overblouse, she yelled, "We're coming out. I had to help my sister with her clothes." Through the slots in the wooded door she could see Zip was nervously pacing about while he kept glancing toward the woods at the edge of the clearing. Christine and Dell came out of the outhouse.

"How bad is it?" Lena snorted in a mock laugh. "NEXT!" Lena didn't wait for Zip's permission. "Be right out." She snapped the door closed and disappeared behind the vertically slatted door.

Christine guided Dell to nearby bench seats. She whispered out of the side of her mouth, "When I tell you, move around to the back of this bench and then head for the woods." Christine was watching the way Zip was focused on the outhouse. She raised her voice only a little, "Why are you so mad at her?"

Zip rolled his eyes, but did not look away from the outhouse. His fingers were nervously massaging the pistol in his hand. "She killed my uncle."

"I'm sorry, Mr. Zip. Why do you want us?" Dell was sounding mature and sympathetic.

Zip made a quick glance at Dell. "You're quite a little girl. I have a niece just like you...she's pretty sharp too. He now fixed his eyes on her. "I don't want to hurt you girls, but I'm in a spot. There are a bunch of police coming up that ridge, and you are the only ones that can keep the police at bay." He glanced back at the outhouse. "I just wanted to make sure she didn't get away."

Zip shot his head closer toward the outhouse. There was a crackling noise coming in that direction. The cliff and the surrounding trees made at difficult to pinpoint sounds. From their position at the bench, Christine and Dell could see Lena; she had broken through the back of the old wooden outhouse. As fast as she could run, she was making her way toward the edge of the cliff.

Dell looked at Christine. They didn't need to speak to read each other's face. Was Lena planning to commit suicide? The girls froze as they watched Zip sprint toward the back of the outhouse. He was having trouble getting traction; several times his knees brushed the surface of the short grass and pine needles.

Christine nudged Dell, "Get ready!"

"Okay!"

It was like watching a play or a football game. Christine and Dell sat on the wooden bench as they watched Lena race for the safety of the cliff while Zip was pursuing her. She had almost reached the end of the cleared area; Zip was a good twelve feet behind her. Christine and Dell seemed to be of no concern to him.

"Let's go, Dell…not too fast, just lay flat on the ground." She grabbed her hand and pulled Dell to the ground. "Now crawl to the brush…fast, Dell" Christine looked over and noticed that Zip had just glanced in their direction, he seemed tortured by conflict. He needed the girls for bargaining, but he could not let the killer bitch get away. Abruptly he stopped and dropped to his knees; he raised his pistol to the cup and saucer stance and fired in the direction of Lena's escape.

The sister could feel the cuts that were happening to their uncovered knees, but they moved further into the brush, heading for the pine trees.

"Police; Police, stop where you are…freeze;"

Chapter 73

The girls froze; were the police talking to them, had they heard them talking or moving through the grass? There was a brief silence and then, from somewhere up in front of the sisters, they heard the sharp report of a rifle shot. The sound rang out in the forest, much louder than the funny pop sounds that were coming from Zip's pistol.

Dell screamed, "They're shooting at us." She started to stand up, but Christine pulled her back to the ground and covered her mouth with her hand.

"They're shooting at HIM." Christine used her chin to point where Zip had been shooting at Lena.

Zip was still shooting when another shot was fired from the woods. This time Zip's right leg folded and he dropped to the ground, the girls could hear him yell, "You shot me!" His tone was one of surprise and indignant complaint. "I've been shot". Then he let out a string of words in a foreign language.

Just a short distance from the girls a group of policemen came charging out from the edge of the forest. They were in black uniforms with chest protectors and carrying assault weapons. "Swat team." Christine announced to Dell.

In a snotty voice Dell said, "I watch TV, too, smarty, I know that."

Ignoring the tone in Dell's words, Christine grabbed the hand of her sister. "Stand up...slowly. We want them to see us, but put up your hands." The two girls felt as silly as they looked. Standing there like two hardened criminal, they slowly moved over to the spot where the officers had come out of the forest.

From behind one of the trees, a voice asked, "Who are you girls?"

"Christine and Dell Malone, we were prisoners." Her voice was meeker than she had intended, and there was a tremble in her delivery. "Where's our dad?"

Dell repeated the same question, it was almost like the sound of an echo, "Where's our dad?"

With the grin that the girls would never forget, the officer moved out from behind the tree. His face was alive with the joy he felt in rescuing the two girls. In an effort to not scare the girls, he lowered his weapon toward the ground and started walking toward the two girls who now looked like a pair of statues. "Are you all right?"

"We're fine, officer." Christine had been taught to never call a policeman a 'cop'; she should always address them as 'officer' because they were 'officers of the law'.

Dell whispered out of the side of her mouth, "He wants to know if we were raped, doesn't he?" She sounded so adult, at least she thought so.

Christine ignored her little sister's attempt at playing adult. She was just going to ask about me, when she saw Rudy and me heading toward them. She waved and yelled, Dad!"

We couldn't get to the girls fast enough. They kept waving their hands and chanting, 'Dad...Dad...Dad', as if they thought Rudy and I were just desert mirages and would soon fade into dusty whiffs. The shouts and movements of the swat team were pushed to the back of our minds for all we cared; they could have been holding a flag football game. As Christine and Dell charged into my body, I gave no thought to the jolt it gave my recently repaired heart…it was the best medicine it could have received: now, all of my kids were safe. I looked over the tops of their heads and read the envy that was flowing from Rudy's eyes. I was a happy man with a wet shirt: the girls were eye-leaking while they nestled their faces into my scarred chest.

Rudy moved on and joined the swat team. By now the team was gathered around the edge of the cliff. Two men were tending to the wounded body of Zip. He was yelling like a wounded javelina, but he sounded like he was going to be fine.

I think that one of the last thoughts I will have will be the look on the faces of my two girls. Their wet eyes glowed like glacial pools on a bright spring day. We weren't doing any talking; I knew they were 'okay'. The girls loosened their vise like grips as Rudy returned from watching the swat team do its work.

Rudy began talking even before he got within ten feet of us. "The guy down there is called Zip. A bullet passed through his liver, but he'll be okay." He paused to give the girls a quick welcome home hug.

"He was okay to us, Dad…for a bad man." Dell offered her appraisal of the criminal.

"There is a blood trail that leads to the edge of the cliff. The swat team is looking for Ms. Pepper. They think that Zip character put a round in her; I think she's dead. She probably fell down the cliff, maybe as far as the flowing stream at the bottom."

Chapter 74

Lena pushed her hand against her mouth; it was the only way she could hold back the coughs. Bubbles of almost clear looking blood were coming out of her mouth. The pain in her right shoulder was beginning to hurt like a hot poker. Her throat and chest rattled when she tried to breath.

Outside of the small animal cave she could hear the police as they looked through the brush and cautiously moved along the loose pieces of rock. It was near to impossible for her to see through the brush that she had pulled in and hastily arranged around the entrance. There were pieces of dog hair stuck to the floor and against jagged chards of rock cutting into her like nicked razors.

"Nothing over here!" boomed a voice that was just outside the entrance to her shallow cave. "I think she must have gone over the side!" The voice was moving away.

Lena wanted to sigh with relief, but it wasn't within her to do so. She was seriously wounded, trapped in a coyote cave, and knew the death penalty was waiting for her if she decided to surrender. She would either have to wait until it was safe to come out, or she would have to give up and hope to be able to escape from prison. *Fat chance.*

Already the sun was beginning to coat the ravine in shadows, she was surprised at how cold it was becoming. Too dark to see her hand, she wiped he palm against her shirt and waited. She felt so alone, deserted by her dead brother, Harold and 'boyfriend', Karl. No body seemed to care if she lived or died. In a word, Lena had lost all hope, then, suddenly, pictures flooded her mind. They were the bodies and faces of the children she, her brother, and Karl had taken to be used for their amusement. For the first time a different scene flashed and she wondered if this was how they had felt: the ones they had held captive; had they also died clinging onto a fading hope?

Something had awakened her. It was too dark to see, but she could feel the breath, and hear the breathing of something. The breath was old, rancid smelling, like one of her dogs. A chilling shock passed through her insides, *COYOTE?* Whatever it was, there was more than one. She must have fallen asleep, or passed out. Lena moved her hand and felt the wet sticky blood that had accumulated in her palm and rolled down her arm. *I've got to get out of here. Coyotes don't attack full grown people...do they?* It was a wishful thought, but she had to believe it. She moved, the animal growled, snarled and shot its teeth into the back of her forearm. She yelled, "Help!" It was a sound that many of her captives had yelled as they pled for mercy, but all they had received were giddy giggles of delight. "Help me! Help me!"

The smile of her blood was attracting to the animals, it meant a meal for themselves and their families. Daily they would have to find food and it was not often they could corner a prey so easily. The hunters were patient, they had their quarry trapped…it was a certain kill. The lead dog had tasted the flesh and blood and found it different, but acceptable. He knew he would have to fight off some of the other younger coyotes, but he had done that many times before.

Her cries for help were lost within the cave, but even if she had stood outside and shouted, there was no one there to help her. The night belonged to the hunter, and the prey had best beware. Lena's arm was bleeding from the coyote bite, she wanted to escape from the hole, but she was weak and she would have to expose her entire body as she came out of the hole. She had not yet considered what she would do once she had managed to get out of the hole: maybe jump? Lena wanted to cry out to God to save her, but she could not, even now, force herself to do such an abhorrent thing.

It was after the third bite she decided she had enough. Mustering every ounce of strength she could, she pushed out her legs and she was out up to her armpits. Quickly, she pulled the rest of her body out of the hole. The dogs were startled and backed away to consider the situation. Lena was struck by the beauty of the night; a cloud covering the moon looked like gossamer lace while the moon's rays cast a movie picture glow over the river below. The dogs were recovering from the initial shock of her size and shape; they were now beginning to strategically place each member around her.

Without hesitation, Lena dashed toward the ribbon of moonlight at the bottom of the cliff. It was a peculiar feeling, not at all like she had expected, she was floating in the air, passing through the night space, like an eagle diving on its evening meal. She felt no pain, no fear, and no thoughts except the sensation of the moment: she was flying. The water would soon be coming to meet her...she wondered if she would feel like a fish. The water looked like flowing gold as she entered into the cool stream.

Chapter 75

It was like it never happened. The following day after the cabin incident, Zip was in a hospital and headed for prison, and our family was in the backyard sipping 'cool ones' with Rudy and Kate. The kids were splashing in and out of the family swimming pool with not a care in the world. I don't mean to say that none of us had some leftover trauma from yesterday, but you couldn't tell it from looking at us.

The cookout grill was the chosen hangout place for Rudy and me. We were in a heated debate about the merits of gas grills compared to all charcoal grills. Rudy grabbed at his chest, I thought he was having a heart attack, a subject about which I now have some experience.

"I have it set on vibrate" He clutched his cell phone from his pocket and continued talking, "I didn't think I could hear it if it rang." With a sly smile he nodded toward the swimming pool and the band of screaming kids. He turned his head to avoid an attack of smoke from the grill. "Yeah? Are you sure? Where did you look?" He glanced at me and said, "They can't find her." Rudy shifted his attention to the cell phone. "She's got to be there some place. You checked downstream; how far?"

For a moment I thought it was some other case Rudy was involved in, but then the reality struck me. He's talking about Lena Pepper. Involuntarily I looked over to check on the kids. If she were still on the loose she could come after any one of us.

The phone snapped shut. Rudy had a bewildered expression on his face. He was speaking, but his cadence was like he was talking to himself. "They found the spot where she was hiding; it was a small cave-like hole used by coyotes; lots of blood." His eyes met mine; they seemed to be asking me to explain the whole thing to him.

"What else did he say?"

"It was a lady officer" As if that were the important point. "Ah, she, Lena, was apparently attacked by some coyotes, but some of the blood looked like it came from a lung wound." He offered an aside comment, "She was probably shot by that Zip guy." Rudy nodded toward my black looking hamburgers.

"Just the way Julie likes them." I quipped as I moved the rest of the burgers to safety.

"Okay, then they tracked her steps to the edge of the cliff." Rudy paused and made a face, "They're sure she jumped...maybe to escape the dogs, the coyotes, but she jumped. That spot is no less than sixty feet high, maybe higher...and into shallow stream water."

I put some hot dogs on the upper level and closed the lid, "Did I hear you say, 'they couldn't find her?'"

"That's what they said. She jumped, but they can not find any trace of her, not in the water or along the shoreline. They dragged the water, but no body. She just vanished into thin air. It's like she was taken up by aliens."

I lowered my head and said, "Don't tell Julie or the kids, I don't want them to worry."

"Okay, but I think they should still be on their guard." Now Rudy sounded like the FBI guy he had been for so many years.

"Are they done looking?" I asked.

"Just about, it's a mystery, Ed, but I don't think we're going to have the answer, at least not for a few days...sometimes we never find out." Rudy shrugged and looked at the grill. "Better serve up the goodies, Ed." Even Rudy didn't like his explaination.

Mechanically, I mounded the burgers and laid out the 'dogs', but my mind was a million miles away, well maybe just as far as Prescott, Arizona.

* * *

The water had been so cold, not at all like the romantic feeling she had as her wounded body fell through the night sky. The moon had seemed so soft and friendly behind the fluffy cloud, and the water looked as refreshing as a TV commercial.

Lena had gone into the water in a feet-first position, her legs had broken at the knees and her butt had struck the rocks at the bottom. She was being pulled into a backwash where the stream had created a mini waterfall. The force was beyond her ability to fight back. With one lung punctured by the Zip's bullet, her supply of air quickly disappeared. She was alone and being forced into a pocket of rocks that had been blasted out by the power of the tumbling water. There she opened her eyes and lamented over her fate, but she could not find time to regret the number of times she had intentionally ruined the lives of other people.

It was to be later in the summer when two high school boys, made their way down the side of the cliff and stripped to enjoy the cool water. They had been swimming and diving for about a half hour when they decided to have a diving contest. One of the boys almost died of shock when he spotted the bloated body of Lena Pepper tightly wedged against the back wall of the nature made waterfall. She would never kill again, or taunt and torture innocent children. Lena Pepper had died as she had treated others and the world would be a better place without her.

Chapter 76

The Phoenix weather was turning to HOT in the valley of the Sun. It's the time of year when we all spend most of our time hibernating in air-conditioned cars, homes and cold shopping malls. Julie and I had been thinking of leaving the kids with Rudy and Kate, just for a couple of weeks, and going to the Pacific Northwest, namely, Seattle-Tacoma area: I have lots of relatives there.

Like a series of slide-snapshots, the events of our last trip blinked through my mind. The way we had innocently ended up with a computer disc that was scheduled to be used by a group of terrorists who were planning to blow up the Palo Verdi Nuclear Power Plant, well, it was scary. Did we really want to fly? Could it happen again? I wasn't sure I even wanted to be away from the kids, but they had no interest in spending the time away from their friends.

We had not yet received the news the body of our nemesis, Lena Pepper, had been found so I was a bit confused when Rudy told me "They had found them." The two guys who were tracking me, Bill and Peter, had been executed, gang land style, but the disc had revealed the off shore bank account numbers of those plotting the Palo Verdi disaster. Like always, some of them were easy to catch and indite, some of them just disappeared, and some of them were too highly placed to be touched. Next time, I would be sure to sit where no one could possibly place something in my luggage.

When Lena's body was finally found, and The Puppy Killer case closed, I was left with just the memory of passing out at the ferry dock at Fire Island. I like to say 'passing out', others say that I had a traumatic death occurrence. Either way, I was fortunate because if I had not 'passed out', the two disc guys, Bill and Peter, would have arranged my death right there on the dock; so you might say that I was saved from being killed by being medically dead.

Life is pretty much back to normal, if having three kids entering their teen age years can ever be normal.

Rudy and Kate are going to spend some of the summer in Virginia; they have a home there and think Heather could use the trip to help her recover. The kids seem to have relegated the kidnapping to the many stories that continue to be embellished with their many acts of bravery.

Through all of the trials and brushes with death, the friendship of Rudy and Kate has really stood out, but my hero is the one who encouraged me and held my hand when I was near death (or as some say, dead). Julie was always there, often so subtle that I neglected to appreciate her tender, fighting spirit, but as we grow old together, I can do without another summer like this last one.

My wife and I plan to grow and annoying to our children.

I really love my wife who is also my best friend.

(Apologies to our faithful hairy friends; Günter and Max.)

THE END

Rescued by Death
By
Raymond Lee Hegstad

Other books by this author:
The Blue Fin
Chocolate Sleuths (1,2,3)
The First Manuscript
Rescued by Death

More books ready to publish.
RLH

Notes about the author

Raymond Lee Hegstad (aka Alaska Makissnee) has authored many titles covering: Alaskan Adventures, children's series, Religious fiction, and crime thrillers.

He was born and raised in Juneau, Alaska, served in the 4th infantry, and graduated from Washington State University before graduating from The American Institute for Foreign Trade (now renamed to The American Graduate School For International Trade).

After many years in the business community, Ray and his wife, Glena, started, owned and operated many Montessori Schools.

He and his wife of many years (Dr. Glena Hegstad) live in the Phoenix, Arizona area. Dr. Glena teaches in Scottsdale, Arizona.

Of their five children, two live in the Phoenix area and one in Oregon, one in Montana, and one finds home in Slovenia when he is not piloting a corporate G200 jet.

www.ingramcontent.com/pod-product-compliance
Lightning Source LLC
Chambersburg PA
CBHW071249220526
45468CB00001B/48

9 781974 317523